STREET TO WALL STREET

2 HOODS

AN AUTOBIOGRAPHY

JERRY A. WOLFF

Patch Reef Press
Highland Beach, Florida

CONTENTS

INTRODUCTION

My autobiography shows how a five-year-old Brooklyn Street kid reaches the American dream despite numerous obstacles. Early on I experienced violence, rage and racism. as well as numerous problems with adults. At the same time, I had a loving family, many friends and some great teachers.

Playing any kind of ball was my outlet. Without sports, the chip on my shoulder would have continued to grow and there is no telling how my life would have turned out.

My education was a roller coaster of success and failure, but I was determined to not let the system beat me. Environment is critical to obtaining a quality education and this is something I believe needs to be addressed at the highest level of government.

My Wall Street career began at seventeen with an unprecedented exposure to the financial world. I was very fortunate to have great mentors who encouraged me to learn, succeed and always do the right thing by my clients.

Along the way I challenged employers and corporations to also do the right thing, but greed and self-interest too often won. I have seen corporate misconduct turn employees into radicals and create a hostile workplace.

Travels around the world revealed a wealth of cultures and opportunities to learn. I hope you enjoy my journey through life.

1

BROWNSVILLE BROOKLYN WAS SPECIAL

Growing up in Brownsville I often felt different than other kids. Still, in many ways we were all the same, growing up in six-story apartment buildings or two to four-story walk-ups. I lived in The Mayflower, a six-story building with twenty-four apartments per floor and ten in the lobby. The location at 9720 Kings Highway was unique as it was on the border of Brownsville and East Flatbush. The building faced the end of Kings Highway and its corner was on East 98th Street, which was Brownsville. The six-story building right ncxt door also faced Kings Highway, but was on the corner of Rockaway Parkway and was designated East Flatbush. Just a few hundred feet separation between the two buildings created two school zones. I went to elementary school in Brownsville, while the kids in the next building went to an East Flatbush elementary school. Essentially, these were two different worlds.

In the 1950s, Brownsville was primarily a Jewish neighborhood with several synagogues, where everyone religious or not celebrated the High Holy days. My parents kept a kosher home as my great grandfather had been a cantor in Russia before immigrating to New York City around 1878–1879. When arriving at Ellis Island, my great grandfather indicated he was a tailor.

Unfortunately, with anti-Semitism around, many Jewish immigrants changed their names and/or indicated a different occupation to get into the United States. Many chose a tailor as their occupation.

My father, David, and my mother, Fay, were born in Manhattan and later moved to Brownsville after getting married. They were married for 63 years before my mother passed away. Both came from poor families and suffered tremendously during the depression. My mother was the youngest of five and her father died when she was just one year old. Her mother, Rose, never remarried and raised the children on her own in Manhattan before moving to Brownsville. My father was the oldest of five siblings which included a step-brother he never talked about. Both of my parents completed school through the 8th grade. They had to find work. My father worked a registry window in the main branch of the Manhattan post office for 35 years. Often, very valuable municipal tax-free bearer bonds came through his window. He said he was provided a gun for protection which he kept at the post office. I never went to see him at work, so I never saw the gun. In fact, I rarely saw my father as his work hours were from 2:00–10:00 P.M.

My only sibling was my older brother Larry by 7 years. In my early years my brother protected me, but we often fought. It was still nice having him around. One of my earliest Brownville memories is at age 3 of throwing a large red, white and blue ball with stars at the front of my building's steps as my mother closely watched and occasionally retrieved the ball. If a baseball scout had been watching, perhaps he would have thought "this one is going to be an athlete."

Growing up in a mostly Jewish neighborhood, we had access to kosher butchers, also fish stores that sold smoked white fish and often had live fresh fish in a tank. I remember at age 4, my mother took me into the kosher butcher and he gave me a small brown teddy bear which I promptly named BuBu. Apparently, someone left BuBu in the store and never came back for him. My mother, on her many visits to the butcher, would complain how chewy the meat was or lodge some other complaint hoping to get a better cut of meat. Of course, she was competing against every other Jewish mother on the block. Believe me, that is tough competition. We had a great kosher deli just a few stores away from the kosher butcher and fish store. All were located on East 98th street. If you wanted a good Hebrew National hotdog, it was going to cost you, 30–35 cents. That was a lot of money back in those days. Also, along East 98th street there was a butterfly store where Nikita S. Khrushchev's son, Sergi Khrushchev a serious collector of butterflies came in 1959 for a visit along with a police escort. It wasn't clear whether his father was with him, but my friends and I were very excited as we stood across the street and watched while these Cold War stars made their appearance.

During the 1950s and 60s there were candy stores on every other corner. Some operated as luncheonettes that offered hot dogs, hamburgers and greasy pastrami sandwiches that were the best I have ever tasted. I loved the 8-cent cherry cokes and cream sodas. Although my parents never drove and my brother didn't get a car until he was around 19, we always found a way to get to a great cafeteria on Pitkin Avenue on Sundays. If we had to walk, we would. The exercise kept all us of slim. When my brother started driving, we added Dubrow's and Juniors in downtown Brooklyn to our dining spots. Dubrow's offered free seltzer. These cafeterias always had great matzo ball soup for an appetizer and coconut cake for dessert. If not, they might as well shut down. Broiled chicken, brisket of beef and chopped sirloin were my family's favorites for those Sunday feasts.

On weekends, my father sometimes took my brother and me to Betsy Head Park or Lincoln Terrace Park. Both were walking distance from our apartment building. Betsy Head was much smaller and had a community swimming pool about 3 or 4 feet deep. I remember at a very young age getting tiny rubber submarines in cereal boxes. These "subs" would float when inserted with baking soda and were part of the fun when I played with other children at the pool. There were always a mix of races and I got along just great with all of them. Betsy Head Park had a few baseball fields, too. Often, you could watch Latin ball teams playing fast pitch softball, game after game on Saturdays. The players were young men and they were super good. They could hit, field the ball, throw and run like something I had not seen before in softball play. It was exciting to watch. This was sandlot softball at a very high level. Lincoln Terrace was a much different type of park. It was large with hills, big trees, baseball fields, hot dog stands and, overall, simply a great park to walk around in. Both parks played major roles in my development.

2

WHO WAS I?
THE DEVELOPING YEARS

Born in late December 1949, I was allowed to enter kindergarten at age four and a half years. There were so many young children living in my building, I never felt alone. My best friend was Jackie Resnick. He was born in February 1950 and had to start kindergarten a year later than me. Jackie had two older sisters (Nadine and Sharon) and lived in a three-bedroom corner apartment with his parents. We both lived on the sixth floor of our six-story building. However, my apartment was much smaller. Rare was the day that I didn't walk down the hall to visit Jackie. After all, he had a set of Lionel trains and plenty of room to have them running on the tracks regularly. They had a piano and a real good stereo system which his two sisters used for dancing to 50s rock music. On the other hand, we only had one bedroom, which my parents slept in. Larry and I slept in a convertible couch in a small living room where the TV, bookcase and a guppy fish tank was located. I slept in a convertible couch from the time I was out of a crib until I was thirteen years old. My brother, being seven years older and eventually 6'2", often elbowed my head in the middle of the night as he turned in the bed. Those hits to the head probably toughened me up for what lay ahead. We shared a dresser that was kept in my parent's bedroom. Often, I found it hard to sleep because some of the woman in the building, including my Aunt Elsie, played cards right outside our apartment door. Their nightly chatter kept me awake and, even though my mother complained, the offenders rarely paid any attention to her.

My mother took me along to our local small grocer to shop for sweet muenster cheese, canned goods, cereals, butter, cream cheese, cottage cheese, White Rock sodas, Hoffman sodas, orange juice, cookies, half sour and sour pickles directly from the barrel and coffee. The sweet muenster cheese and those pickles were great. Bierman's Bakery, a few doors down on East 98th street, was where we bought fresh bread, cakes and black & white cookies. Actually, I enjoyed shopping with my mother. I liked observing shoppers and I began to study prices on various items even though I was only about 5 years old. Numbers were of interest to me. Everything seemed logical and real with numbers. Who would have known that years later, numbers would become a key part of my career?

I always enjoyed being around and playing with other children. It was fun and exciting to see what other kids in my building were up to and if they were interested in anything that I might want to do. It didn't take long to figure which ones would become my friends or playmates. Most of us were only a year or so apart in age, and mostly from middle or lower middle-income families. There were some very cute 4 and 5 years-old girls that I was attracted to. One of them, who lived just below my apartment on the fifth floor, was named Hillary, but everyone called her Ferny. At 5 years old, I fell for her and often serenaded her from the stairway near her apartment. However, she was always inside when I did it, so she never knew my special feelings. If she had stepped out, I probably would have stopped singing, as I was extremely shy about singing in front of anyone. Then there was Merrill, a beautiful, skinny girl who was tall like me and lived on the fourth floor. Both her parents were very tall and good looking. Her father likely was a white-collar worker, because whenever I saw him during the week, he would be wearing a dark navy suit. I always felt the parents kept a close eye on her and didn't allow her very much time to play with the other kids. Then, there was Elaine and her cousin Gwen along with numerous other children in the building. I will always wonder what happened to all of those wonderful kids from The Mayflower. Most moved away before my family decided to get out of what was to become a crime-ridden building and neighborhood.

It wouldn't be long before I was to begin kindergarten in September 1954 at P.S. 183 in Brownsville. I overheard discussions between my father and mother about her taking a part time job. For the most part, I ignored those conversations.

3

KINDERGARTEN THROUGH SIXTH GRADE P.S. 183

I n September 1954, I was getting ready for my first day in kindergarten. Most mornings my mother walked me to school together with my friend and classmate, Lenny, returning to pick us up around 2:00 P.M. Lenny was about five months older. He lived in a two-story brownstone down the block from me. His mother was a stay-at-home mom and I got along quite well with her. His father was much stricter than my parents and worked in a grocery store in Harlem. Sometimes I felt a bit nervous around him. Lenny's younger brother, Phillip, was on the quiet side. I noticed he liked to listen and observe, but rarely participated. Lenny and I would go on to play a huge role in each other's lives.

On this first day of kindergarten, I meet my teacher, Mrs. Blatt. She was near 65 years old and never smiled. It seemed as if her main concern was getting through the day and often seemed to be burned out. There were probably about 20–25 kids in our class. Most seemed pretty relaxed, considering this was their first day away from family. Having grown up in an area with so many children around, we were less suspicious of each other. Brownsville, at the time, was a neighborhood of racial diversity so we kids were more accepting from the get-go. We spent the day coloring, singing songs, doing some arithmetic and, most important, enjoying milk and a cookie late in the day. Afterward, we sat in tiny wooden chairs, put our heads down and closed our eyes. We also ate our homemade lunches in those same chairs.

Once my mother saw I was comfortable in kindergarten, she began to work part time as a stenographer. Even so, she was rarely late picking us up. The pickup spot was the basement level. One winter day, I wore a tight pullover sweater to school and I was having trouble getting it over my head. I watched Mrs. Blatt helping several other children with their sweaters and jackets. I kept trying to seek her help, but I was ignored. Out of frustration, I flung one small chair at her feet. Fortunately, she did not notice my action. I gave up seeking her assistance and managed to get my sweater over my head without her help, but I was upset with myself for throwing the chair at her. I knew that was wrong. That episode marked the beginning of an attitude change. If you want something done, Jerry, do it yourself. From that day on, I became more independent.

When I got home from kindergarten, I wanted to play ball in the long hallway on the sixth floor, either with Jackie or by myself. Some days, I would place a folding table in the hallway outside my door and play grocer. To this end, I saved empty cereal boxes, orange juice containers and cartons from milk, sour cream and cottage cheese. I would then gather a few children from the building and pretend to "sell" the various food items. Each child was given some Monopoly money to spend. I always felt it was a fun way to learn to count and understand money. The children enjoyed playing both roles of customer and, at times, grocer.

As I approached the age of 5, my mother allowed me to take to the streets on my own. She limited my boundaries to our building and our long block that we cornered. Jackie's mother, Beatrice, would allow Jackie to join me, provided that he stayed with me. She trusted that I would make sure nothing happened to him. Being two months older and having started school before him, she felt I provided the protection of an older brother.

First grade was very different than kindergarten. We no longer were forming circles and having stories read to us. The focus had now changed to learning and developing some discipline. Fortunately, I had a great first grade teacher, Mrs. Goldstein, who got married during the school year. She was a young, beautiful, sweet and a caring individual. All of the students loved her. She taught us the basics in math, writing, reading and how to be comfortable in a classroom. I listened carefully to her lessons and felt that I was keeping up with the class quite well.

Late in the school year my mother announced that she was going to work full time in Manhattan for an import-export company named Harry Alter. This meant she would not be home until 6:00 P.M. or later. I was not surprised, but I was upset by her decision. I guess my parents determined the only way to improve their standard of living was for mother to work full time. I remember my Aunt Jean getting into an argument with my mother over her working full time. My parents felt that I was capable of walking the six blocks to elementary school on my own. At age 6, I felt ready too. If I were to get into any trouble after school, my Aunt Jean, who lived down the hall from us, would probably be around. My brother, Larry, was in Junior High School, but had a limited number of friends. So more than likely, he wouldn't be too far away.

The good news with my mother going to work full time was that I became very independent and street wise. The bad news with my mother going to work full time was that I became very independent and street wise. Most of the kids that hung out on the streets were basically good kids. It wouldn't take long for one to learn who the bullies were and who was trouble.

During the 1950s and 60s, Brooklyn was a major playground for any kind of street ball. I lived in the street. We played punchball, stickball, stoop ball, three box baseball, slap ball and numerous other games. If you could afford the 25 cents for a ball, you purchased either a Spalding or a Pensie Pinkie. They were top quality balls. Although, being just six years was too young for organized game, I already knew, from repeatedly throwing a ball at a wall, that I would soon be able to demonstrate my athletic skills. I enjoyed watching and learning from older kids how to play punchball at a high level.

In my family baseball was the great American sport. My father and I loved the Brooklyn Dodgers, while Larry was a hardcore Yankee fan. If my mother favored one team over the other, she never let on. I guess she wanted some harmony in our small apartment. As far I was concerned, anytime the Yankees lost was a good day for me.

In the mid-fifties, Converse Chuck Taylor All-Stars sneakers were a hot item for kids playing sports. Irving's on Sutter Avenue was the only shoe store around that sold them. The cost was $7-$8 a pair. Irving always threw in a pair of colored laces on the house. They fit great and I was thrilled every time I got a new pair. They needed to last 8–9 months before my parents would pay for new ones. With the amount of baseball, punchball and basketball I was playing, the sneakers would have a one-inch hole in the lower front within six months. I had to apply Johnson & Johnson adhesive tape to cover the holes to make them last a few more months. Otherwise, I would have to pay for a new pair out of my money.

I made it through another hot summer in Brooklyn and was ready for second grade with Ms. Barbara Bosworth as my teacher. She was a lot older than Mrs. Goldstein and had many similar characteristics as her. She was kind, caring and enjoyed teaching. In all eight categories on my report card, she graded me "good" for all three grading periods. The nice part of the elementary school report cards was the teacher's comments. She noted that I was "a very quiet child and gets along very well with his classmates". A report card like mine pleased my parents. The good grades alleviated any concerns about allowing me to roam the streets looking for a friendly game of ball.

Ms. B. Stern was my third-grade teacher. Unfortunately, I came down with chickenpox later in the year and missed a total of 41 days of school in the third-grade. She was not happy with me being out so much. My grades fluctuated between fair and excellent. Once again, I was criticized for being too quiet and not participating in class. She noted that when I read a book, I kept the book very close to my face. I'd started wearing glasses at four, but I hated them and didn't always wear them in class. That began to have a negative impact on my reading ability. Even though she was not one of my favorite teachers, Ms. Stern's insights would become a big plus for me later in my education. We also had a few troubled students who would not hesitate to steal a pen off my desk. In particular, there were two girls I had to keep an eye on. That made me feel uncomfortable in the classroom. After one of them stole a Parker Jotter pen of mine, I had an altercation with her. I hated losing my cool and did not allow that to happen again, at least in that classroom.

Mrs. Cohen was my fourth-grade teacher and once again informed my mother I was "too quiet" in class. My grades were okay, but, like my past two teachers, she wanted me to partic-ipate in class discussions. In light of this repeated criticism, I decided to change my attitude. That was a huge turning point in my personality and education to come. Mrs. Cohen wanted my class participation and she got it. She gave me the confidence to speak my mind in front of my classmates. I hope she did not regret it.

In the summer of 1958, I went to Tilden High School Day camp. It would cost my parents about $80.00 for four weeks. Even though I had been quiet in the classroom, my participation in sports was whole-hearted. Baseball was my true love. I lived for competition. I learned to play chess by observing the older kids play. Even though I had never read a book on chess, I still managed to become an above average player.

My first serious encounter with violence took place at around nine years old after a chess game with Alan, a boy close to my age. The act took place in the foyer of his apartment on the third floor of the building where I lived. I had just beaten Alan in chess and was headed back home. When I turned my back and put my hand on the door knob, he picked up a razor blade that was lying on a lamp table and slashed the right side of my face. Fortunately, he just missed cutting my right eye. I ran screaming to my apartment for help. It was a weekend, so my mother and father were both home and patched me up. It took weeks for the wound to heal. That was the last time I had anything to do with that kid. Sometime later, though, I came across the same boy in an alley where I was playing in a punchball game. I saw him urinate on a player's jacket (who knows, it may have been mine). Obviously, this boy had mental issues.

That Fall, I started my own baseball team, which I named the Eagles. Now came the hard part of putting a team together to play at Betsy Head Park in Brownsville. I knew who the good eight and nine-year-old players were and was able to recruit the best. My team was a mix of all races. Through school sports, they all were friends of mine. My mother purchased blue baseball caps for nine players and she sewed the letter E for Eagles at the front of the cap. I loved her for that. Now we were a real team. I arranged to play two different teams that were in our age group after school. We beat them so badly, no one wanted to play us again. That was the end of the Eagles with a 2–0 record. Naturally, I was the pitcher. All of this was accomplished without any parental supervision/interference/deposits for playing fields. I might add there were no parents in the stands to witness our triumphs.

The fifth-grade teacher, Mrs. Salstein, was at times difficult. I did not agree with her grading process. Even though she seemed to like me as a student, I felt some of her concerns were unfounded. She gave me an excellent rating in Social Behavior for "accepting constructive criticism." Her concern with my fourth-grade reading level was legitimate. However, for two thirds of the year she rated me only fair in Mathematics, but then reversed herself and gave me an excellent on my final report card. Strangely, she claimed I had difficulty with number facts, while at the same time stating "he understands number combinations." I still have no idea what she meant by that. I always felt my mathematical skills were at a much higher level than everyone else. She noted my work and study habits were excellent.

Being a talented athlete, often I could be found in the after-school center playing in class tournaments. In 1959 my class team was the champion in both punchball and kickball. Some of those teammates had also been on my Eagles baseball team. At our fifth-grade monthly auditorium meeting, we were given our individual championship certificates. It was exciting to hear our names called out, as each of us went up to the front to receive our winning certificates. Those wins had weight: there was no such thing as a runner up prize. Mrs. Salstein was proud of us and noted it on our report cards. I still have those original certificates. Mr. Safran was the teacher in charge of the afterschool center. He saw I was a very good athlete and he put me in charge of handing out the basketballs and other sports equipment.

Aside from helping out in the afterschool center, I also volunteered for School Safety Patrol as a crosswalk guard and was awarded a certificate of merit by the Automobile Club Of New York on November 6th 1959. I was proud of this award, because I knew I was protecting the lives of other school children. As a crossing guard I was given a white crossing belt to wear. I expected other children to follow my instructions and rarely did I have anyone create a problem. It was a huge responsibility for a young boy just approaching his tenth birthday. However, I was up to the challenge.

I had an issue with a girl named Joy who lived on a lower floor in my apartment building. She was very emotional and, for some reason, she seemed to dislike me. One day I was on the sixth floor, waiting for the elevator. When the doors opened, Joy was inside along with her younger sister, who was sitting in a grocery cart. Normally, she never came to the 6th floor. When Joy spotted me, she went into attack mode and flung the cart into me. I took the hit and pushed it back at her. She began to cry, even though she did not appear to be hurt. A few hours later, I was throwing a ball in the hallway and I heard her father yelling "Where is that, Jerry? I'm going to hurt him," and more threats in that vein. I ran to a nearby broom closet and hid in it until I felt comfortable to come out. I was scared of him and had no idea what Joy told him I had done to her. A couple weeks later, I was walking to a luncheonette around noon. From behind, I felt hands go around my neck. It was Joy's father threatening me stating "if I ever touched Joy again, I will kill you." This man in his thirties must have been stalking me for days. After that incident, if I ever saw Joy walking down the block, I crossed the street or went the other way. I did not know what Joy or her father was capable of, nor did I want to find out.

The sixth grade was my breakout year. I was thrilled to have Mr. Safran as my teacher. He was over six feet tall, a strong man who didn't take any crap from punk kids. He already had my respect from working with him in the afterschool center. He was very pleased with my knowledge of Latin America and my ability to interpret maps and graphs. One time at the afterschool center he showed me his Lincoln penny collection. I thought it would be a great hobby and immediately starting collecting coins. I lived across the street from the East New York Savings Bank. I'd walk in with, say, a ten-dollar bill and walk out with twenty rolls of pennies to begin my treasure hunt. A couple who lived on my floor had an infant girl and a wonderful male dog named Shane, who was an intelligent half beagle and half terrier mix. I got my first dog walking job earning 10 cents a walk. Generally, I walked Shane three times a day. Those monies, along with delivering groceries for my local grocer, helped me start up a coin collection. On some weekends I helped the grocery delivery guy, Howie, when he had an overflow of bags or boxes that had to be carried to 3rd and 4th floor walkups. He couldn't leave the food in the wagon while he hiked up or it would have been stolen, so we got the job done together and split the tips which often included return deposits on soda bottles.

As good as school was going, 1960–61 turned out to be a very violent year outside of school. One snowy winter day after playing ball at the afterschool center, I was approached by my friend Lenny and two other boys I knew from the block. They started a snowball fight with me. It was Lenny, Terry and Mark against me. Three against one may seem unfair, however I could throw harder and more accurately. At one point I picked up a cake of snow and smashed it on Mark's head. He was laughing and all of us were having a fun time. Enter the adults. . .

Mark's mother was watching from her second-floor window and began screaming. I always felt she was very strange as she rarely left her apartment. I told her "We are just playing," but she continued to yell at me. Terry's father strolled by and, without knowing any of the facts, took her side. He told me to "get off the block." There were a few moments of silence as I went to pick up my school briefcase, which was lying in the snow. As I turned to head toward my building, Terry's father pushed me from behind and after several pushes, he knocked me down. Lying in the snow I looked up at him and said "fuck you." He then pushed my face into the ice and left me with a cut close to my right eye. I was petrified that a six foot 35-year-old man would do that to an 11-year-old. I went home with tears in my eyes and no one to talk with. Later I told my father what had happened but, as far as I know, he never spoke with Terry's father.

After that incident, I had nothing to do with Terry or Mark. Previously, there had been bad blood between Mark's mother and me. Sometimes, I walked Shane on a lot across East 98th street from where Mark lived in a two-story building. His mother would often yell out nasty comments about my walking the dog. Generally, I ignored her, even though she threatened to call the police. We sometimes played punchball in the alley next to her building and I felt she didn't want us there. However, she didn't complain, because her son played with us, so it was difficult for her to harass us without telling Mark to stop playing. She hated me so much that when an elderly couple in a nearby building was robbed, she told the police she "saw me" climb the wall and stand on a planter to commit the theft. The police never bothered to speak with me, because her accusation was so bizarre.

Spring 1961 was finally here. Leaves were returning to the trees. It was a fun time to head to any park. We had a day off school and I joined two of my classmates, Hoy Yee and Robert Arkin, for a walk around Lincoln Terrace Park where I would be playing baseball in the Youth Service League. The local Democratic Club sponsored a baseball and basketball league. I played in both leagues from ten through fourteen years of age. Their letterhead sported the motto: "Keep the Normal Child Normal." As the three of us walked around, I located a hot dog stand and purchased one.

We were walking in an isolated grassy area when we were approached by ten kids. Two boys held real bows and arrows to my head while four others jumped me. One of them took 30 cents from my jeans pocket and knocked the rest of my hot dog on the ground. Since I was a lot taller than my friends, they chose me to attack. My two friends were watched by the other four. Our attackers left and ran up a hill without physically harming anyone, but left a fear which I will never forget. A few moments later a police officer walked by and, teary eyed, I told him what had happened and that I could see a few of the culprits up on the hill. The officer then told me, "When I was your age, I would have kicked them all in the balls." Following those words, the gutless officer walked away and did not approach the attackers.

That mugging incident, along with the threats and injury by two adult men, left me with a profound lack of respect for adults and authority figures for the rest of my life. I tend to regard authority figures with great suspicion. I never felt police were there for my welfare. Adult males had shown they had no scruples when it came to attacking an eleven-year-old boy. They did not want to hear my side of the story. It was quite a lesson to learn at a very young age. Almost thirty years later, I was visiting Lenny, a participant in the snow ball fight, and as we discussed it, his voice broke and became that of a young boy as he recounted the violent episode. That attack on me was never forgotten.

I was somewhat shy around girls, but beginning to take a strong interest in two of my classmates, Barbara J. and Linda E. My sixth-grade friend, Dennis B., was a very good athlete, good looking and smart. He always tried to be one up on me. Together we were two of the most popular kids in school. When he knew I was interested in Barbara and Linda, he also developed an interest in them. If I joined any kind of service squad, he would find his way on it and become captain. We were both extremely competitive and perhaps it made us better in the long run. However, we got on each other's nerves. This rivalry climaxed with a fist fight arranged after school in an ally way. Dennis was physically stronger and had a weight advantage. When the fight began, at least twenty school mates were on hand for the battle. I had more friends than him. Many of my black and Puerto Rican friends showed up to cheer me on. At first, I held my own, but when we were forced to move the fight to an open lot three blocks away, I was knocked down by some of his punches. At least I walked away with my pride. I will never forget the friends who showed up to cheer me on in my fight. After that day, Dennis and I rarely talked. Sometime, after the sixth grade, his family moved from

Brownsville, while I went to Arthur S. Somers Junior High School in East Flatbush.

Despite all the problems that year, the sixth grade was a wonderful growing time for me. My classmates Gregory Wise, John Walker, Kenneth, Darrell Rice, Raymond Mack, Willie Morales and numerous others helped our class win the P.S. 183 punchball championship. On June 30, 1961, I received three Honor Certificates from the principal, Charles E. Warshauer. Two were for Monitorial Services and one for my service on the Audio-Visual Instruction Squad. All sixth-grade students were given three exams just before the end of the school year. If you did very well in all three, you would have the opportunity to combine the 7th and 8th grades into one and skip a year. I had the highest math score that year, just beating out a Chinese girl. My I.Q. was also high enough to meet the skipping requirements, but my reading level was not. Thankfully this issue was addressed in the seventh grade at Somers.

As the school year ended, local gangs began to appear in Brownsville. There was a Puerto Rican gang known as the Roman Candles, along with a black gang known as the Frenchmen who wore black berets. In the summer of 1961, I was playing punchball with several kids in the P.S. 183 schoolyard when the Frenchmen ran through the front gate with bats and chains and began to attack anyone around. I was playing in the outfield and ran out through the backside gate. I was unharmed; but I was sick inside to see a close friend was part of the gang. Raymond had been a superb athlete, a kind and gentle person. During the sixth grade, he played the lead role in the school production of the *King and I*. He was extremely talented and bright. I knew his family had been having a tough time. When I visited his apartment one of his windows was broken and you could feel the winter cold coming in. I can only hope he got out of Brownsville, away from the gang and used his intelligence to make something special out of his life.

In the summer of 1961, I spent another four weeks at Tilden High School Day Camp. I had grown five inches that year to 5'6". Following my love of baseball, I began to concentrate on my pitching and throwing arm. Although hitting was not a major strength, my singles, walks and on-base production were very good. I was selected as a starting pitcher by camp counselors. When I didn't pitch, I spent time playing third base, shortstop or left and center field. When playing the outfield, my counselors taught me how to throw to the cut off infielders, to always throw hard and to keep the throws down. My throws became timely and accurate. I knew I had acquired a new range of baseball skills, that would help me in the Youth Service League next spring.

4

ARTHUR S. SOMERS JUNIOR HIGH SCHOOL P.S. 252 1961-1964

In the seventh grade I lost almost all my friends. Previously, East 98th street was the border that determined if you were going to a Brownsville elementary school. Junior High, changed that. If you lived on East 98th street, you went to an East Flatbush Junior High School. Almost all my P.S. 183 friends would go to Markus Junior High School in Brownsville. Most I would never see again. On the plus side, I would attend a new school with a good teaching reputation only three blocks from my apartment. As an outsider, it would be up to me to make new friends.

Since I was a very good athlete, it did not take long before I began to make friends at the Somers night center basketball courts. The Somers student body was mainly white, which required me to make a few mental adjustments. I felt more at home on the weekends when I played basketball in the Youth Service League. The kids in this more racially diverse league came from East Flatbush and Brownsville. All league games were played at Somers, for me an easy walk.

I was assigned to a basketball team called the Colts for the 1961–62 season. The ages for my team were 11–14 and we were a mix that included blacks, whites and a Latino. I wasn't a starter, but I usually got to play about five minutes per game. We had a great team and finished the regular season with nine wins and two losses, both losses by one point. The coach's son played on our team and was given the sixth man position, even though I knew I was a better player than him.

Our team finished second in the league, and played a memorable one game championship against the 11–0 Owls led by Billy Batson, who at age 14 and 6'5" tall was virtually unstoppable. The Colts were led by Perry Walker and Austin Carr, our two best players. The week prior to the championship, the coach's son broke his arm and was unable to play. That opened up the sixth spot for me. I won't tell you that I was saddened by his injury. My mother, father and brother were all at this game. For the first time I would be playing in front of my entire family. I managed to take one shot in the game. I swished it through the hoop and felt a second of greatness, when one of the referees called a walk. Under today's rules, it would have been a three-pointer. Instead, the ref's call made it no basket and a turnover. I was disappointed, but managed to keep my cool.

In the final minute, we were down by three points and the Owls were taking the ball out from the side. Perry Walker stole the inbounds pass and threw it to Austin Carr for an easy layup going to the basket. Down by one point with about 15 seconds left, Perry Walker stole the inbounds pass again and drove to the basket for the winning layup as time ran out. I remember ecstatically jumping up and down on the sidelines with my teammates. How thrilling it felt to win and share that victory with my family. The underdog Colts were now the 1961–62 Youth Service League Junior Division basketball champions. Albert M. Leavitt, President of the league, handed each of us our trophies. For me, it was the first of many to come. Unfortunately, my mother chose not to attend any of my future athletic events. I wish she had. She claimed she didn't want to make me nervous, however I feed off the crowd. She never had a chance to see what kind of athlete I became.

Around 1962 Jackie and I took a couple of buses to bowl at the new Gil Hodges Bowling Lanes in Brooklyn. We were provided with a pencil and a big sheet of paper to keep score. After bowling, I spotted the former great Brooklyn Dodger Gil Hodges at the counter and got him to autograph a piece of my bowling sheet, which I still have. It was one of the last things Jackie and I did together before Jackie's family moved to Queens.

Things were looking good in school, as well and I was very excited about going into the seventh grade. Fortunately, I was assigned two excellent teachers. Mrs. Weinberg was my English teacher in a specialized class to help students improve their reading level. She had a tough job. There were some delinquent kids in this class who were rough, lacked discipline and simply did not want to learn. It required a great amount of patience on her part and at times I felt her frustration. Thanks to her, by the end of the class year, my reading level and my concentration were at or above grade level.

My other special teacher was Mr. R. Friedlander. He taught both my Mathematics and Social Studies classes and my final grades were 97% and 95%. I received Achievement Certificates for both courses. I also received certificates from both teachers for outstanding school citizenship. I made some new friends playing ball, but it never felt like Brownsville. Somers kids were into cliques, and being an outsider, I didn't always feel welcome. I did all my studying and homework on my own. My priorities were to continue getting good grades and follow Mr. Friedlander's advice: "Jerry, make sure you go to college." I never forgot those words.

During the year, we began to hear footsteps on our building's roof, usually after 6:00 P.M. when it became dark outside. We called the police, but it would take 30–40 minutes for them to show up. By then, the would-be robbers were long gone. Thieves would use either the numerous fire escapes or roof entrances to escape being caught. It was not uncommon to hear youths communicating with each other on the fire escape as they checked out potential targets. When we heard someone on the roof, I would go to my dresser and get a couple of baseballs to protect us from the intruders. If they were home, my father and brother would grab baseball bats. We would then join the 6th-floor tenants in the hallway until the police arrived. Our building's fearless superintendent was always contacted immediately when we suspected intruders. He was tough and gave the appearance of a Coney Island Carnie.

He lived on the ground floor and never hesitated to go up on the roof with a flashlight. Sometimes his wife even joined him. One snowy evening at around 10:00 P.M., we heard footsteps on the roof, called the police and watched our superintendent and wife enter the roof. Within seconds, we heard what sounded like a gun shot. Moments later, our superintendent came down the stairway from the roof holding the arm of a white man in his late thirties wearing a blue winter jacket. He claimed to be "checking out the architectural design of the East New York Savings Bank" across the street, which had a circular structure, highly unusual for a bank. The police showed up and took him away. No gun was ever found, but we believe either he or an accomplice fired a shot to warn the other that someone was entering the roof. Two days later, I spotted the same man at a local bus stop. The police had released him.

A few months later, a Hispanic man was spotted defecating near an entrance to the roof. A neighbor called the police and he was taken into custody. We never found out if his intent was to commit a break-in. I remember holding a baseball and preparing to throw a baseball at him if he approached me from the roof stairway. Thankfully, that did not happen.

Then came the robbery. My Uncle Hymie invited my family to a house warming in Bayside-Queens, a very nice neighborhood.

It was a large party held on a Saturday winter evening. My brother, Larry, drove all four of us to the event. We arrived home after midnight. My father stayed with Larry as he parked the car. My mother and I went to the apartment and as soon as I put the key in the door, I knew something was wrong. The lights were on and a hook was latched on the inside of the door. Not thinking, I pushed open the door and went inside. Fortunately, the thieves were gone. My mother followed me in, as we both began to shake when we realized what had happened.

Larry and my father joined us shortly after. All the damage and theft took place in my parent's bedroom. The thieves took a butcher knife from the kitchen which they used to ply open a locked dresser where my father had placed $300 just a few days earlier. The badly bent knife was lying on my parent's bed. The window to the fire escape was completely broken. My 15 U.S. silver dollars were stolen from the dresser I shared with my brother. Almost all my family's photographs were damaged beyond repair. The criminals crumpled and threw the pictures all over. They stole jewelry and any cash they could find. The television was too heavy to carry down a fire escape six floors. No clothing was taken either, because it was a sure way to attract police attention.

Sports were my comfort zone from these neighborhood nightmares. In late spring the Youth Service League baseball season started play at Lincoln Terrace Park. I was assigned to a team called the Hawks. We had brand new uniforms. My teammates and I were thrilled. The league required a deposit each season for uniforms: $10 for baseball and $5 for basketball. As long as you returned them washed at the end of the season, you got your deposit back. Generally, the uniforms were replaced every five or six years. It was not unusual to wear a uniform that was torn, discolored, had holes in it or was about to fall apart, so it was great when you started a season off with a new uniform.

Once again, I had to deal with a coach whose son automatically became the starting pitcher. On opening day, my team was down by six runs going into the final inning. My coach pulled his son out and gave me a chance for the final inning. I pitched a perfect inning, including two strikeouts. We came to bat and scored seven runs to win the game and I was the winning pitcher. I kept the game-winning ball. Never asked if I could, but I felt I deserved it. The coach continued to have his son pitch almost every game. I never got to pitch again that year and generally played third base. At the end of the season, my father attended a one-game elimination playoff, which we lost 1–0. The opposing team's pitcher threw a no hitter, while the coaches' son threw a two hitter in the loss. I was hit by a pitch and made it to second base, but never got a chance to score. Had we won, we would have played for the championship.

In the Youth Service League, the policy was to give trophies *only* to the championship and runner-up teams. I support that concept. Awarding trophies just for showing up does not build character. I know some parents will disagree with me, but I believe awards should be earned. It diminishes the thrill of winning when society awards trophies for losing. It makes it all seem bogus. The practice encourages an attitude that can show up later in the work place and in a person's life. "Give me a raise, I'm here." It sends the wrong message.

Eighth grade was similar to the seventh in many ways. I continued to get very high grades in Science and Mathematics. My math teacher, Mr. Marks, gave out postmarked foreign stamps to students who volunteered correct answers during class. I collected the most of these colorful stamps. Even though they hadn't any dollar value, I enjoyed the competition. Feeling some students were not happy with me, I gave others a chance to get a stamp or two by not raising my hand every time.

When, we had our finals for math, my teacher marked my test first, and informed me I had scored 100%. He asked if I would take home the students' exams and grade them. I was surprised he had chosen me for such an important task, which I immediately accepted. My friend Lenny, one of my classmates, was extremely concerned about his math grades. Within an hour of my getting home and working on grading the exam papers, Lenny arrived at the door asking how he had done. I remember telling him not to worry. I knew he was bright and would do well, but he would have to wait until tomorrow to find out his grade. The next day, Mr. Marks thanked me. At the end of the school year, I received certificates in Mathematics and Science.

During the 1962–63 school year, I continued to play Youth Service League basketball and baseball. I had grown 10 inches in two years and was now at least six feet. I played basketball at Somers Junior High almost every weekday night. My growing so quickly and playing ball all the time created problems with my left knee. The knee started to buckle often, similar to a trick knee. Several times on my three-block walk home at around 9:00 PM., I'd fall in the winter snow as the knee gave way. I never told my parents, as I feared they would not allow me to continue to play ball.

In one of my Youth Service League games, I scored almost twenty points during the first half. There was a tall kid on the other team who dribbled the ball with a high bounce down the court, leaving himself vulnerable to steals. I stole the ball from him three straight times and drove to the basket for easy layups. He told me "Do it again, and I'll get you." On the next play, I stole the ball again and when I went up for the layup, he smashed me from behind into a gated concrete wall closet behind the backboard. My left knee crashed into a master lock and I went down in extreme pain. When I got up, I went after the other player, but was immediately grabbed from behind by my teammates. I took two foul shots and my coach removed me from the rest of the game because he did not want me to get in a fight. When I got home, I iced down, but the damage had been done. Again, I did not tell my parents about the incident as I was looking forward to next week's game.

In the summer of 1963, there were a couple of classmates, Ray and Sam, with whom I occasionally played punchball, stickball, chess or penny poker. They were part of a clique and though I earlier tried to be friends, we never got close. That summer, for unknown reasons, these guys assaulted me in the schoolyard. I was by myself when Ray and a pal approached. Ray claimed I had said something derogatory about his father's baldness. I told Ray, "I don't know what you're talking about," and, as I tried to step aside, he punched me in the nose. I was stunned and fell down. Having been hit in the nose, my eyes began immediately to tear. It was a one punch fight—fortunately my nose was not broken— that I never saw coming.

Later that summer, again in the schoolyard, I was attacked by Sam, Ray's friend. Punches were thrown and Sam got on top of me and began to rub the top of my hands against the asphalt. Both hands were heavily scraped, bloodied and missing skin. After those two incidents, I had nothing to do with either them or their clique. I heard a few years later, Sam had joined a gang called the Clarkson Avenue Boys. I was told he slit someone's throat with a knife and was being held at Rikers Prison for the murder. The stories are unconfirmed, but perhaps I was lucky just getting my hands scraped and bloodied. I don't think I told my parents about that incident either.

Mrs. Ratner was my ninth-grade homeroom and typewriting class teacher. When President John F. Kennedy was assassinated on November 22, 1963, all students were told to go back to their homeroom. Mrs. Ratner was crying as she revealed that President Kennedy had been assassinated. Some students began to cry too. All of us were stunned. We were told to go home as the school was going to shut down until further notice. I felt very depressed. None of my family were home and I needed to be around people, so I walked about a mile to the Colony Bowling

Lanes. I bowled two games by myself and then just sat there killing time. When it started getting dark, I walked home and waited for my mother and brother. We sat in the living room the next few days watching the news and trying to understand how and why someone would kill our president.

It would be several weeks before things started to get back to normal. The ninth-grade was a very important year, because now my grades counted for high school. I knew if I was going to get into a free New York City college, they had to be very good. My grades stayed at a high level all year and I was awarded the Junior Arista designation May 8, 1964. Only 20–25 students in the entire school were given that honor. In the auditorium we were called up by name and given a certificate and a blue-and-yellow lapel pin honoring our achievement. I was very proud of my academic accomplishment and felt I was on my way to college in three years.

During the 1963–64 school year, I continued playing Youth Service League basketball. My shooting skills were developing and I was starting to average 12 to 14 points a game. The League had assigned me to a losing team—we won just one game—but I was playing very well and was selected to be on the All-Star team for the second straight year. My brother came to watch me play in that game and was treated to a great double overtime victory by my team. I scored fifteen points, with four of them coming in the overtime. After the game, we drove to a coin show in Bay Ridge, Brooklyn.

My parents understood how important it was to go on vacation. Miami Beach and the Catskills were their favorite spots. The Catskills often exposed me to spoiled brats. During the day, softball was the big game for teenagers and adults. The older guests either relaxed at the pool or played cards all day. The nightly entertainment was a mix of well-known and unknown entertainers.

One day I got to play centerfield in a softball game at Brown's Hotel. It was a match of the Guests versus the Staff. Jerry Lewis, who was the Brown's nephew, along with entertainer George Kirby and comedian Nipsey Russell were on the staff team. In the sixties Jerry Lewis was a very good athlete, but he often cursed out the opposing team's players which I didn't find amusing. Late in the game, with the bases loaded and two outs, a Staff team member hit a deep fly ball toward right centerfield. I ran hard and caught the ball among a thicket of trees. Everyone was surprised when I emerged with the ball in my glove. The hitter was called "Out!" and Jerry Lewis cursed me out. My catch won it for the Guests as we held onto our one run lead.

5

CRIME, AND THE MOVE
TO 636 BROOKLYN AVENUE

I t was becoming obvious that the neighborhood had changed over the past few years. Families in my building were moving out in droves. Most left to better sections in Brooklyn and Queens. The few wealthier families went to Long Island. With minor exceptions, I would never see any of them again. My Aunt Jean and Uncle Irving moved to a large development in Queens. Uncle Sammy and Aunt Elsie with their two sons, Harvey and Robert, had already moved out.

For the first time, my parents began looking for another place. Aside from rent concerns, they did not drive, so it was essential that a subway be nearby. They started to look at apartments in Brooklyn and Queens. I believe they used the Sunday New York Times rather than a real estate agent. They were so eager to get out, that when they located a co-op in Jackson Heights, Queens, they signed a contract without consulting Larry or me. They knew I would have voiced my unhappiness with a contract that had specified a closing date just a few months before I would complete the ninth grade. In addition, the nearest subway at the new place was over a mile away, which would have put us in a double fare zone. That meant a bus would be needed to get to and from the subway. The Jackson Heights location did not make any sense.

After a few weeks, my parents cancelled the contract and lost their small deposit. I never knew what they were thinking, as they rarely discussed things with me. There were times, I felt more like a boarder rather than a son. They accepted me as a very independent child. I could do almost anything I wanted, as long as I didn't ask them for money. That was fine with me. I knew where I stood: when it came to household decisions, I was the low man on the totem pole.

The search for a new apartment continued. We looked at the Ebbets Field Apartment Projects which were built after the Brooklyn Dodger stadium was torn down February 23, 1960. The apartment rooms were very small and the neighborhood did not seem any better than Brownsville, though there was a subway nearby.

In 1964, my parents purchased a co-op on the seventh floor of a 16-story building located at 636 Brooklyn Avenue. It had many conveniences. Larry and I would finally have a bedroom to share and we each would have our own bed. The subway was four blocks away and a Great A&P supermarket was across the street from the station. George W. Wingate High School was directly across the street from our building and the Kings County Hospital emergency entrance was three blocks away. It all sounded great. However, my parents never researched neighborhood crime or school quality. Would it be better than Brownsville? It didn't take long to find out my parents had made another bad choice.

6

GEORGE W. WINGATE HIGH SCHOOL 1964-1967

My family spent the summer of 1964 getting settled in our new apartment building. Once again, I felt as if I was starting over. As an athlete, it did not take long to find a few new friends. There were several Jewish, Italian and Asian, as well as some African American families living in our 16-story building. We were surrounded by two story family houses in what seemed like an Italian neighborhood. I soon discovered the Italian families sent their kids to Catholic schools. None went to Wingate High School. I would soon find out why.

I spent most of the summer playing basketball, punchball or stickball with neighborhood kids on the Wingate outdoor courts or in an alley way. The kids I played were my age range, give or take a few years and very competitive. I was very skinny and immediately got the nickname "Bones", which never bothered me.

In September I was starting a new school, George W. Wingate High School. I received a notice to report to a homeroom class with Ms. Feldman, an Art Appreciation teacher. Within five minutes of taking my seat, I was asked by a tall black kid seated next to me, to give him a quarter, when I replied "no," he responded with a solid punch to my shoulder, which Ms.

Feldman witnessed, though she said nothing. I wondered, what the hell am I doing here? Is the entire school a bunch of delinquents? I was scared.

Fear was replaced by fury when, moments later, I received a copy of my class schedule. I freaked out when I saw that Wingate had listed me as an Art Major. That was totally ridiculous. Geometry I and Spanish were not listed on my class schedule. I had been a top math student, and needed to be taking academic courses. I went up to Ms. Feldman and advised her that my schedule of classes was a "huge mistake." She told me to go to the guidance counselor to get it straightened out. I went to his office and was told "there wasn't any room in Geometry or Spanish." Rather than go to Art classes, this so-called counselor requested that I sit outside his office each day until he could "work it out." It took two weeks before I was assigned to a Geometry and a Spanish class. I told my parents what was going on, but rather than go to the school, they trusted it would all work out.

When I finally got into my Geometry class, the teacher, Mrs. Friedman, announced there would be an exam the next day. After class, I explained to her that, due to a mix up in my course schedule, I had not been in a geometry class for the first two weeks of the term. I could not possibly be prepared for the exam. She said to me "that's your problem". I guessed at the answers the next day and got a 19 on the exam. Overnight I went from being an Arista and top math student to a disaster. I was angry and sick to my stomach. I failed the course with a 55 on my report card. My three years at Wingate seemed like a jail term. Although I took Geometry I over again and passed the course with an 85, my attitude toward school had changed dramatically. I still loved math and completed two terms of geometry, intermediate algebra and trigonometry, then passed the New York State Regents exams for all three. That said, my changed attitude was reflected in my other classes where I received mediocre grades. Getting into a free NYC college was a rapidly fading opportunity.

My concentration shifted to sports. I spent weekday nights playing basketball at the Wingate night center and earned a spot on the team for three years. I rarely started, but usually got to play some minutes each game. I tried out for Wingate's bowling and baseball teams, as well. I made the bowling team all three years, but the coach constantly criticized my form. This resulted in lower confidence and below average bowling scores. The Wingate keglers were given special transportation passes each year, so we did not have to pay for subway or bus fares.

One day I met a lady in my building lobby who asked me if I would be interested in walking and feeding her cocker spaniel, Brandy. This was a very sweet dog, so at 25 cents a walk I couldn't resist. The only problem I ever had with Brandy was as soon as she heard my key in the door, she got very excited and often wet the floor. The woman and her daughter moved out a year later, so that ended my dog walking venture. Instead, I wound up sharing a New York Post delivery route with my friend, Alan. That helped bring in a few extra dollars.

In my sophomore year, I tried out for the Wingate baseball team as an outfielder, but it wasn't until my junior year that I made the team as a pitcher. The coach was Ira Wiedman. In the past, several players from the school had made it into the minor leagues and one, Frank Tepedino, played in the majors. Wingate field was a nightmare. There was no money for upkeep and it was full of holes and ditches with large rocks. During games, the coach would often have me warm up in 40-degree weather and then not use me. It was frustrating to do more warming up than actual pitching, though occasionally he would let me complete an inning. When I did pitch, the batters had a hard time hitting my stuff. There were two or three senior pitchers due to graduate, so I was looking forward to being a starter in my senior year.

My East Flatbush neighborhood had a past history of being called Pigtown, a derogatory name dating back to the 1800s. There were a few Italian gangs around, and I got the feeling that those kids were not the ones going to Catholic schools. More than likely, they had dropped out. They liked to go around with baseball bats or chains as weapons. Some of my friends and I already had been assaulted by them. The gang members were known to hate blacks. Jews were not beloved, either.

At age 16, my friend Jeffrey Frisch and I were approached by four or five gang members while we were standing outside my building. A few of them held baseball bats and as soon as they crossed the road, they yelled out that we were "Christ killers" and started to run at us. While Jeffrey was chased past our building, I ran to the front glass door entrance being held open by a 15-year-old girl named Carey. She'd been outside and seen the attack. As I turned to get through the door, a baseball bat just missed my head and connected with my right shoulder. In pain, I went to Jeffrey's apartment and told his parents what had happened. Then a bloodied Jeffrey came through the door sporting a large bump on his head. He, too, had been hit with a baseball bat. His parents called the police who asked "how old are the kids who did this?" Jeffrey's father "replied 15 to 18 years old." Because of their age, the police refused to come out and file a report. As long as no was killed, it seemed they could care less.

I'd also seen Italian gangs with bats and chains chasing groups of black kids on Brooklyn Avenue. They'd run through an alley that dead-ended in an 8 to 10-foot wall next to Wingate baseball field. In one fluid motion, the black kids ran at the wall, planted one-foot mid-way and then vaulted up and over to the grandstands on the other side. Their superb climbing skills were like something choreographed out of *West Side Story* and would be the envy of any Marine. Their Italian pursuers did not demonstrate the same talent, so no one was harmed.

I began to realize why many of the Italian kids in my neighborhood did not go to Wingate. About 70% of the students in Wingate were bused in from Bedford Stuyvesant. Almost all were African Americans. It became clear, my parents had chosen another dangerous neighborhood. To me it was a war zone, where I found myself looking front, behind and side to side when walking anywhere. Since I'd been assaulted many times, I developed a strategy I hoped would keep me alive. There were only three options that might work if I was threatened: I could run, I could give up money or I could prepare to fight. Over time I used all three strategies and survived.

There was still a month or so left in baseball season. Twice, after pitching to a few batters or simply warming up, I experienced sharp pain in my right shoulder. The pain got so severe, I would wake up my father at 1:00 a.m. and have him walk me three blocks to the Kings County Hospital emergency room. Each time I arrived, there was a man bleeding and handcuffed to a table guarded by one or two police officers. Both times, a doctor asked me what the problem was. I told him "I pitch for Wingate High school and have massive pain in my shoulder and can't sleep." He came back out and handed me one narcotic pain pill and told us to go home. I could feel the warmth of the drug go through my body and would feel fine the next morning. No paperwork was done. I was never x-rayed. I would not find out until I was 50 years old, that I had a dislocated shoulder from the night the Italian gang had hit me with a baseball bat.

I never told my coach what had happened. I didn't like him and didn't know how he would react. Probably, it was a judgement mistake on my part. Maybe I would have received some care. I had been written up in a local newspaper as a promising pitching prospect for my senior year. But when he came up to me at the end of baseball season in my junior year and asked if I was going to pitch my senior year, I told him "No." I did not tell him why, nor did he ask. My baseball career was over at 16 years old. I never played in a baseball game again.

I lined up a great summer job. My friend Warren's father was an accountant for Haber Typographers located on West 29th Street and the Avenue of Americas in Manhattan. Warren told me he was going to work the summer there as a messenger for $1.10 an hour minimum wage. His dad got me a job there, as well. My responsibilities as a messenger were to make sure the packages got delivered and picked up. Avoid rain, but always complete your mission. The deliveries were all time sensitive.

It was fun roaming the streets of Manhattan during the mini and micro-mini skirt era. At the age of 16, I couldn't think of a better way to spend a summer making a few dollars, learning the city and seeing beautiful young ladies everywhere. Some of Haber's clients included Columbia Pictures and magazines like *Glamour*, *Parade* and *Cosmopolitan* so I saw models and actresses as I made my routes. Sometimes, I made extra money because we were given a transit fare if the distance from Haber to your destination was at least eight blocks. When it was just a few blocks more, I walked the distance and pocketed the fare. It was quicker and more fun than waiting for a train or bus. Sometimes I would purchase a Sabrett hot dog drenched with sauerkraut as a snack. This would be my reward for walking.

It was always great to see Times Square and Broadway, plus you never knew what you might experience on the streets. At the time *On a Clear Day You Can See Forever* was playing on Broadway and I remember walking behind a young man who broke out singing the title song. I followed him for over a block. It was obvious from his great voice he was in the show. I love Broadway music, so it was quite a treat and in New York it is literally in the air.

One late Friday afternoon, I was asked by my supervisor to make a delivery to *Parade* magazine. I arrived past 5:00 P.M. and very few workers were around. I was told to go down the hall and drop the package off. When I got to the door it was closed. I knocked, but no one answered. Scared that I would fail to make delivery, I turned the door knob to open the door and I was in for a surprise. There was a couple in the nude on a couch getting it on. The man nervously asked me to leave the package on the floor. I did and promptly left with a big smile on my face. What a way to end the work week.

Most of the money I earned that summer went into my coin collection. September and my senior year at Wingate were near. I couldn't stop thinking about my future. It was unlikely I would get into a free NYC college. I had allowed Wingate to take control of my education and perhaps my life. I was angry, sick of the gangs, fed up with my teachers, and at times just didn't care. The few white kids I knew had gotten their parents to pay the $25-$35 cost for the College Board Exam Study book. I didn't bother to ask my parents for a dime. Most of the black kids were like me: they knew better than to ask for money from their parents. When it came time for me to take the exam, I opened the test and, without reading most of the questions, just selected an answer—right or wrong, it didn't matter. The chip on my shoulder was firmly in place. I was the first student in the classroom to finish the exam and left. I had just blown any chance for a college scholarship. Mentally, school was over, but I had to graduate.

Sports helped me get me through the rest of the year. I had made the Wingate bowling and night center basketball teams for the third straight year. I had the same annoying bowling coach and failed to improve much over the prior two years. In a game against Brooklyn Technical High School, I opened the first two frames, meaning I didn't get a strike or spare. The coach pulled me from the game. That was unheard of and I felt like shit. It certainly did not help my confidence. My basketball team had a very exciting year. Richard Tepedino (cousin of Frank Tepedino, the baseball player) and I were the only white kids on the team.

Our coach was an ex-marine and worked as an orderly at Kings County Hospital. He was about 6'3" and a solid 220 lbs. with a disciplined coaching style no team member ever questioned. He did not care if our opponent scored 60 points as long as we scored 80.

Just prior to our third game of the season, coach approached us during warmups and told us one of our players had been shot in the head and killed the night before. I remember one of the players saying "He was a bad guy. You knew something was going to happen to him." We went on to defeat the opposing team and bring our record to 3–0. It was like nothing had happened. That's how it is when you know you are living in a bad area. Today, a school would have had ten psychiatrists ready to provide services. After that night, we never discussed the deceased player.

Coach drew up plays on a chalk board. The team was very athletic and could shoot the ball. He wanted us to grab the rebounds and run the ball down the opponents' throats. It worked. We went 8–0 for the season and played the championship game against an all-white Canarsie High School night center team. As soon as we arrived in their gym, I felt very uncomfortable. The two refs were white. All their fans were white. The game had been scheduled behind my coach's back and without his input. Instead of ours or a neutral court, Canarsie was the site. Was this game fixed?

I did not start. Still, I respected my coach and felt he was the best coach I had ever played for. From the very beginning of the game, the refs were calling foul after foul on my teammates, most of them outrageous. With a minute to go in the first half, my coach called the team off the court and went up to one of the refs. Coach grabbed him by the front of his collar and said, "You make one more fucking call like that again and I am going to shoot your ass." From the sidelines, my teammates looked at each other in shock and wondered if we were about to forfeit the game. Neither of the two refs called a technical and we continued the game. I guess they were too scared. In fact, the next few calls went our way.

The second half was no different. The refs continued to hit us with fouls while rarely calling any on Canarsie. Four of our five starters fouled out. I was put in with about four minutes left. I hit a shot from inside the lane, but was taken out by my coach because the game was close and I was never a great ball handler. We were down by one point with less than a minute left in the game. Their player charged into our defender, knocking him to the floor, however the ref called the foul on my teammate and Canarsie made their two foul shots. We lost the championship by three points. Canarsie scored 40 of their 60 points from the foul line—unheard of in basketball. It left no doubt the game was fixed. The league was determined to not let a black coach with a predominately black team beat a white team in a championship game. Up to this point, we never knew who sponsored the league (the Knights of Pythias). I always thought it was the NYC Public School System. I especially felt bad for my black teammates, because more than ever I understood the racism they faced every day.

My coach and another player lived in my area, so we all took the same buses back to our hood. We walked about a block or two from the last stop, when my coach said "the ref was lucky I didn't shoot his ass." He proceeded to take a Saturday Night Special out of his pants pocket to show he wasn't kidding about the gun. He then put the gun away and we continued to go our separate ways home.

About a month later, a trophy award night was held in a large conference room at the St. George Hotel in downtown Brooklyn Heights. Wingate was first up to receive trophies. They were made of cheap plastic with a coated-to-look-like-metal player holding up a basketball. The title on our trophy read "Grand Lodge John F. Kennedy March of Youth Incentive Award" and had the Knights of Pythias coat of arms. The Canarsie players were each given a beautiful 2-foot trophy made of marble and wood. My teammates and I were getting angry and were ready to give our trophies back to the sponsors and tell them where to shove them. I began preparing myself for a brawl, just in case trash talking or shoving started in the next few minutes when we lined up for the buffet. Luckily, nothing happened. After that evening I rarely saw any of my teammates or the coach again.

There were still a few months to graduation. I had room on my schedule for an elective and took a Distributive Education course which taught me about the tanning process of leather goods. That class provided knowledge that helped turn me into an expert world shopper. Whether it was leather bags, clothing or semi-precious stones, I developed an eye for quality. My future wife, Catherine, would become the beneficiary of my "A" grade in that class.

Graduation was scheduled for late June 1967. I'd hated Wingate throughout my three years there and didn't want to go to the ceremony, but my mother insisted. She never understood the damage Wingate had contributed to my education and attitude. At graduation there were a half a dozen kids who received honors awards and scholarships. I had to settle for an uncertain future. For about thirty days, I went back to work at Haber Typographers. I felt that would give me enough time to figure out what I wanted to do. College was out. I didn't have the money and I would never ask my parents for help. Whether they thought I had failed, the issue never was discussed.

In spite of all that had gone wrong at Wingate, I had confidence in myself and knew I was much smarter than my grades had shown. Math was my strength and I knew it had to be my key to success. I stopped working at Haber Typographers to concentrate on a career. I also began checking the classified ads in the New York Times.

I noticed a job listing with Cosmo Personnel agency in Manhattan. It was for an IBM trainee and fee paid. I called and was told it required a strong math aptitude. I told them I would be there within an hour. On arrival, I was informed that job was already taken, but another position was available with a stock brokerage firm, Walston & Company, in their stock record department. The job would pay $70 a week, but was not fee paid. If I was hired, I would owe Cosmo $140— two week's pay—money I didn't have. I agreed to the interview after signing numerous contract pages with Cosmo. Even though I did not know a thing about Wall Street, I figured what do I have to lose going on an interview? I took the subway to Walston and instead of an interview they gave me a standardized exam. It didn't seem hard and I felt confident I could do well. Midway through, it hit me that I'd have to pay out $140 if I got the job. I decided to take my time and did not finish the test in the time allotted. Consequently, I did not get a call back.

At dinner that night, I mentioned my interviews with Cosmo and Walston to my father. He asked me if I was "interested in Wall Street" I told him "It sounds exciting and I'd like to find out more." Pop was retired from the post office and was now working on Broad Street in a prestigious law office as a law clerk. He told me "He delivered securities to George Walsh, a senior partner at Paine Webber, Jackson and Curtis." Would I be willing to meet with him, assuming he could get me an interview? I said "Yes."

I met Mr. Walsh at his office the second week in August. I remember the view of the river was magnificent. He gave me 30 minutes of his valuable time. I was only 17 years old, but I felt I made a good impression. As we talked, my confidence grew. His gorgeous secretary brought me down to Human Resources, where I was given the identical exam, I'd taken at Walston a week earlier. This time, I zoomed through it. The next day, I received a call offering me a job in their margin department at $75.00 a week (no agency fees). I was thrilled, accepted the offer and began my career August 14, 1967.

7

WALL STREET 1967: WITNESSING HISTORY

I began my career at the dawn of the Wall Street transition, computer age. Years later, I realized I had been a pioneer in experiencing the early stages of computers.

On my first day at work, I was told I would train with Mark Cimino, a senior margin clerk who was responsible for handling the Paine Webber partner brokerage accounts. I also would spend half of the day with the in-house runner, who took papers and securities to all the different departments. The in-house runner left me off at three departments: dividend, stock record and P&S (purchase and sales, where all trade confirmations were processed). This was so I could learn how these departments functioned. It was a great opportunity to learn brokerage operations at every level.

I will always be grateful to George Walsh for believing in me and giving me my start. I was not aware of anyone else in the margin department receiving such hands-on training in other departments. I found myself troubleshooting for the margin department on operational problems. I believe George played an important role. Then Mark began educating me on how the margin department worked. For the first few weeks, I sat by his desk and watched him do his job. Mark was a charming person who knew how to handle the partners in the firm. When tensions or deadlines surfaced, I never saw him lose his temper. He had great patience and was fun to be around. I shared my section of the room with Bob, the assistant manager, and Charlie. All three were Italian and often sent me to pick up lunch at a local sub shop that made great Italian heroes. They always paid for my meatball hero and a soda. It was delicious.

Trading volume started to surge at the New York Stock Exchange (NYSE) and Over the Counter (OTC) markets. Margin clerks had to hand post on three-foot lined account pages which were held in a drawer rack. Security transactions, dividends, cash balances, securities received from and delivered to clients were posted daily. If a client was trading on margin (credit), the margin clerk would have to keep additional records documenting margin calls, Special Miscellaneous accounts (SMA) and buying power calculations. Those records had to be current or run the risk of Federal, NYSE security law violations. There were also brokerage house requirements on margin accounts.

Just prior to Thanksgiving 1967, the trading volume was at least 10 million shares a day. The brokerage firms could not keep up with the paperwork. Trades were not being settled between brokerage firms. Stock deliveries were failing all over Wall Street. Operations were chaotic and the brokerage firms were desperate. The NYSE decided to shut down the exchange on Wednesdays and stay open the rest of the week from 10:00 A.M to 2:00 P.M. This would help give firms enough time to get their paperwork in order and begin the firms' transition to computers.

Computers were not available yet. RCA (Radio Corp. of America) was one of the first to manufacture computers for use on Wall Street and there were enormous problems with their systems. I remember seeing RCA workers marching in the Wall Street vicinity holding protest signs and chanting "2,4,6,8" slogans. It seemed to me the RCA employees were either on a slow-down strike or on strike all the time, while I was working a 70-hour week on the clock.

We could get the daily computer runs from 10:00 A.M. to 4:00 P.M. or not at all. I would punch in at 7:00 A.M. and leave most days at 7:00 P.M. and work every Saturday. For me, at age 17, it was great. Paine Webber also paid for a night course at the New York Institute of Finance on "Work of The Credit Department." After I passed the course, I was given a $10 a week raise to $85.00 plus overtime after 40 hours. At time and a half, I was able to double my pay after working 67.5 hours.

True, I didn't have much of a social life, other than basketball, but I was happy to earn and save whatever I could. The entire margin department worked on Saturdays. Charlie would bring in a record player with Frank Sinatra, Dean Martin and Frank Valli record albums. Mark, Charlie and Bob led the chorus. We were having a ball enjoying the music and making overtime. Mark always would remind me of two words "The Money". There were many Saturdays, I would come home at 5:00 P.M. and, forget dinner, just sleep through to the next morning.

At this point I was given Kansas City, Topeka and Wichita branches to take care of, so I had my own "racks." These were small branches that had mostly conservative investors. There were not a lot of margin traders. Ninety percent of those clients had paid-in-full "cash" accounts. I found the branch operation workers to be cordial and very business-like.

Thanksgiving weekend was near and the word was out, don't make any travel plans. Our first computer system was going" live" that weekend. We were expected to work at least 18 hours straight, if needed—and we did. On November 25, 1967, the computer runs were delivered to the margin department and it was our job to make sure it matched what was on our posting sheets. We checked positions, cash balances and margin accounts. Immediately we saw that the computer runs did not pick up the correct information on any of the margin accounts. Key margin percentages were wrong and had to be individually adjusted. We had to go back and manually adjust SMA and buying powers on each margin account. It was helpful if you had a very good understanding of math and were a team player because we all pitched in to help each other.

For the next several months, I concentrated on servicing my branches and learning as much as I could about margins and the industry. Senior margin clerks with four or more years' experience were earning $150-$200 a week plus overtime. Many doctors and CPAs were not earning as much as my coworkers. My plan was to keep learning and make a career on Wall Street.

Having turned 18 in December, I registered with the Selective Service System as required by law. The Vietnam War was heating up and President Johnson was increasing the number of troops to over 500,000. The Tet offensive began in 1968 with numerous attacks against the South Vietnamese and U.S. soldiers. The nightly news focused on the war and how many of our soldiers were killed that day versus the North Vietnamese Army (NVA). The reporting almost always showed a disproportionate number of NVA casualties versus American deaths. To me, the numbers didn't seem true. My friends and I were all worried about the draft. Some were in college and had a 2S draft classification, which as long as they completed at least 12 credits each term, meant they could not be drafted. Their deferment had a four-year limit. On the other hand, I was 1A and could be called up at any given time.

My margin department manager, Dennis, was also concerned. In late March, he called me into his office for a "quick meeting." I thought it was to give me another raise. Instead, he said he had received complaints from branches about my work and suggested I look for another job. I was in shock and said "Let's call them now and find out what the problems are, because no one has said anything to me from the branches." He quickly backtracked and said "I think you're just waiting around to be drafted." He then suggested I take what time I need to find another job, be it "a week or a month did not matter." I wondered about other possibilities. Dennis was Irish and had never been friendly. I never heard him say a racist word, but of the 30 or 40 employees in his department there may have been just one other Jewish employee (taking off for Yom Kippur was the tipoff). Then again, perhaps the direction came from the partner whose office I walked into at Christmastime, I was delivering a personal check and caught him and a young lady on a couch in a very compromising position. I'd been discreet, but I knew my time there was over.

8

HAYDEN STONE INC.: CAREER ACCELERATES

Within a week, I was hired as a margin clerk with Hayden Stone Inc. at $100 a week, an increase, and not as much overtime. I was glad to be there and began making friends quickly. Fred Broder, a manager interviewed me and I was introduced to Bill Nesbitt, my future supervisor. Bill and I hit it off and within three months, I was given a raise to $120 a week and the title of assistant supervisor which some called lead margin clerk. I would provide support to Bill by supervising 7–10 employees. At 18. I was the youngest in our group and no doubt some resented me. I had to grow up quickly.

Our group was a mix of margin clerks and cash clerks. The cash clerks had not been trained to handle margin accounts and were paid less regardless of how long they had been in the business. Bill asked me to work with a couple of young female cash clerks. Lilly Preston was a single, sweet and smart—a tall thin black lady who wanted to learn everything I could teach her. I also tried to train an Italian lady who had more important concerns, namely that she was pregnant. She often came in late to work. My immaturity showed when I made the mistake of mentioning that I was not happy with her coming in late all the time and that I was not thrilled with her work. Justifiably, she verbally took my head off with a few kind Italian "F" words. That was an important lesson learned: you don't piss off pregnant women. I felt ashamed of myself for not being more considerate and never repeated that action again during the rest of my 48-year career.

While working in the margin department, I made friends with department managers and clerks from other back-office areas, just as I had been previously encouraged to do at Paine Webber. Learning something new every day became part of my routine. My confidence was building: a real career had begun. Most supervisors did not have a college degree or background, but were earning a very good base salary of $200-$400 a week. I wondered if that would be enough to satisfy me in the future. I loved the concept of being wealthy someday and enjoying life to the fullest. I knew that would require an education. I also felt a strong desire to get out of Brooklyn. Crime was getting worse.

One night I ran into Peter, a former Wingate classmate, in a local pool hall. He mentioned that he and his cousin had registered to go to Florida's Miami-Dade Junior College North Dade campus in August. I told him I had seen the school's new South Dade campus, located in Kendall, a much nicer and safer neighborhood than the North Dade campus. I suggested that I'd consider rooming with them if they switched to the South campus. Shortly after, I applied to Miami-Dade JC South and was immediately accepted for the fall term. Saving money became a priority. I would need a car, board, books and living expenses, as well as off-campus residence since the school had no on-campus dorms. All this would be on top of out-of-state tuition. My parents were not going to pay for me to go to Miami, nor did I want a dime from them. Crime was getting worse in Brooklyn and I wanted out.

On Thursday, April 4, 1968, Martin Luther King Jr. was assassinated. Riots broke out in many states. It was a very sad day for our country. The next night, two friends and I went to shoot pool at Spot & Cue near Flatbush Avenue. When we headed back to our apartments, about a mile walk, we saw a bus approaching and decided to take it. As I was running, a young white man in his late 20s threw a punch at my face. I deflected his fist with my forearm. The man then pulled a gun from his jacket and said "I'm going to shoot you." I ran a zig zag to the bus and hoped he would not shoot. Thankfully, there was no gunfire. Once again, I never bothered to tell my parents, as I did not want to worry them or have them try to control my lifestyle.

I stayed in touch with Peter as summer approached. Peter and his cousin agreed to register at the Miami-Dade Junior College South campus and split the cost of an apartment with me. In August, we would be flying to Miami and beginning classes. I would not meet his cousin until the day we were flying out.

Having been promoted and doing very well at Hayden Stone, I hated telling my supervisor, Bill, I would be leaving for college before the end of August. Bill was a great guy and understood I had to take this opportunity. My parents were not thrilled with me going to Miami, but knew they could not stop me. I was 18 and had just enough money saved to purchase a new 68 Mustang, plus cover my expenses without needing their support. That money had to last through April 1969. I would not return back to New York until my two semesters were completed.

9

MIAMI-DADE JUNIOR COLLEGE
AUGUST 1968–APRIL 1969

In August 1968 I met Peter and his cousin at La Guardia airport. We flew to Miami where we stayed with a family friend for a few days, registered at Miami-Dade JC and then found an apartment on Flagler Street a few blocks from Le Jeune Road in Miami. That would be my home for the next 8 months. With cash, I purchased a new 1968 Ford Mustang, small V8 engine, dark blue exterior with white upholstery and a wood trim steering wheel for $3,180. I expected one of my roommates was going to purchase a car, but neither did. I felt some hostility from them. They expected me to drive them to classes and all over, however our class schedules conflicted, which often forced them to take buses to and from the campus. They had day classes while I had an evening geology class and early morning math class.

While on campus, I noticed a sign inviting tryouts for the men's basketball team. Before trying out, I was required to have a physical done at the office of Cal S. Kellogg, M.D. in Miami. During his examination, he determined that I had a systolic heart murmur aggravated by exercise. I was 18 and had several examinations in Brooklyn, but was never told I had a heart murmur. Based on his diagnosis, Dr. Kellogg did not allow me to participate in the tryout. I requested he write down my diagnosis which I kept for future reference. He also suggested that I get a second opinion. I took his advice and was referred to the Miami Children's Hospital for further examination. They found that I had a structural murmur and said I could continue playing ball. Unfortunately, it was too late to try out for the team.

One evening, I came home from my geology class. It was around 10:30 P.M. and when I opened the front door, I heard loud music playing and the lights were turned low. When I opened the door there were about ten people inside, I had never seen before. Almost all were smoking grass. Orange glow paint was all over the living room and kitchen. The toaster had a peace sign painted in the same orange glow paint and several walls had similar markings. I was shocked, but stayed quiet until I could speak with my roommates and find out what the hell was going on. They informed me that some of the individuals were neighbors, friends and friends of friends. Several days later, I was informed by my roommates that one of the pot smokers at the party was moving in with us. My bedroom would still be mine, but if I didn't like it, I could leave. I'd lose my share of the rent and security deposits. Having no place to go, nor the additional money needed, I chose to stay. The rent would be shared by all four of us.

I was told my new roommate had been a medic in Vietnam. They did not bother to tell me he was heavily into marijuana and LSD. From the day he moved in, my association with my roommates deteriorated further. Peter's cousin hung around with our new roommate. One day I caught the cousin taking money from my wallet and he threw a punch, cutting my face with his diamond ring. Peter came in the room and broke it up. I knew then, I would have to hide my wallet and stay away from the cousin. Any chance of friendship was over.

Lenny, my dear friend and kindergarten classmate from Brooklyn, was living with his parents and still had two semesters left at Miami Dade JC before moving on to the University of

Florida in Gainesville as an engineering major. His friends from Miami High School became my friends, especially on weekends. On many Friday nights, we would drive over to the University of Miami campus and see what events were going on there. Sometimes they had a rock group playing music at the main pool area. No one ever asked for IDs so we participated with the UM students. One night we drove in Lenny's car. I had never danced in my life and always used my problematic left knee as an excuse. There was a band dressed like the "Young Rascals" and playing their songs. As the hour approached 11:00 P.M., Lenny said "Jerry, I have seen you play basketball and with all your moves I know you can dance. If you don't dance tonight, you are walking home." I knew he meant it and, spotting a tall pretty Cuban lady standing on the sidelines, I asked her to dance. She accepted, and I discovered not only did I love dancing, but I was good at it. That would be the last song of the night, but a new me had been unleashed.

There were Greek fraternity houses just off the UM campus. On Friday nights we would do a drive-by and listen for the sound of live music. If we heard a band, we parked and headed on in. Once again, no one ever asked for an ID, so we crashed the parties where there were kegs of beer and great live music. Sometimes a student would ask me if I was "rushing." I didn't know what it meant, but I have Russian heritage, so I said "yes." This was 1968, perhaps the greatest era of rock music. Bands were playing super dance music. As I did twirls, slide stepping and used all my movable parts, my dancing skills improved. I kept asking girls to dance, but rarely attempted to talk with them after the dance was over. I took care not to disclose that I wasn't going to U of M. Lenny was happy, too, because my dancing made it easier for him to also ask girls to dance.

My grades were good, and I felt my confidence was back after blowing up my grades at Wingate. I interviewed for a part time job with Burdines, Jordan Marsh, Sears and several brokerage firms. Unfortunately, none had interest. I did not want to go back to Brooklyn if I could make enough money to stay. My room-mates were struggling with their grades. Peter was just hanging in while the others were doing even worse and moreover didn't seem to care.

I hung around with Lenny and a close friend of his, Andy, during the Christmas break. Andy lived with his mother at the Sheraton Four Ambassadors Hotel complex on Biscayne Blvd in downtown Miami. I often had clothes in my trunk, so I was ready for any event, day or night. During my holiday visits, if Andy wasn't home, I parked my car near a construction site down the block from the Four Ambassadors and, since it was rare for anyone to walk by, my car became my dressing room. President Richard Nixon spent time with Bebe Robozo on Key Biscayne. Some of his secret service agents and national report-ers, including Robert Pierpoint who was covering the president, also stayed at the Four Ambassadors. I was approaching 19 years old when I met Mr. Pierpoint's daughter at the hotel. I believe she was around 17 at the time and quite pretty. I had two tickets to the Jackie Gleason show and we set up a date to go see the show together. She cleared it with her parents, but then backed out at the last minute. There had been a kidnapping of a well-known local developer's daughter (Barbara Jane Mackle) Dec 17, 1968 so I could hardly blame the Pierpoints for their caution as they didn't know me.

New Year's Eve Dec 31, 1968 arrived. Lenny, Andy and I had no dates. No problem. We heard live music coming from a big house near the Sheraton Four Ambassadors and decided to crash the party. Rick Shaw, a popular DJ, was at the party. No one was paying any attention to us. I was sitting by myself on a chaise lounge beside the pool when a gorgeous lady, beautifully dressed in a blue gown, walked up to me. She was the hostess of the New Year's Eve party. She said "You look sad. Don't worry you and your friends can stay. It's New Year's." She gave me a quick kiss on the cheek. It was a great start to 1969.

I was enjoying college and really did not want to return to Brooklyn at the end of the semester. I tried to interview as an intern at several stock brokerage firms in Coral Gables. Not one even bothered to meet with me. All I ever heard was "We have no openings." I learned years later that there are always openings in the stock brokerage field for the right candidates.

There was nothing in the world like spring break 1969 on Fort Lauderdale beach. Lenny and I would drive from Miami to Fort Lauderdale in my 1968 Ford Mustang every couple of days searching for love, sex, anything. We approached college age girls on the beach and started a conversation. Usually, there were makeshift stages set up on the sand for rock groups to entertain. We danced with our new acquaintances on the beach, but got no further than good conversation and vibes. I guess that was good enough, because we kept driving back, ever hopeful.

The drinking age in Florida was 18, which led to many wild parties on the beach and at local bars. There were wet t-shirt contests a few times a day that brought many drunk guys and girls together. Somehow, Lenny and I always seemed to wind up with the more conservative, sober females which may account for our long conversations, dancing and nothing else. That was cool too, as we both began to lose our shyness.

After eight months, I would soon be heading back to New York and living with my parents again. With tuition, rent and a new Mustang I bought and paid for in hard earned cash. I was going to run short. I needed $50-$100 to get back to Brooklyn. I heard there would be a talent show Friday night with a $50 first prize on an outdoor stage at Miami Dade JC. Desperate, I decided to enter the competition. You could perform solo or with a group, sing, dance, tell jokes, play an instrument, in short, do almost anything perceived as "talent."

There were 18 contestants. I was number 6 and planned to sing *Exodus*. I brought an instrumental album with about 15 songs on it, among them *Exodus*. Up to this point I had never sung in front of people, but liked to sing and felt I had a good voice. When that Friday night arrived, I developed a sore throat and was drinking hot tea all day. Lenny brought a mutual friend, Tom, a Syrian Christian, to hear me sing. What happened didn't go as I envisioned.

Exodus was the second song on the album and I planned to use it as my background music. A stage helper placed the needle on the record at the end of the first song and out came the *Theme to the Magnificent Seven*, often played in Marlboro cigarette ads. As I glazed into the lights, seeing the first two rows of the audience, I heard—the wrong music. If I wasn't nervous before, I was now freaked out. However, when the music for *Exodus* did begin, I started off with a strong voice and immediately the crowd went quiet. I felt good for a moment, but then my sore throat caught up with me and my voice started to crack. Worse, I could hear the rumblings in the until-then-silent audience. The fourth and final stanza has the same tune as the first, but the words are different. For some reason, on this final stanza, I found myself singing the words of the first. So, I stopped singing and did an exit stage left in embarrassment as the music played on. No one seemed to realize what had happened but myself. Lenny and my Syrian pal often reminded me of my talent show fiasco.

I wasn't going to win anything so I called my parents and asked them to send me $100. On my return to Brooklyn in April, I was rehired by Hayden Stone and paid them back immediately. I didn't want to owe money to anyone.

10

RETURN TO HAYDEN STONE INC.

My parents were thrilled to have me back at home and hoped I would stay. I contacted my former supervisor, Bill Nesbitt, and asked for my old job back. Management was concerned I would save some money and then head back to college in Miami again so they wanted proof that I was serious about remaining in New York. They insisted that I register with Kingsborough Community College in Brooklyn for a night class in the fall term and demanded I show them an acceptance letter. I was back at my job as assistant supervisor one week after returning from Miami.

Within a few months, Stan, also in my department, had set up a bachelor party for one of the young margin clerks I supervised. The event was held at the Riverboat Restaurant on a lower level of the Empire State Building. A steak or lobster dinner, including all drinks, would run about twenty dollars. There was a live band and dance floor for the eleven margin clerks to enjoy. The bachelor and I were the only attendees not married. The *maître d* made the mistake of placing us at a long table near the woman's bathroom.

With unlimited drinks being served, it wasn't long before young ladies coming out of the bathroom were being invited to join our table. Two sisters and their lady friend decided to hang out with us. Stan, who had a beautiful wife, told the sisters that

I was "very shy" and suggested they dance with me. It was the best line ever. The younger one immediately put her arm around my shoulder, got me up from my chair and suddenly I was out on the floor dancing with both sisters. Once it was clear I could dance and wasn't at all shy, the younger sister took control of the dance floor and me. After some "dirty dancing", we headed for a corner of the restaurant and began to make out passionately. The *maître d* came over and asked us to stop, which we did momentarily, but were soon back at it. This time the *maître d* threatened to kick us out, so we stopped and I set up a date for the following Saturday. She lived with her family in Rockaway Beach, Queens, about a 90-minute drive from my apartment in Brooklyn.

I picked her up at her house and saw her sister again, though I don't recall meeting her parents. We chose a drive-in movie for our date. I have no memory of what movie we saw, because we continued where we left off from the Riverboat. As things got hot and heavy, she mentioned that her father was a police officer. The first thought I had was "If I continue, will he shoot me?" I felt as if someone had just thrown a bucket of ice on me. I liked the young lady, but dating a policemen's daughter seemed dangerous to me, so I never called her back.

Woodstock music festival was held August 15 to 18, 1969. I wanted to go and asked a few friends, Alan and Ken, to join me. Regrettably, both declined. I did not want to go by myself so I missed out on one of the greatest rock concerts ever. Even with all the rain and traffic problems the attendees had to put up with, I am sure it was worth it.

Because I was no longer a full-time student, my 2S draft classification became 1A. The military needed more soldiers as the Vietnam War intensified. On December 1, 1969 they held the first Vietnam War Draft Lottery, using 366 blue plastic capsules, (one for each day of the year). Birth dates would determine how soon the selective service would call you up for a military physical.

I remember it had snowed in Brooklyn that lottery evening. I was driving back from my class at Kingsborough. Over the car radio I heard each date called out. I kept hearing December dates announced. Since my birthday is December 23, every time I heard December, I almost lost control of my car. When I finally got home, my parents, brother, Aunt Jean and Uncle Irving were all listening to each announcement in the living room. Moments later, my birthdate, December 23rd, was called at number 162. Strangely, 22 December balls had previously been called. I was in shock. Did someone manipulate the lottery? Even so, I was a strong believer in the laws of our country and would take my chances with the draft if I was called up.

Bill decided to run a Christmas party for co-workers, friends and neighbors in his small Brooklyn apartment. When I stepped through the door every square foot seemed to have someone either standing, sitting, lying down or dancing. There must have been 50 to 75 people there at any given time. When I went to the bathroom, there was one guy in the bathtub, sleeping off whatever he had to drink. I made my way to the kitchen for another beer and soon was dancing to Iron Butterfly's "In A Gadda Da Vida" for over 17 minutes with Lillian Preston. I was ready to pass out myself and take a nap on the couch, if I could only find space. I had not felt a sense of unity like this, since I played basketball with my Wingate High School night center team. That party gave me a special feeling only a real team can provide. From that day on, I took extra enjoyment coming to work each day, even though I had not had a salary increase since rejoining the firm.

As market volume picked up, internal auditing and quarterly cycle counting of securities became extremely important to balance the books. Every quarter I would be asked to work a weekend in the secured cage area counting securities and checking to see if what I counted for various individual stocks matched what was supposed to be in segregation or in the box (known as seg and box). If a security was listed as seg, it meant that if a client's account showed there were 500 shares of a company on the client's statement, then there must be 500 shares on hand in Hayden Stone's name (known as street or nominee name) to account for those shares. If the computer runs showed a stock was moving through the box, it meant the shares were either in transfer to a client, transfer to a stock transfer agent, being received into an account or returning from an agent. I counted securities that had to match the seg position on the stock record books. If the number of shares counted did not match, an audit would begin to find out why. This was not an easy task. Cycle counting almost always took place on holiday three-day weekends which provided for overtime. I rarely missed a cycle counting. Only a select few from the margin department were asked to help.

11

HAYDEN STONE INC: FINANCIAL DETERIORATION

On December 17, 1969, I was one of sixteen employees chosen by Frank Merli, a senior vice president, to join a special staff created to handle "Audit" resolutions for the firm. With our addition, this was a 33-man team, including four group leaders, each supervising seven to eight members. The entire group was the "cream of the crop": vice presidents, department managers, supervisors and the most experienced individuals from every back-office department.

I soon found out the firm was in financial trouble and could not locate approximately $30 million worth of various securities. The last cycle count was a disaster. However, the problem had been going on for years and was not addressed. With my previous audit experience and time in almost every back-office position at Paine Webber, I was a great fit for the group.

We were told we would receive, in addition to our regular salary, half of 1% of what we recovered. That sounded great to me. I was out to prove something: that at age 20 and as the lowest earner at $120 per week, I was as good as—if not better than – the highest paid members of our group. Did I mention I love competition?

The first thing that came to my mind was, how does $30 million in securities disappear? It didn't happen overnight and had to have been going on for years. There had to be an internal and external problem taking place. Fortunately, daily stock records and cycle count audit runs were available for many years. Our group leader assigned each of us a list of three or four companies that showed shortages. I usually started my research on the companies that were the least actively traded and went back as far as I could into old cycle count audits to see where the shortage started.

In one situation there was a Sunoco Preferred stock shortage of 2,000 shares. This was not an actively traded security, so I thought this might be easier to solve. Back in the 1960s most clients did not trust stock brokerage firms and almost always had purchased shares transferred into their name through a transfer agent. From there, it would be changed into the client's name and sent back to the brokerage, where a picture of the certificate would be stored on microfiche before being sent to the client. When the Sunoco Preferred shares left the firm, stock records should have shown the shares being delivered and removed from the client's brokerage account. Instead, they showed the stock being delivered and removed from the firm's name (segregation) instead of the client's account. There had been a break in the computer system showing 2,000 shares not matching and I suspect a clerk mistakenly corrected shares in the wrong account.

As a result of this error, the client had received the 2,000 shares owed him, but his statement still showed the 2,000 shares in his account. The transfer process normally took two to four weeks for the shares to be delivered from the client's account to the address on file. In this case, the client never informed Hayden Stone he had received his shares and the account continued to show 2,000 shares for several years and quarterly dividends, to which he was not entitled, were added to his account.

However, the client never requested the shares or the dividends, so both were still in the account. After I discovered the error, the 2,000 shares and mistaken cash dividends were removed from his account. The total recovery value of the shares and cash was close to $80,000.

I received immediate praise for my catch and shortly after received a check for almost $400. I was thrilled and inspired to do much more. There was a huge shortage in Motorola shares on the books. I made this my next challenge. This would turn out to be much more difficult to solve because Motorola was a very active stock and showed numerous entries on the daily stock records. I devoted a great amount of time, going back over 7 years of stock records and microfiche trying to determine where manual and computer errors had occurred. I managed to recover hundreds of shares that were posted to the wrong accounts. Still, the time I spent on Motorola did not provide the returns I hoped for.

After Motorola, it made sense to primarily concentrate my efforts on finding shortages of less active stocks. Using my forensic style of auditing, and having full access to all departments, I tried to ascertain how entries were being made. So important was our mission, that every department was told to fully cooperate with us.

What I discovered was somewhat shocking. When a certificate registered in the name of Hayden Stone was sent to a transfer agent to be re-registered in a client's name, the certificate and one small sheet of paper with the transfer instructions on it were stapled together. It became a problem when the clerk at the transfer agent detached the instructions from the old certificate. Papers got displaced and the transfer agent rarely called the brokerage firm to let them know that they no longer had the transfer instructions necessary to re-register the shares. My theory was that the transfer agents often kept the securities in safekeeping until someone claimed them, if they were ever claimed at all.

During the late 1960s and early 1970s, many corporations split their shares or paid out stock dividends instead of cash dividends. More and more stock certificates were floating between stock brokerages, banks and clients. With the added volume in the stock market, the brokerage firms continued to lose millions of dollars, as the computer software could not keep up. Anyone with a high school education, even without any experience, could get a job in the back office. Problems multiplied and many stock-brokerage firms, big and small, were forced to merge or go bankrupt.

In one instance, I had a hunch that a local transfer agent (as I remember, Chemical Bank) had not sent stock dividend shares that were owed to our firm and clients. I decided to walk over to the bank and investigate. After asking a few questions and informing them I was employed as an auditor by Hayden Stone, they guided me through an open cage area where securities were scattered on top of numerous desks. As I waited to speak to the person in charge, I wondered why no one bothered to find out what the hell I was doing there. Obviously, security was near zero. Instead of throwing me out, they had one of their clerks work on my idea: that they owed us stock. It turned out my theory was right. Shares were issued and sent to us several weeks later.

Sometime in February, I received a letter from the Selective Service System Local Board No. 44, 271 Cadman Plaza East, Brooklyn, New York 11801 asking me to report to Fort Hamilton army base for a physical March 20, 1970. With my draft lottery number of 162, I did not expect to get called up so soon. Through the grapevine I learned that two of every five draftees who had their physicals at Fort Hamilton were sent to Vietnam. It made me extremely nervous. I developed a severe cough. I felt it was from lack of sleep and fear of the unknown, but I chose not to take any medication.

When I arrived for my physical March 20th, I found myself in a large room with about fifty other recruits. I was given a plastic bag for my valuables and asked to undress down to my underwear. In this uncomfortable state I spent most of the day as I went through nine stations. I was also given a clip board for the medical staff to record test results, mental capacity and, very important, any health issues that might disqualify me.

I had been told by friends, "If you have any doctor notes, provide them immediately at the first station." A colonel M.D. entered our room and asked anyone who had any medical notes or special conditions to "speak now." There was fifty of us, but I was the only Caucasian. The rest were either African American or Latin. I raised my hand and gave the colonel two notes from doctors. One was a copy of my heart murmur diagnosis from 1968 and the other was regarding my severe left knee problems. The colonel requested I squat down on the floor and walk about fifty feet. No sooner did I squat down and placed pressure on my left knee, it caved in. The colonel immediately stopped me and asked me to get up and go back to the bench. He wrote "has a heart murmur and walks with difficulty" in red ink. He then gave me back my clip board. There were two guys near me that had the words "tracks" in red on their medical record sheets. It was obvious the army was going to disqualify them as drug addicts. Noting the red on my sheets, a couple of other guys remarked "Hey, man, wish I had one of your things."

As I moved from station to station, I managed to get three more items written in red on my medical records. Aside from my nervous cough all day, my blood pressure was 180 over 120. I had protein in my urine and having lived in Miami for eight months, my skin was somewhat tanned. This prompted a question: "have you ever had hepatitis?" I did not know what hepatitis was, so I responded, "I don't know, I have had health problems from time to time." The medical clerk recorded that I may have had hepatitis. Even though I was over 6'2" tall and weighed about

137 pounds, my weight was considered normal. I could not help thinking about Arlo Guthrie in the 1969 movie *Alice's Restaurant*. He had a crazy army physical and mine seemed almost a carbon copy of his.

The ninth station was a written exam. We were told if you failed it, you would be held overnight until you passed. I managed to pass, even though I tried not to. I was then informed, without explanation, that they wanted to see me again the next morning. I assumed I was going to be found unqualified for the army. Upon my arrival, I was told to see one of their doctors. I was given another urine and blood pressure test. The results were normal. The doctor examined me and said "you can go." He pointed to the door, and I asked "what does that mean? What is my status?" He told me "You will be classified 1Y." I knew then, I could only be called up in a national emergency, which was fine with me. I celebrated with my family that evening. I was now free to plan my future.

Brokerages continued to have challengers with many running short of capital. In 1970 The Securities Investor Protection Corp (SIPC) was created by an act of Congress to protect the clients of brokerage firms forced into bankruptcy. SIPC acted as a non-profit corporation, funded by member broker-dealers, registered under the Securities Exchange Act of 1934. SIPC provided insurance to brokerage customers up to $500,000 coverage for cash and securities held by the firm (although coverage of cash is now limited to $250,000). If my memory is correct, initially SIPC covered cash for up to $100,000 out of the $500,000.

Around late June 1970, I met Judy in a Brooklyn nightclub. She lived with her parents in a Queens single family home reminiscent of the one in TV's Archie Bunker Show. Judy was an attractive 5'4" Polish blonde who was working daytime and going to school at night to become a nurse. At the end of our first date, I knew I was falling in love. I was Jewish and she was Catholic, but when I told her my religion and asked if that would be a problem, she said "no". Neither of us went to religious services so I believed her. I felt relieved and couldn't wait for our next date. We began to see each other regularly right up until early December. We often went dancing, dining and to movies on Friday and Saturday nights. In summer, we would head to the beach on a good weather Sunday. We did some double dating with friends. I don't recall us ever having one argument. Since we both lived with our parents, we often heated up the back seat in my 1968 Ford Mustang. I placed a purple shag carpet in my trunk and set up a small wine bar. When we were parked, I would pour some wine into two glasses from the Brotherhood Winery, an upstate New York vineyard.

Judy's parents were reserved around me. Whenever I picked her up, they were cordial, but never once asked me to stay for dinner. Judy's bedroom was upstairs and I never made it up the stairway, either. I was a bit suspicious as to why I was never invited up, but never questioned her on it. We were both twenty and, although young, I was making decent money and had a bright future, while Judy would do well when she completed her nursing degree. It never crossed my mind that anyone would come between us.

As summer moved along, I continued to have success in auditing and ranked number one in the group for recovering assets. I noticed my bonus checks were paid at one-third of 1% instead of the half of 1% previously promised. As the lowest paid in our group, I felt I was getting shafted and asked for a raise. Management had put a freeze on raises throughout the firm and I was told to be patient.

With a few brokerage firms approaching bankruptcy, the New York Stock Exchange requested that all brokerage firms set up special auditing departments to make sure their books were in order. In late September, I saw a want ad in the New York Times by F.I. Dupont & Company seeking to hire eight auditors for a new department. I set up an interview with their personnel department. I was interviewed by a slim, well dressed and very educated young black personnel manager. I provided a resume and indicated what I was currently earning. He said "I can't believe you are earning $120 a week." I pulled out a copy of my latest pay stub. Without any further questions, he offered me the job at $141 a week. I told him I would accept the position and could start after giving two weeks-notice. He said "that would be just fine."

I really did not want to leave Hayden Stone, but I was frustrated. I gave my two weeks-notice. At the same time, I told management "Get me a 10% raise and I will stay." On my final day, I worked right up to 5:00, hoping they'd come back with an offer. They didn't, so I started my new job Monday morning.

12

F.I. DUPONT: ENTER ROSS PEROT

In the new auditing position, my margin career appeared to be over. F.I. Dupont was located at 2 Broadway, blocks away from Wall Street. When I arrived at the office, I was introduced to seven other auditors, all newly hired to form a group as mandated by the New York Stock Exchange. There were two male Vietnam vets, one black and the other Puerto Rican. Rounding out the group were two women, three additional males and myself. We were a mix of races and religions. There was a wide range of experience and education among us, but could we work as a team? I was concerned how well I would get along with the Vietnam vets. I had failed my army physical and was for the most part against the war. I always supported the troops, not the politicians or the generals, who I felt were misleading us every day.

We were taken around to the margin and stock record departments. They were better computerized than Hayden Stone, though they still had the same problem of not knowing where numerous securities were. Their previous cycle counts of securities also had big shortages. I got friendly with Steve and Mary, two of my group members. I had quite a bit more experience, but I was willing to teach them and together we formed our own team. I thought this would work well when we went to do research in other departments. It would be more difficult for a department manager or supervisor who did not want us around, to bully three workers versus one. Frequently, we were treated more like NYSE auditors than F.I. Dupont employees trying to clear up a company mess. It became clear that top management did not inform everyone about the trouble F.I. Dupont was having.

On most days, I joined Steven and Mary for lunch. There were some very good sub places available and it was always fun to walk around Battery Park and people watch. We had an hour for lunch and were hired for a 35-hour work week with no overtime. There was no clock to punch. Steve and I became very good friends and Judy and I would often double date with Steven and his fiancée, Linda. Mary was of Polish descent, like Judy, and I always felt I could talk with her about anything.

Our auditing team began to run into numerous issues with our back office, especially the stock record department. No one had told us that records over two years old were kept in a warehouse on Hudson Street, New York City. Our audit group was told to start working in the warehouse and the place was a mess, full of dust and poorly kept. We would go to work in jeans, as dressing down became a necessity. There was some good news. Several of us were into basketball and there was a park nearby. We often shot hoops at lunch time. This brought our group closer together. Under poor conditions, we worked hard for a few months and were then told to return to 2 Broadway. F.I. Dupont was merging with Hirsch & Company. Within months, another merger followed, with Glore Forgan & Company.

Over a three-day weekend, our auditing group was asked to help with the conversion of the three companies' records into the F.I. Dupont system. Even though we'd worked a full day Friday, management wanted us at the office Saturday by 5 or 6 A.M. Steven and I decided it made no sense to go home and come back so early so we came up with a plan. I took my 1968 Mustang with me to work that Friday and we ate dinner in mid-Manhattan. Knowing we had many hours to kill, prior to going back to the office, we hit several bars and got somewhat polluted. As the night moved along, we stopped drinking, went for coffee and sobered up. At around 3:00 A.M. we got back to my car and drove over to Wall Street to get a few hours of sleep, lying on top of some office tables. It was not very comfortable, but it was better than the floor.

On Saturdays it was legal to park near the Treasury building. As I parked, a policeman appeared and said "you can't park here." I responded, "Read the sign. It says I can." The officer said "Do you see the cameramen in front of the Treasury building? They are filming." I said "Yes, and they can film my car, if they want to. Otherwise, I'll have to park five blocks away to get a free parking space." The officer advised me if I didn't remove my car, he would ticket me, because "Mayor Lindsay supports the filming industry." I drove off steaming.

Early that morning, the computer runs arrived, showing new account numbers for the Glore Forgan & Company and the Hirsch & Company client accounts which had been converted into the F.I. Dupont system. Our job was to make sure there were no duplications. It was a large task for our auditing group. Fortunately, everything went very smoothly as there were no duplicates. From that point on, my group worked more on merger issues, rather than the stock record auditing we were hired to do.

As we neared Thanksgiving Nov, 26, 1970, the New York Times reported that H. Ross Perot had provided F.I. Dupont with a $15 million infusion. The additional capital was needed to keep F.I. Dupont in business. The collateral was provided in a complex financial manner that appeared designed to provide some cash or tax benefit for Perot, which also left him in control of the company.

While the power play was going on at F.I. Dupont, my mother had come down with a bad case of the flu and was unable to have a Thanksgiving dinner. I mentioned that to Judy, hoping that her parents would finally invite me for dinner. The invitation never came. In the prior few weeks, I felt Judy was acting a little cold, but I thought she might not be feeling well. That weekend we saw each other, but neither of us brought up the subject of Thanksgiving.

Christmas was less than a month away and I purchased a gold ankle bracelet for Judy. I kept the gift in my car trunk. A few weeks later, while sitting in the front seat of my Mustang, Judy said to me "I feel we should break up." I didn't want to believe it. I asked "Is there another guy?" She responded "No." Then I asked "Did religion or your parents have anything to do with it?" She said "Both." I felt sick inside, so sick I don't recall asking her how *she* felt about the breakup. I knew I loved her and to me that was all that mattered. I went to the trunk and handed her the ankle bracelet. She was surprised and perhaps saddened. I don't know. We wished each other the best and that appeared to be the last we'd see of each other.

The next day, I called Mary, my co-worker and friend, asked if I could drive over to her place and talk. She said "ok." She had a nice cozy apartment in Brooklyn. I told her about the breakup and how bad I felt. I desperately needed someone to talk with and Mary was perfect. She really listened. After an hour or so, I thanked her and left.

Looking ahead, how was I to know that in four months I'd fly down to Puerto Rico and, while on vacation, go to a Bobby Vinton show at the flashy El San Juan Hotel. I was escorting a date, a tourist from Connecticut I'd met at the hotel. We were both very well dressed as we waited for the show doors to open and it was then I ran into Judy and her girlfriend in the lobby. I guess if you have to encounter an old girlfriend, this is the way to do it. Judy said "I thought you would be in Florida." I asked where they were staying. It turned out we were both in Condado Beach. After the show I said good night to my date and took a taxi back to Condado Beach, where I walked the streets for a few hours, my head spinning. I'd assumed I'd never see Judy again. Now she was here and without her parents. If I had her alone was there still a spark? I did not know which hotel she was staying at. PAN AM had booked me in a mosquito-infested guest house, but I used the Condado Beach Hotel as a hangout for ping pong by day and the casino at night. No one ever questioned if I was a guest. That's why a few mornings later I spotted Judy and her girlfriend about to check out. I asked for a few private moments with Judy in the lobby. After we talked for about ten minutes, I realized it really was over. Her personality, even her look, seemed different. Perhaps our break up had taken a toll on her as well. I wished her well and actually walked away with a smile on my face. I never saw her again.

Between the new management with H. Ross Perot and losing my girlfriend it was not a fun time. No sooner did Perot take over the company, than my audit group was informed our lunch hour had shrunk from one hour to 30 minutes and our work week went from 35 to 40 hours without any additional pay. That did not go well with most of us. After all a deal, is a deal, though I guess not on Wall Street. I proposed that our group form an eight-person union. Several, however, did not want the risk of losing their jobs so my idea was finished within ten minutes of discussion.

Things got worse. At one point, I recall a supervisor requesting we come to work in white shirts. I was told "Ross Perot considers that look more professional." I never met Perot in person, however I heard he made his fortune with Electronic Data Systems (EDS), which he founded in 1962. EDS made him a billionaire and was eventually acquired by General Motors. All his success in the computer field could not save F.I. Dupont. There were rumors that Perot lost between 60 and 70 million dollars on his F.I. Dupont investments.

On a sunny late fall day, Steve, Mary and I went to lunch at one of the Italian sub shops and ordered a bottle of wine with our food. We were all feeling pretty good after lunch and strolled the Wall Street area. As we approached the block where the police officer and I had gotten into an argument over where I could park, Steve reminded me of Mayor Lindsay's support for the movie industry. Immediately, I went into a rant and rave about the mayor. In just one minute I had an audience of over 100 people listening to what I had to say. New Yorkers are like that: very curious people who don't want to miss out on anything. It was easy to see how a politician or radical could obtain followers just by ranting and raving in a street. Just get a platform and you're all set.

New Year's Eve 1970 arrived and I was feeling depressed over the breakup with Judy. I decided to grab a bottle of wine from the Brotherhood Winery and take the IRT to Times Square. I wanted to start the New Year fresh with ideas and hope for the future. I drank about half the bottle while on the trains. I arrived around 8:30 P.M. and it was very cold. I was wearing a winter jacket, wool hat and gloves and hoped my clothes would keep me warm until midnight. I was wrong. My bottle of wine was soon finished and I kept ducking into places to grab a bite and stay out of the cold. Around 11:00 P.M., as we got closer to the ball dropping, I bought another bottle of wine and shared it with anyone who wanted a sip. The crowd was huge and even though I had grown up with so much violence, I felt a special warmth towards other people that evening. At least for several hours, my anger had left.

As a lover of Broadway music. I thought of Leonard Bernstein's *West Side Story*. That play will always be part of my soul. Its music, especially Something's Coming, Tonight and Maria, seemed an expression of my life. After all the wine I had, I was singing those songs out loud.

I could feel happiness and excitement brewing as midnight approached. I positioned myself to see the ball come down. As the countdown began, the crowd pushed and shoved. The ball had dropped, but I didn't see it come down. A few seconds later, someone knocked my wool hat off my head as everyone headed for the subways. There was no chance of recovering my hat as I would have been trampled. After all, New York is New York. Just go with the flow.

Somehow, I managed to make it to the IRT station. I was supposed to switch trains at the Utica Avenue station for the Flatbush Avenue line, but I fell asleep and ended up at the end of the line at New Lots Avenue in my old Brownsville neighborhood. A blast of cold air from the open windows and doors woke me up. A black police officer looked at me questioningly. New Lots could not have been my stop. Whites simply did not live there. He found out where I was going and told me to stay aboard as the train would be turning around. This time I stayed awake until I reached the Utica Avenue station and changed to the Flatbush line.

It was past 1:00 A.M. when I walked up the steps from the Winthrop Street train station and felt a flurry of large snowflakes hitting my face. January 1, 1971 had arrived.

For my New Year's resolution, I decided I would make this a special year full of changes, starting with my job.

13

HORNBLOWER & WEEKS, HEMPHILL, NOYES: "I SEE YOU PLAY BASKETBALL"

I was 21, working for F.I. Dupont & Company and saw absolutely no chance for advancement. Worse, the company seemed likely to go into bankruptcy in the near future. The auditing task I was assigned was boring and there were no incentives for doing a great job. It was time to make a move from auditing back to what I really enjoyed: the margin department. Having been away from margins for almost a year, I spent several hours brushing up on security law requirements in preparation for an interview.

Hornblower & Weeks, Hemphill, Noyes ran an ad looking for senior margin clerks. I bypassed Human Resources and set up an interview with the manager of the margin department, Mr. Jiminez. I liked him from the start. He was a young man of Mexican descent who had a very pleasant smile. On the employment application I wrote my desired weekly pay as $160.00 and listed my outside interests as basketball, baseball and numismatics. Instead of asking about my margin experience, he said "I see you play basketball. Are you any good?" Not knowing where he was going, I replied "I can play". He then said 'We play basketball, and are you able to work a couple of Saturdays a month to review your branch client statements?" I said "No problem." He said "You want $160 a week salary. When can you start?" I said, "In two weeks." He said "looking forward to working with you." I thanked him and left.

I decided to give F.I. Dupont one week notice instead of two and head down to Gainesville to spend a week with Lenny at the University of Florida, where he was studying to become a nuclear engineer. Even though he was into his books until 2:00 A.M., he was struggling with grades.

During the week, he loaned me his car and provided an ID that gave me access to the University Center. There were a few bowling lanes and several ping-pong tables available. One day, Lenny joined me for a couple of ping pong games, in which I trounced him. The UF ping pong champ and runner up were playing on the next table. Lenny suggested I play one of them. He wanted to see me get my head handed to me and I lost 21–5 to the runner up, so Lenny had the last laugh.

It was Friday, the day before I was flying back to New York. I had rarely seen Lenny during the week. I found out there was a keg party in one of the women's dorms that night and insisted he join me: "There will be no studying tonight." After a few beers, I met a student named Wally (nickname for Gwen). We talked for a few moments. Then Lenny walked over, I introduced him and left to wander around the campus looking for other parties. I eventually found my way back to Lenny's house. Months later I found out he and Wally were ride sharing back to South Florida on their breaks. Eventually they moved in together and his grades got much better, plus he wasn't studying until 2:00 A.M. any longer. Having a good woman around took the pressure off.

Back in New York, I enjoyed working for Hornblower & Weeks. The firm had most of the good ingredients that Hayden Stone had, minus the bad. I felt right at home and, excluding overtime, was earning the most money per week ever. Work was fun again.

Management assigned me several California branches and I was responsible for supporting their margin and cash account back-office needs. The three-hour time difference coast to coast did not have any effect on my working hours. I also met a few former Hayden Stone employees working in the margin department.

One Thursday afternoon, Jimenez stopped by my desk and asked if I was coming in Saturday to work on the monthly client statements. I said "Yes." He said "Bring your sneakers." That Saturday, I wore my sneakers and brought along shorts. After punching the clock at 8:00 A.M., I grabbed a coffee and donut from Chock Full O' Nuts and began reviewing the monthly statements. At 10:00, Jimenez walked by my desk and told me we were heading to the courts. About ten others got up from their desk and headed for the door. At that point, I asked "Do I have to punch out?" No, was the answer, we are driving over to some outside basketball courts near Chinatown. I quickly put on my shorts and hopped into one of the cars.

We split into four teams and played each other in rotation. There was a wide range of talent and age on the court. After playing for close to two hours, I felt that I was the second or third best player and knew I would fit in just fine. Weather permitting, we played once or twice a month. When we got back to the office, most of us would grab a Sabrett hot dog from a nearby stand, then work until 3:00 P.M. Since no one punched out when we went to play ball, I felt like a paid athlete at $10-$11 per hour— not bad.

My search for love continued and during this time I met a Jewish elementary school teacher at a nightclub. She was short, thin and loved to talk. I liked her a lot, but never got the sexual vibe I needed for love. She lived with family. For a few months we dated every Saturday night and would either go to a movie or dancing. After taking her home, often we made out on her couch, then talked for hours, sometimes until 4:00 A.M. She was bright and

I enjoyed being with her, though I didn't see her as my wife. One night I invited her to my apartment and she refused because my parents would not be home. Even though I assured her "nothing was going to happen," she said no. I needed someone who could trust me and believe my word. A few weeks later, I broke off the relationship. It was best for both of us.

I was relaxed and made new friends at Hornblower & Weeks. Herman Garcia, an experienced margin clerk, became one of my best friends. Herman was a mix of Puerto Rican and Italian with the look of Tom Jones and an easy manner that went a long way when we hit the nightclubs. Herman shared an apartment with a female roommate in Staten Island, a short ferry ride from Wall Street. Often, we would meet up on Friday nights at the Revelation or Penthouse nightclubs in Bay Ridge, Brooklyn. The Penthouse was known for its great dance floor, while the Revelation was more of a hangout bar.

It was there, when I met up with a good-looking Italian girl. After a few dates, she was open to having sex. I lost my virginity in my parent's apartment while they were away. It was one of the most awkward experiences I ever had. I was led to believe she was experienced and could provide some guidance. Though I used protection, I was never sure it was on correctly. After a few more dates, we stopped seeing each other.

My job was going well and I was promoted to assistant supervisor and given a $10 a week raise to $170. A few months later, Jimenez called me into his office and asked "Would you like to take a job as operations manager in our San Diego branch at $150 a week?" The San Diego branch manager had called and the job was mine if I wanted it. They would cover my travel expenses and help me find housing. It sounded like a great opportunity, but I had never been to California and was concerned whether I would like it out there. I thought it over and decided to decline the offer.

After work one night, I was walking from the subway when I passed an elderly woman from my 16-story apartment building. She was carrying groceries and it was a short distance from our backdoor entrance. I said "hi" and walked on. As I put my key in the lock, I heard screams. I immediately ran back and found the lady on the ground with her groceries scattered all over the street. As I helped her up, I spotted the two young men who had knocked her down and stolen her purse. They were about a half block away and I chased after them.

Just then, a police car came down the street and I ran after them yelling "Stop!" which they failed to do. I followed the two muggers until they ran into an alley. Then I ran into Kings County Hospital where they called the police. When another police car arrived, I guided them to the alley where the muggers ran. The police refused to go after them or investigate the condition of the victim. A week later I brought a few friends into the alley and we found a severely damaged purse with nothing in it. I assumed it was the stolen purse, but did not know the ladies name, so we threw it in the garbage. I was upset because maybe the lady would not have been attacked had I escorted her the short distance to our building.

Once again, I felt the police had let me down. Here I was, unarmed, chasing two muggers who could well have been armed, while two armed officers refused to pursue them. My attitude toward law enforcement sank to a new low. I knew I had to get out of that neighborhood and soon. I felt my life was in danger every day and that I could not count on the police for protection.

Life had to go on, though, so one Friday night, I drove over to the Penthouse, where I met a gorgeous Puerto Rican girl dressed in red hot pants named Maria. I saw her dancing with her sister and decided to cut in at the end of the song. Her slim body and sharp hip movement on the dance floor were exciting to watch. As she got into the music, I did my best to match her enthusiasm. During our first few dates, her older sister tagged along like a chaperon. I liked Maria a lot and felt we could be sexually compatible. She was great to kiss, but things never got more intimate.

I talked with Herman Garcia about the possibility of moving in with him and his female roommate. I wanted out of Brooklyn. Herman and I even discussed working in London as we noted many ads in the New York Times for experienced brokerage back-office personnel. The cost of moving would have been our expense so we never followed up.

Moreover, I loved working at Hornblower Weeks. The margin department was well managed and everyone seemed focused on doing their job without the normal office bullshit. Personal business discussion was kept to a minimum. Before committing to anything with Herman, I had to determine where I wanted to live and what I wanted out of life. I had one year of college and often thought about continuing my career in Florida. Hornblower had some offices there, but I was not aware of any openings in their operations.

I called Fred Broder, one of the Hayden Stone margin department managers who had originally hired me in 1968, and asked him to check on available openings in South Florida. He knew my vast experience and that I would be a big plus to any branch operation.

In 1970 Hayden, Stone & Company was acquired by Cogan, Berlin, Weill & Levitt. The result was CBWL-Hayden Stone. CBWL had been creditors to Hayden, Stone during the late sixties stock brokerage crisis. I was not surprised by the acquisition, having witnessed Hayden, Stone's problems prior to my move to F.I. Dupont.

A few days after our talk, Fred informed me of an opening for an assistant operations manager position in the Fort Lauderdale branch. That would be perfect. The only problem was the salary: $110 a week versus the $170 I was currently earning. Unlike New

York, I would not have to pay state or city payroll taxes in Florida. Also, the cost of living would be far lower. With this in mind, I asked Fred to set up an interview with the operations manager and I would drive down to Fort Lauderdale. I had a week vacation available and it was late August, a quiet time in the market.

I packed my car with a bunch of clothes, so I must have felt pretty confident about getting the job. My interview was with Thomas Goin. Tom was Irish and from the Bronx. He had just taken over the operations manager position and had been a senior margin clerk on Wall Street. We had a lot in common. We both grew up poor in violent neighborhoods. Tom was about six feet, 155 lbs., built lean and tough. He was the kind of guy I'd want on my side in a fight. He mentioned that he had his share of fights growing up. I liked him from the start and felt we would get along great. We'd be handling a 35-broker office and I knew I could count on him to have my back.

14

CBWL-HAYDEN STONE FORT LAUDERDALE: "WHO'S THE F-ING HIPPIE IN THE CAGE?"

Tom wasted no time offering me the job. After filling out the many forms, I let him know I could start in mid-September, as I needed to move and square away my finances. He was fine with everything.

From the branch, I drove a few blocks to Lauderdale-By-The Sea and parked my car. I stripped down to the bathing trunks under my suit and ran on to the beach to celebrate. My face was shining with happiness. I had made my wish come true. Brooklyn and I had separated forever, at least geographically. My parents were somewhat upset when I broke the news. Still, they raised me to be independent from age 5, so they were not surprised.

I had stayed in touch with Maria. She and her sister were flying down to Florida for a short vacation. When they arrived in Florida, I gave them a walking tour of Miami Beach. After a fun day, we kissed each other and that would be the last I would see of them.

While driving back to Lenny's house where I was temporarily staying, my car radiator blew up on I-95 South. I drove off an exit which put me right in the heart of Overtown, Miami. It was

Saturday night at around 11:00 P.M. and this was not the kind of neighborhood I wanted to be walking around in. I saw a closed AAA-authorized gas station and managed to get my smoking '68 Mustang into their parking lot. I only had about $15 on me and no credit card. I started to call Lenny from a phone booth, but before I could complete the call, a young man approached yelling threats. I ran away before completing the call. It was past midnight and I did not want to wake up Lenny and his family, so I decided to walk to Coral Way in Coral Gables where I felt safe. I spent the night walking around, dropping into the local Denny's and drinking lots of coffee.

At around 7:30 A.M. I walked southwest about 3 miles to Lenny's house, called the gas station to let them know about my car and asked when the radiator could be replaced. They were fast: it was ready later that morning. All was well. A few days later, I left my car at Lenny's and flew back to New York.

I gave Hornblower three weeks-notice as I planned my relocation to Florida. They were sad to lose me, but wished me the best. After packing a few more items, I said good-by to my family and friends, then flew back down to Miami.

I began looking for an apartment rental near Fort Lauderdale Beach. I drove through several neighborhoods looking for rental signs. I found a fully furnished efficiency which included electric for $170 a month at 90 Hendricks Isle, just off East Las Olas Boulevard. The owners were a nice young couple from Connecticut and had recently purchased the eight-unit building. The location was on a picturesque finger isle, a mile from the beach and about ten minutes from my new office on East Commercial Blvd. Some called it the Venice of America. There were huge yachts docked up and down Hendricks Isle. I couldn't believe how lucky I was to find the perfect location for a single guy.

On my first day driving to work along A1A, I was pulled over about a half mile north of Sunrise Boulevard by a Fort Lauderdale policeman who stated "You went through a red light."

I looked back and said "what light?" I knew there weren't any lights after Sunrise Boulevard until you got near Oakland Park Boulevard. What the hell was he talking about? He then told me "Do not question me. I don't want to see you again on AIA with New York plates." He did not give me a ticket, but this was not southern hospitality. I was a bit shook up, but brushed it off before reaching the office. From that day on, I used Federal Highway U.S.1 until I got my Florida plates.

When I arrived at the office, Tom introduced me to the operational employees working in the cage. I had a small desk in the same area. Later that day, Tom would acquaint me with most of the financial advisors (a.k.a. account executives) and inform them I would be servicing their accounts for any operational issues that may arise. That would include making sure their clients paid for their trades and met margin calls as needed. Over time, I found that some of the hot shot advisors did not appreciate me hounding them to get their clients' funds into the branch that were needed to meet NYSE requirements. Also, a few of them were major commodity traders. Those accounts constantly had commodity margin calls. Commodity trading was like going to Las Vegas. You could win big, but in most cases the clients lost money.

Robert (Bob) Bannister, our branch manager was tall, with short hair and always conservatively dressed. He reminded me a bit of President Richard Nixon. At that time, I had long brown hair and was wearing a polyester knit suit in maroon. When Bob first spotted me at work in the cage, he asked Tom "Who's the fucking hippie in the cage?" Tom let him know I was the new assistant operations manager and advised me of Bob's comments several months later. By then, Bob had gotten use to me and respected my work. For me, that was all that mattered. So, when Bob married a gorgeous girl in Miami, he invited the entire office including me, to their wedding.

Tom was having a house built in Palm Aire and asked if I could put him up for a few weeks. I said sure, if he didn't mind sleeping on the floor, as I was living in an efficiency. He chose to take me up on my offer. Tom's wife and son were still in New York waiting for their house to be completed.

Tom was a diabetic and liked to drink. That was a combination that spelled trouble, especially considering our work. The brokerage industry was a pressure cooker at all times.

One Sunday night we went for drinks at TJ's Lounge a few doors down from our office. At the bar we met two young African American ladies and had a chat. They were heading over to the Chateau Madrid Lounge and asked if we'd like to join them. We were short on cash, so Tom went back to the office and put an IOU in the petty cash box for about $30, which he reimbursed on Monday. We drove over to Oakland Park Boulevard and North Federal Highway to join them.

The Chateau Madrid was a late-night club located on the top floor of a circular eight-story building. They served food, drinks and often had live bands. That night they had a great R & B group performing to a mostly empty lounge. The two ladies were waiting for us at the entrance and we got a booth, ordered drinks and joined another couple on the dance floor. When we walked back to our booth, we heard shouts from about five Latin men sitting at the bar telling us "You no can sit together." At first, we ignored their racist shouts, but they kept it up. In defiance, we got back on the floor and did some bump and grind dancing, which further inflamed the racists. They yelled at us to get off the dance floor, but we only went back to our booth when we were worn out from dancing.

Tom started to have a problem with his diabetes and went up to the bartender for a glass of water and a bite of something to help get it under control. The bartender, egged on by the Latin patrons, refused Tom's request, so he picked up a chair and threatened the bartender. A tense situation was developing and

I pictured an angry mob throwing us through the large glass windows of the eighth floor. Fortunately, the bartender came to his senses and provided Tom with what he needed before anyone got hurt. We paid our check and said good night.

During the week, I arranged a Saturday dinner date with my dance partner from that night. She liked Chinese food and I recommended an old-time diner located on a traffic island on South Federal Highway just north of the Fort Lauderdale Airport. The place was empty. When we sat down, there were three waitresses standing near the back of the diner talking and staring at us. It was obvious they did not want to serve a mixed couple. After over fifteen minutes waiting for a menu, my date and I left. It was 1971, but racism was still rampant throughout Florida. We drove over to Lester's Diner on State Road 84 and had dinner along with one of their bottomless cups of coffee.

After dinner, she proposed heading back to her house off West Sunrise Boulevard. Upon arrival, she poured a few drinks. As we began kissing, she suggested we head to her bedroom where I could get undressed. When I was down to my underpants, she emerged from the bathroom in skimpy lingerie. We continued to kiss and caress. The second I was about to remove my briefs, her phone rang. It was her ex-boyfriend who told her he wanted to see her now. She apologized and told me "You better leave." With no hesitation, I dressed and was out the door in a couple of minutes. Otherwise, my exit may have been through the window.

It was a night to remember. It began with white racism and finished with a failed attempt at having sex. I felt I had missed out on something good, but on the plus side, I didn't get killed.

Tom often said if you want sex without obligations, date older women. One night at TJ's, I met a 26-year-old widow who lived in Hollywood with her five-year-old son. She seemed reserved, almost sad and I learned she was recovering from a hysterectomy. We began dating and, although she wanted to have sex right away, it had to wait due to her recent surgery. On our third date, after dinner at a restaurant, we went back to her single-family home and had sex on the couch. I felt she was very nervous and concerned whether she had healed properly so I took things slowly and she seemed to be ok. After a few more dates, she told me she needed to find a man who would settle down with her and be a father to her son. At 21, I was not ready for anything like that, so we ended our relationship.

Tom's new house was complete and his family joined him from New York. He seemed happier and more relaxed. Before they had arrived, Tom had a DUI and was locked up in the Lauderdale-By-The-Sea jail for one night. He was a diabetic and at one point they deprived him of insulin. This led to a fight between Tom and one or more officers. When I saw him, he was bruised all over from numerous kicks and punches he'd received during his stay. Years ago, that small town was known as a ticket trap. You could get a ticket for being five miles over the speed limit or changing lanes when the right lane suddenly became a designated turn lane. The flawed road design probably made the town enough money to pay all the judges' and police officers' salaries.

My nephew, Glen, was born just before the Christmas holidays and with my birthday coming up, I flew to New York to see family, friends and former co-workers at Hornblower & Weeks. There would be several parties at my old firm to attend. I let Herman Garcia know I was flying in so he'd let me know when the margin department had their party. Christmas, Hanukkah and New Years in New York City is the best. No matter your religion, there is something for everyone to enjoy at that time of year.

I arrived at LaGuardia Airport wearing a long overcoat and holding a straw hat, hand made on Fort Lauderdale Beach. There was a gypsy cab at the terminal who offered to drive me to my parent's apartment in Brooklyn. Just minutes earlier I'd been turned down by a licensed taxi driver. It was after dark and he didn't want to go into that neighborhood.

At the building, my brother was just getting out of the elevator as I was getting in. He looked like hell. His newborn son was fine and being watched by our Aunt Esther, but his wife was not well and was at Kings County Hospital. He left and I went to my parent's apartment on the 7th floor. They were thrilled to see me and we got caught up. I saw Glen the next day, then went with my brother to see his wife who was struggling with many issues.

Thursday, December 23rd, was my birthday and the Hornblower margin department was having their Christmas party. Dressed up in my long gray overcoat and wearing my straw hat, I hopped the IRT to Wall Street. The stares I received were of curiosity, amusement and bewilderment. The passengers must have wondered if a new kind of nut case was riding the trains. No one bothered me or said anything. It was probably my safest subway ride ever. I was smiling knowing that what I wore represented winter cold in New York and year-round heat in Fort Lauderdale. I had chosen a sunny new life.

When I showed up at the Hornblower margin department I was greeted with hugs and kisses. They missed me and I missed them. It was only midday, but the Christmas celebration was already in full swing with drinks and food everywhere. Being my 22nd birthday didn't hurt either. The more everyone drank, the more kisses I got, a great deal for me. My straw hat was a big hit. After all, they knew I was a little bit crazy and liked to have fun.

Hornblower shut down their offices early as the stock market would be closed Friday December 24th. I joined Herman Garcia, for the short ferry ride to Staten Island where he lived. When we left the office, we were feeling no pain, but by the time the ferry left the port, I sobered up as soon as the winds hit my face. A few hours later, I took the ferry back to Manhattan. Sadly, I would never see my friend, Herman, again.

Before flying back to Fort Lauderdale, I spent a couple of days with my parents. I was concerned about my brother and his family health issues. All I could do was provide emotional support. I couldn't wait to say "goodbye" to New York and return to my new life.

There were three reasons I moved to Florida. The first was to get away from a crime-infested environment. Second was to leave the cold weather. Third, was to return to college as a full-time night student, which I didn't believe I could accomplish in New York.

Back in Broward, I declared Florida residency by filing an affidavit of domicile and acquired state license plates for my Ford Mustang. Now I was officially a Floridian.

15

BROWARD COMMUNITY COLLEGE JANUARY 1972–DECEMBER 1974: "HE'S A BUM"

B roward CC Davie campus was about a 30-minute drive from my office. I enrolled in four courses which ran 7:00 to 9:00 P.M. Monday through Thursday. Having Tom as my boss helped. His philosophy was simple: get the job done. He wasn't going to hold me to the time on the clock. If I had to leave an hour earlier to do some last-minute prepping for an exam, Tom would cover for me. If I was needed to help him with a project, I always found time.

English 102 turned out to be the strangest and most diffi-cult course. The teacher, Ms. Koenig, was single, an attractive, dyed blonde in her thirties. For her first class, she invited a male poet acquaintance to give us a reading in a small auditorium. The thickly bearded poet, began by updating us on his personal history.

He told us he had been married with two young children and had chosen to leave his family and a job where he had earned over $100,000 a year. His new life was traveling to college cam-puses all over the country and reading his poetry. The piece he recited centered on his thoughts of committing suicide. I lis-tened in disgust. It seemed as if he was using my classmates to work out his mental problems. He needed help for sure, but we were not going to provide the answers.

He left and we returned to our classroom. Ms. Koenig asked what we thought of him. I was in the back of the room and waited for someone to respond. When no one did, I made the mistake of raising my hand. "I think he's a bum who gave up all responsibilities to have a good time traveling to college campuses seeking women and drugs." As I remember, he confessed a taste for the latter, as well. Several students laughed, but I wasn't trying to be funny. I thought Ms. Koenig wanted an honest answer. From the look on her face and the sudden silence, I realized he may have been something more than a "friend." Time ran out on the class and I could not wait to get out of there.

My English class became a nightmare. Ms. Koenig had me read out loud from William Shakespeare's "Hamlet" in several classes. She seemed intent on humiliating me for calling her poet friend "a bum." However, her strategy backfired because I enjoyed playing the roles even if I didn't always pronounce the words correctly. The better I did, the more disturbed she seemed to become.

Ms. Koenig required a term paper which would be a major factor in our final grade. You were allowed to select your own topic, pending her approval. I was working full time in the stock brokerage industry and asked her if I could choose that as my topic. She said "Yes." Her only other requirement was that it be about ten pages long. That wasn't a problem for me. I had access to books at work and, given my prior Wall Street experience, I felt this would be easy. So, I was shocked at our final class, when she handed back the papers and at the top of mine was "F" and the word "plagiarism" both in red. At the time, I didn't know what the word meant and asked another student for a definition. I was incensed and as soon as the class was dismissed, I asked her what was plagiarized? She claimed the copy was too good and had to have been taken directly out of a book. I said "Show me what I plagiarized." She refused. Instead, she said "I'm going to the dean's office" to which I said "Great, I'm coming with you". She insisted I wait in the hallway. She returned within five minutes and she said she would change the "F" to an "incomplete." I added seven to ten more footnotes, though I felt they were not required as the information was common knowledge in the industry. But apparently this satisfied her and she gave me a "C" for my course grade. I doubt she ever spoke to the department dean, but I decided not to file a formal complaint for a better grade. I continued to take two to four classes for the next couple of semesters.

In the spring of 1972 Tom approached me with an opportunity I couldn't turn down. Business was slow and I was about to be let go. However, one of the firm's biggest producers (trading both stocks and commodities) appeared to be having a large number of clerical errors and needed help. The firm wanted someone who was licensed to become his protégé and clear up his paperwork problems. Without a four-year degree or NASD license, CBWL Hayden Stone would not sponsor me for the New York Exchange license.

We had a new branch manager whose brother-in-law was also a branch manager in a small over-the-counter brokerage named C&M Securities located in downtown Miami. He agreed to hire me and, as a favor to our branch manager, sponsor me for the NASD exam, which I successfully passed. I worked with C&M for about four months and learned some sales techniques. I stayed in touch with Tom and waited for his call to return to CBWL Hayden Stone in my new protégé capacity. Late that summer I got the call and was welcomed back.

I would be working with a big producer, Mike, and earning $800 a month, a huge salary at the time, which came out of Mike's paycheck. He was single, a generous, hardworking man, who I believe was independently wealthy. Mike liked to trade in and out of various commodities for his clients and himself. At times he seemed brilliant, a word I don't use loosely, so I tried to learn as much as I could by watching him closely. When his clients visited the office, Mike always introduced me as "an associate." I spent about a month poring over workbooks for my New York Stock Exchange license, which was required by NYSE member firms. This was in addition to the NASD and Florida State licenses I had already obtained at C & M Securities.

One Friday night, I stopped by to see my friends Joe and Barbara at their apartment. Both had once lived in the next-door apartment to me at Hendricks Isle. Joe was working late and Barbara offered to make me spaghetti, which I could not turn down. After dinner, I decided to go to TJ's for a few drinks. While standing at the bar I noticed two well-dressed women walk in. Both were very pretty. One was a 25-year-old blonde, who I found out was divorced with a five-year-old daughter, while the other appeared to be three to four years younger and was magnificent in a low-cut designer dress. Her name was Jean and I found out that her mother, once a designer for Oscar de la Renta, had made the dress for her. We danced some and when it was time to leave, she asked me to drive her home. Jean lived with her mother, step-father, brother and step-sister in Plantation. As I spent more time with Jean, I noticed the other woman who had driven herself home that night, also seemed to be part of the household.

When I pulled up that first night to Jean's driveway, we got into some very heavy necking and agreed to go out the following night. When, I arrived at her home, she had a girlfriend there eyeing me up to see if I was appropriate for Jean. I guessed I passed the test, because Jean went to bed with me that night and it was very special. At that point I saw her the next night and then we began seeing each other four to five times a week, even living together for a few months. I was totally in love. But Jean wasn't ready to settle down with one person, so, as much as I loved her, it was a very difficult period. Over the next two years, we were on and off. We always remained friends and I even took her to Montego Bay for a weekend after we finally broke up.

I registered for several more night classes at Broward Community College for the fall term. I saw a notice announcing walk-on tryouts for the men's basketball team. My dream was to play college basketball. I had been running about a mile or more per day and felt I was in good shape, so I showed up for the tryout. The coach had 10 guys on scholarship and two non-scholarship openings available. I scrimmaged with the team and, although I took just one shot—a running hook shot, which I made—I out-hustled several of the 18 to 19-year-old players. Afterward, the coach called the players over to the bench and praised my effort. "We had a guy who showed up today and out-hustled almost every one of you." Later, the coach and I talked about my personal situation. He offered me one of the two spots available and I was thrilled, however I would have to switch to daytime classes and quit my job. A week earlier I had taken the NYSE exchange exam and expected the results any day. Moreover, I had very little in savings and wouldn't be eligible for a scholarship. I told him my situation and said I would call him as soon as I had the results. Two days later, I learned I passed the exam. I called the coach and thanked him for giving me a chance to play on his team. I told him "You have no idea how badly I want to play for you, but I need to earn a living and don't want to go into debt." He wished me the best. That would be my last shot at playing college ball.

At work, my focus was on helping Mike with his clients. During that era, I felt commodity trading and rules seemed to be weak. After all, I had been hired to help Mike avoid commodity trade errors. But were they errors? I noticed Mike would place an order for, say, 25 to 50 contracts of a specific commodity (cocoa, silver, hogs, cattle, corn, wheat, etc.). He would buy long (meaning he'd own the position) or sell short (meaning he'd sell a commodity he didn't have a position in with the idea of buying it back at a lower price later on for a profit). Normally these orders were for around seven discretionary accounts, meaning the client had signed paperwork giving Mike discretion for their commodity trades.

When Mike placed a buy or sell order for the contracts, the trade was almost always done on one order ticket. He would sometimes wait up to 30 minutes after the trade executed, before giving me a list of client account names and numbers to match the executed order. I would then bring the list to the wire operator to input back to the home office.

1972–73 was an era of very volatile commodity prices. A prime example was the U.S.-Russian wheat deal in 1972 in which the USA subsidized the Russian purchase of 10 million tons of wheat. Consequently, wheat and corn prices were often up at the maximum of the daily exchange limit. Inflation was hitting the U.S. consumer hard.

As a result of such volatility, you often knew whether a commodity trade placed at 10:00 A.M. was a successful trade by 10:20 A.M. By closing out the position, you could create a nice profit. Therefore, by submitting the list of account names and numbers on buy or sell short orders twenty to thirty minutes *after* the executions, a trader could determine which clients received his winning or losing trades. Although, I believe what Mike was doing was probably unethical, to the best of my knowledge, back in the early 70s the practice was not illegal.

When a client complained about a number of losing trades, Mike would have me put some of the trades into the house error account and have the trade losses charged to him as errors. Slowly I realized why I was hired to work with Mike. The firm wanted to believe what he reported to be errors were actually errors. I knew they were not, but couldn't say anything at the risk of being fired. At this point, Mike wanted me to get licensed in commodities. I worried the firm would use me as a scapegoat to protect Mike if I got my license, so I intentionally failed the exam. After giving up my chance to play college basketball, the last thing I wanted to do was risk losing my NYSE and NASD licenses. I certainly didn't want to be implicated in a trading scandal.

One evening in 1973, I went to the Banana Boat lounge on East Commercial Blvd in Fort Lauderdale. There was a woman sitting on a bar stool who had been doing some heavy drinking. As I walked by the bar, she got up, put her arms around me and began to kiss me. I had never seen her before, but what the hell. She was a few years older and after talking for a while, she asked me to drive her home. As soon as we got there, she began taking off her clothes and invited me into her bedroom. When I woke up the next morning her cat was in bed with us. She wasn't bad looking, but she'd looked even better the night before. I learned she had a son who was staying overnight with a friend or maybe her ex-husband. After three or four dates, she was exploring the idea of me moving in together, but I was not interested.

Our final date was a bombshell. We'd just had sex and were lying in bed, when she told me she was a paralegal. She said her law firm was filing suit on behalf of one or more commodity clients who had lost money with a brokerage firm. I asked her who the firm was and she named the firm and account representative. I thought I was about to have a stroke. She had named Mike.

I spent the weekend trying to figure out what to do next. Could I afford to give up the $800-a-month salary if I left Mike? Should I let Mike know about the pending law suit? Should I inform the new branch manager of what I knew and would he allow me to go on my own as a personal representative or would he fire me?

Watergate was all over the news and business was slowing down as traders were more concentrated on the news than buying stocks or bonds. On Monday, after weighing all my options, I told Mike I was going to split from him and go on my own. He was in disbelief that I would give up my salary. I never let on about the pending lawsuit to anyone. The manager, Creed, was upset with me for leaving Mike, but agreed to continue me on commission. Life was about to change once again. My new office was a small cubicle in a loft overlooking the boardroom. I was lucky: the young gentleman sitting to my right was the regional municipal bond trader. He taught me almost everything he knew about municipals. It was great having another mentor shoulder to shoulder, as I soaked in everything he had to say.

One day at the office, a young stockbroker approached me for a most unusual favor. He had been told that I lived alone and I believed he lived with another woman. He mentioned two friends, Las Vegas showgirls, were arriving in Fort Lauderdale for a few days. He was planning a threesome and asked if he could use my apartment. As a sweetener, I was told I'd be welcome to "join in." The only problem was I had an important economics exam the evening of the rendezvous. His friends showed up at the office the morning of the main event and they were absolutely gorgeous. One looked like Abbe Lane, the singer who had been married to Latin bandleader Xavier Cugat, while the other was a beautiful blonde. Both had great figures and would be returning to Las Vegas the following day. I gave the broker a spare key to my apartment and told him I should be back by 9:00 P.M. After finishing my exam, without even pausing to review my answers, I hurried home. All I found were disheveled bed sheets with sex stains and the three of them gone. The next day I got my key back with barely a thank you. I asked why didn't they stick around until I got there and was told they were "done." All I could think was how much I had sacrificed for an economics exam, which, by the way, I passed with a B. Fifteen years later I ran into that stockbroker at a business event and, when I brought up that evening, he looked at me blankly and said "I don't remember." But I do.

The Yom Kippur War began Oct 6th and lasted through Oct 25th, 1973. Israel was attacked primarily by Egypt and Syria. In addition, eight other countries provided military forces against Israel. The United States provided major support for Israel, while the Soviet Union helped supply its enemies. Israel survived the war, but it wasn't without a great number of casualties on both sides.

On October 10th, 1973 Vice President Spiro Agnew resigned following reports of bribery, extortion and tax fraud. Gerald R. Ford took over as Vice President on December 6, 1973.

In mid-October, I dated a Japanese teacher for about five weeks. She liked dancing, was a talented artist and enjoyed going to places like the Vizcaya Museum & Gardens in Miami. I loved her sense of fun. She had graduated from Boston College and was living with her American parents. She informed me early on that she was going to spend a year in Japan teaching English, beginning in December 1973. We chose not to get intimate, but got to know each other, with the idea of resuming our relationship when she returned from Japan. We got along so great I felt it was worth seeing where we would be after a year apart. Before departing for Japan, she gave me a piece of her artwork as a "thank you" for the time I'd spent with her.

As all this was happening, the Arab nations within OPEC placed an oil embargo on the U.S. that lasted from October 19, 1973 into March 1974. Gasoline prices skyrocketed at the pumps, while everyone waited in long gas lines hoping to get ten gallons of gasoline before the tanks ran out. While the gasoline crisis was going on, we were still dealing with Watergate and the Vietnam War. On March 13, 1974 the Dow Jones Industrial Average stood at 577.60 at the close of the business day.

The United States was headed into a recession with high inflation, so I had to ask myself, "how do I do business?" I wondered if it had been a smart thing to leave Mike and go on commission versus the $800 salary. I was scared that I might fail and have to return to New York and the back offices of Wall Street. The stock market was sinking day after day with very little volume being traded. I spent most of my work day cold calling on municipal bonds. I would offer free booklets on municipals and call back a week later after mailing them out to prospects. Most individuals hung up the phone as soon as they heard I was a stockbroker. Other brokers I knew were working two jobs. One ran a bar at night. Others worked in family businesses, as well. Branch managers knew how tough it was. The established stockbrokers had clients that could keep them in business, while most like myself did not. At least I did not have a family to feed.

I still had to eat. While working as a stockbroker full time and attending college at night, I worked part-time as a pizza delivery man. Within two to four months after we had parted ways, Mike left the firm. I can only assume he was asked to resign because of his pending lawsuits. I called some of Mike's clients I had previously serviced and, from time to time, they threw a few trades my way, helping me get through June 1974. I was on a draw of $600 a month. In order to earn that $600, I had to produce at least $1,800 in gross commissions. I managed to do that in June 1974 with a $2,000 gross commission month, but because I hadn't earned my draw for the prior several months, they chose not to pay me anything for June, not even the minimum wage of $300 for the month. I protested and got the $300. After my battle with management, I resigned and concentrated on college where I was entering some of my tougher math classes.

There was a broker who dealt in commodities and stocks in the office named Jack Efird. Jack was an honest broker and I knew I could trust him to take over my 15 to 20 active accounts. Joseph P., the new branch manager, approved the account transfer. Jack and I remained friends for many decades. Jack rarely solicited those accounts, but managed to do a small amount of business with them. This would prove to be a smart move, because less than a year later, I reclaimed those accounts from Jack when I went to work for Southeast Securities Inc.

On August 8, 1974, President Richard M. Nixon resigned. Vice President Gerald R. Ford would now become the 38th president of the United States on August 9, 1974. Even though Watergate and the OPEC oil embargo were over, our nation still faced huge uncertainty. The U.S. economy was stagnant at best and it would be some time before oil prices got back to normal.

Around October 1974 I was hired as a trainee by Management Recruiters, a personnel firm. My salary was $75 a week, plus commissions. I could earn commissions by getting a signed contract from a company to hire one of our firm's applicants. I spent most of my day cold calling major corporations trying to get an "in" with their personnel or human resource departments. Due to the recession, there were very few management jobs available, as everyone was trying to hold onto their positions. As a result, I failed to make any commissions, though my company had no problem keeping me on. They hoped the economy would get better. It didn't.

During the second week of December, I stopped by the Banana Boat Lounge for a drink and ran into one of the guys I had played basketball with. He was sitting with Cathy, a pretty blond Delta flight attendant, who asked me to join them at their table. When he left for the evening, she invited me to a party to be held at her home the following Sunday, December 15th. She gave me his telephone number and told me to call him for her address and directions. I was looking forward to seeing her and wondered whether she was flirting with me by extending her invitation. On Sunday I called my basketball acquaintance and asked him for Cathy's address and what to bring. He told me that the party was going to be small, just Cathy and him and another couple. From his tone, I could tell I was not welcome. No address was provided and I never ran into Cathy again.

Who could have known that my life would change forever because of a guy who was afraid of possible competition?

16

CATHERINE ENTERS THE PICTURE

Rather than let my disappointment get the best of me, I decided to go to Pete & Lenny's Disco in Fort Lauderdale that Sunday night. I arrived well dressed in a British style wool blazer at 9:00 P.M. It was nearly empty when I noticed a group of seven or eight young men and women enter the disco and head to the other end of the bar. One tall blonde in the group caught my attention. I wanted to dance with her, but I was concerned: one of the guys might have been a boyfriend and I wasn't looking for a fight, so I waited about 10–15 minutes before approaching her. If any of the guys in her group were with her, it didn't appear that anyone was paying her any special attention. I made my move and asked her to dance, which she accepted. We danced to two songs. The last one was Rock the Boat by Hues Corporation and afterward I bought the two of us a drink and joined her and her group.

Her name was Catherine and she had moved to Fort Lauderdale from Laguna Beach two years earlier. I was surprised I hadn't seen her in a lounge before. It turned out she had an artist friend visiting from North Carolina, and a group of friends decided to hit a few lounges in Fort Lauderdale. Catherine was not into the bar scene like I was. In fact, if I had been at Cathy the flight attendant's party, I most likely would have never met her. Catherine told me the group was heading for another bar.

I was not asked to join them so I asked for her phone number which she refused to write down. Instead, she quickly rattled off a number. I told her I would call her Tuesday night. She probably never expected to hear from me.

Shortly after they left, I went to my car and wrote down the number: 305-523-9176. Catherine had no way to know that I was a numbers person. I may not remember names, but I have a great memory for numbers. I saw my mother the next day and mentioned to her, I had an interesting night and met someone special. Tuesday evening, I called and Catherine picked up. I was happy she answered and even happier when she agreed to go out with me to see a band called the Impact of Brass. I had seen the group in Miami a few times when I went to Miami Dade JC in 1968–69. They played Chicago-style music (lots of brass) and were well known in the Miami area. Catherine claimed to be familiar with the group, though in reality she'd never heard of them. This was about to make for an interesting first date.

Saturday night I picked up Catherine at her apartment near Ft. Lauderdale beach and began my drive to the Crossway Motor Inn in Miami, where the Impact of Brass band was playing. It hadn't crossed my mind that going all the way to Miami for a first date and then pulling into a motel parking lot might frighten her. Worse yet, we were only five minutes from Miami International Airport on Le Jeune Road. In the lobby I walked up to the front desk to find out the location of the band. Catherine thought I was trying to get a room for the night and perhaps rape her. We walked down the lobby hallway to a closed door where a man standing outside advised us there was a three-drink minimum per person. I paid for the six drinks and the attendant opened the thick door behind him. We could see and hear the Impact of Brass immediately. I noticed the relief on Catherine's face. However, her stomach was so upset, she could only have one drink. Over the next several hours, I wound up drinking five

Heinekens. She loved the music, but didn't reveal until months later how scared she had been.

After driving her home, we kissed at the door and I told her I would call her during the week and perhaps we could together enjoy the bottle of wine I brought her. Christmas was a few days away and after Catherine agreed to see me again, I bought her a crystal penguin as a Christmas gift. We started seeing each other several days a week and spent New Year's Eve 1974 together having dinner on Commercial Boulevard at the Raindancer, then celebrating at Stan's Lounge on the Intracoastal. Although I slept over that night in her bed, we did not go all the way. Still, I felt we were getting closer and would both know when it was the right time.

In late January, a French-Canadian co-worker, suggested I give Catherine a French maid black lingerie outfit as an enticing gift. It worked. A month later I moved into her apartment and our relationship blossomed. Shortly after, we spent my last $75 on a one-night stay in Key West. It was our first trip together away from home and everything went quite well.

With the economy in a severe recession, I knew I had to leave Management Recruiters and start a new career, where I could have stable earnings and still have opportunities to grow.

17

YOU'RE HIRED

February turned out to be a combination new beginning and re-entry into my old stock brokerage life. In the Sun Sentinel classifieds, I found a job listing for a construction reporter with Dodge Reports (a division of McGraw Hill). The company was interviewing that day at their Wilton Manors office and agreed to meet that morning. There was another listing that also caught my eye: for a small, family-run NASD member firm named Southeast Securities Inc. The company was headed by Ted Kata and his wife, Mary. Three wonderful daughters, Anita, Arlene and Andrea "Andy", all going to college, helped with the back-office paperwork. The brokerage was run out of a duplex style home that Ted owned and was, by coincidence, also located in Wilton Manors, just 3–4 blocks away from the Dodge Report office. I set up a 3:00 interview with Ted.

After meeting with Dodge management, they offered me the job and I accepted. They liked that I had sales experience, an Associate degree from Broward Community College and could type. The salary was not good, but the benefits were great: a company car which I could use for personal needs, health coverage and help with college tuition. My job would take me out of the office about 60% of the time while covering building departments from Fort Lauderdale through Lake Worth. I reported on upcoming housing projects, commercial buildings and government related buildings. Those reports were sold to subscribers who might bid on a job or inquire if their services were needed. Subscribers included general and sub-contractors, along with material suppliers.

After landing the Dodge Report job, I still interviewed with Ted Kata at the brokerage. I wanted to see what Ted had to offer. He sounded like a real nice guy. On my way over, I got a flat tire on my 1968 Ford Mustang. I called Ted and said I would be there as soon as my tire was fixed. He said "Yes, no problem." I got there around 4:00 and we chatted for over an hour. I went over my stock brokerage experience, explained my financial situation and advised him of the Dodge Report job offer I had accepted earlier in the day.

Ted had about five to six older stockbrokers working part-time at his duplex. I let him know I would be on the road 60% of the time and could come by to do business during lunch or after work or whenever I could get over to his office. I wanted to keep my brokerage licenses active and needed to be registered with a broker-dealer. Ted hired me and we drank a Polish beer as a toast to my future with his firm. I immediately felt at home. I would spend all my leisure time reconnecting with the stock trading accounts I had left in the care of Jack Efird at CBWL Hayden Stone eight months earlier. All of these clients returned to me and were happy to hear I was back in business.

Wow, what a day. I now had two jobs and, once again, a new beginning. All I had to do was keep Dodge Reports from finding out that I had a part-time job just a few blocks away. My training at Dodge included being taken around to all the cities and towns I would cover. I was part of a five-person office which included a receptionist and a salesman. There were two other reporters who covered architects and engineers in Broward and Palm Beach County. I found my job was very easy and, while on the road, I often stopped in at various brokerage offices to see the tape in the boardroom and keep up with the stock market.

There were no cell phones in those days. If a stock caught my attention, I would stop by Southeast Securities at lunch and call a client or two with a recommendation. I made a few extra dollars in commissions that helped supplement my Dodge salary.

After receiving my first few paychecks, I took Catherine for a long weekend to Great Harbour Cay in the Bahamas. A few years earlier I had obtained a free voucher for a 4-day, 3-night stay in a villa at the island's only resort. The voucher was still valid. We were supposed to listen to a 90-minute sales pitch, but the resort was having financial problems and did not put us through the hassle.

The only airline that flew to this small island was Mackey Airlines, a Fort Lauderdale-based airline founded by Col. Joseph C. Mackey. When I booked, I was under the impression it was a non-stop flight; however, I was wrong. When the 40-plus passenger, twin engine Convair 440 left Fort Lauderdale for Miami, I found out we were also stopping in Miami and Bimini before going on to Great Harbour Cay. Shortly after takeoff to Miami, the plane started to shake and the air conditioning was turned off. The single flight attendant was buckled up and looked concerned. No announcements were made. We approached the Miami runway and seemed to be about 30 feet from the ground when the plane went back up. No one understand the turnaround. Finally, we were informed that due to mechanical difficulties, we were heading back to Fort Lauderdale. By now, the plane was really shaking and the look on the flight attendant's face was one of outright fear.

The plane landed safely in Fort Lauderdale and we were asked to disembark. There were a few men wearing red jackets standing near the plane who rushed us inside the airport. I overheard one of them say that one of the two engines had failed. I was relieved to be back on solid ground, but was concerned that my trip had blown up and angry at the lack of information. Inside the terminal, I immediately went up to the agent behind the counter. He informed me we were now booked on a non-stop flight to Great Harbour Cay leaving in about four hours on an eight-seat Cessna. I asked the agent if one of the two engines had failed and he acknowledged "Yes." I said "Why didn't the plane land in Miami?" He responded, "because our mechanics are in Fort Lauderdale." At that point, I went crazy as I realized the airline jeopardized the lives of its passengers to save a few bucks. Catherine yelled at me to cool it and someone else tried to calm me down from going over the counter. In the end, I stopped myself or no doubt I would have been arrested.

Later that afternoon, we flew on to Great Harbour Cay and had a magnificent weekend. The villa, food and entertainment were great. The pure white sand and clear water was delightful. We were alone and had a chance to enjoy each other in privacy. When we got home, we realized we had experienced something very special that ranged from fear of dying in an airline crash to loving each other even more.

Both my new jobs were progressing and, although I had hardly any money, I proposed to Catherine in August 1975. She accepted. Maybe what did it was that poem I wrote a few months earlier:

> The Sleep
> by Jerry Allan Wolff
>
> As I go to bed each night
> There is the closing of the light
> I can feel the loveliness of touch
> My body excites to a rush
> The dreams of violence I cannot stop
> Surroundings do not allow for such a sleep.

Catherine was so impressed she even had me send it into Harper's Magazine, and even though they didn't say "yes", she did. We went to Carroll's Jewelers in Fort Lauderdale and picked out a lovely diamond engagement ring. The cost was $400. I put

$40 down and paid off the balance, $30 a month over the next year.

A month prior to our wedding, we flew out to Los Angeles so I could meet her parents and three younger sisters for the first time. Her sister Elizabeth (also known as "Liz" or "Leez") had purchased four $5 tickets to the Lakers-Celtic game through Ticketron. The night of the game, I advised Liz to get there early because it was a big game – it was Christmas time— and we may have problems parking. I didn't know that Liz was chronically late, and believed her when she said "Don't worry, we won't have any problem." Wrong. We had to park over ten blocks away from the Forum in a neighborhood that was not the safest. We arrived at our seats just as the game tipped off. There was only one problem. All of our seats were taken. Ticketron had sold duplicate tickets for our seats. The usher told us to go the ticket office to get things straightened out as fans yelled "Sit down." We went back to the ticket office and after arguing with the office manager for ten minutes, he told us the four people in our seats had been moved and we could go back. Once again, we hiked back to our seats and found them still occupied. Fans continued to yell at us and we went back down to the ticket office. I spotted the office manager hiding behind a cabinet and I lost my cool when he sent out a young woman to tell me they would not provide us with any seats. They claimed Ticketron was responsible and there was nothing they could do. I advised them that Ticketron was acting as their agent, a fact they didn't want to hear. I began knocking on the glass ticket window as Catherine's sisters edged away from me. I yelled that they were committing fraud. Finally, we were given four different seats in the top row of the "nose bleed" section of the Forum. We sat down with just one-minute left in the first half. From that distance I could hardly see the players as I did not have my glasses. I wrote a letter to Ticketron and months later Liz got a $20 refund for the tickets. Most important of all, her sisters realized I would stand up for my rights and welcomed me into their family.

Before we left Los Angeles, we took a drive to Laguna Beach and in one of the town's hippie boutiques purchased a flowing cotton dress made in India that would become Catherine's wedding "gown." It was quite a bargain at $16.

We chose January 24, 1976 for our wedding to be held at Colee Hammock Park in Fort Lauderdale. It was the site where the Colee family was killed by Seminole Indians in 1842. The location is on the New River surrounded by trees trailing Spanish Moss. We had 40 guests. My co-worker and friend, Richard A. Mills, a former college basketball player and Fort Lauderdale City Commissioner, arranged for Judge Floyd Vance Hull to marry us, and I paid the judge $15. We catered New York style deli from Pomperdale in Fort Lauderdale and ordered a wedding cake for pick up from a local bakery. Taylor Rental was our source for tables and chairs. We donated $50 to the First Presbyterian Church, 401 SE 15th Avenue, to use their parking and provide access to their bathrooms. I also called the city to make sure the sprinklers would stay off during our wedding. My best man, Joe, along with his future wife, Barbara, served cocktails. "Barb" had been a barmaid at the old Bachelor III nightclub in Fort Lauderdale. The wedding started at 2:00 P.M. and if you arrived two minutes late you missed the ceremony. Judge Hull asked Catherine and myself a couple of questions. We both said "I do," and we were done. Neither of us had any additional words for our ceremony. Friends of ours, Tom and Sarah Flood, arrived at 2:02 and were shocked they had missed the ceremony, but I think they enjoyed the celebration in the park.

18

HIGHER EDUCATION AT FLORIDA ATLANTIC UNIVERSITY

A year earlier I had completed my Associate of Arts degree at Broward Community College. Now I felt ready to go back to college at night for my Bachelor's degree. At the brokerage, Arlene Kata suggested I take a course at Florida Atlantic University (FAU) to see if the environment was a good fit. She suggested a financial course that was held on Saturdays. The professor, Dr. Thomas Laird, was just the kind of teacher I needed. He gave me the confidence to continue my education. He encouraged class participation and I felt he respected my views. This respect was something I often did not get from other teachers who regarded me as challenging the status quo. Dr. Laird gave me a "B" and I felt ready to start taking a couple of courses. Over the next few years, I took two more classes from Dr. Laird and will always be grateful to him for being the right professor at the right time in my life.

Several years earlier, Catherine had completed a Bachelor of Arts degree with a major in English from California State College at Los Angeles. I suggested that while I was going for my Bachelor degree in Business Administration, she should work for a Masters of Arts degree from FAU at the same time. She agreed, providing I would drive her to the Boca Raton campus, where most of her classes were held, while most of my business courses were a distance away at the Ft. Lauderdale campus. I felt this was fair, considering she was working full time as copy chief for Levitz Furniture, a major corporation in Miami.

This worked great with Catherine getting all As in her classes, while I accumulated credits maintaining a B average. Considering virtually all our classes were at night, it was no easy task after working full-time jobs during the day. We were young and weren't afraid to work hard and maybe stay up late.

In late 1976, we vacationed for a week in Mexico City, staying at the centrally located Hotel Reforma, a lovely old building. Every morning the elevator operator would hand me an American newspaper as we went for breakfast. We were there at a historic time around November 22, 1976, the Mexican Peso had a dramatic 64% decline in value overnight from 12.50 pesos to 20.50 pesos to the dollar. Currency exchanges were forced to close during that economic crisis. We had just arrived, so our dollars were in high demand. I remember having dinner at Delmonicos, a renowned restaurant. We had delicious steaks, potatoes, and an excellent bottle of Bordeaux and the cost was only $20. I gave the waiter a $10 tip which was greatly appreciated. Service had been impeccable.

While in Mexico, we toured the ruins of Teotihuacan, an Aztec Pre-Columbian masterpiece of pyramids, including the Temple of Quetzalcoatl. The next day, we drove to Taxco and stopped to tour the Cacahuamilpa Caverns, magnificent cave systems that go deep underground and were not completely explored. The altitude was almost 6,000 feet above sea level so our guide gave us a few minutes to stretch our legs before entering the caves. I played a short basketball game just outside the caverns with a few locals, but was immediately out of breath. Even more breathtaking, though, were the cavern interiors.

We arrived in the beautiful colonial town, Taxco, well known for its silver crafts in .925 pure sterling silver mined in the

surrounding hills. We discovered a spectacular array of jewelry, goblets, sculptures and the distinctive Castillo family silver designs featuring wildlife animals, reptiles, birds and even
fish. After purchasing two silver goblets we roamed Taxco's
cobblestone streets surrounded by Spanish colonial architecture including the 18th century Santa Prisca church in the main
square. I wish we could have stayed longer, but we left promising
ourselves to return.

On March 6th, 1977, I attended a gold summit held at the Pier
66 hotel in Fort Lauderdale. I felt all my previous forebodings
on the United States economy had been given an even sharper
definition when I attended a brilliant seminar by Robert Paul
Yamin, President of International Commodity Investments, Inc.
The guest speakers, Pik Botha, South African Ambassador to the
United States and United Nations, along with Mr. John de Loor,
South African Ambassador to the International Monetary Fund,
presented their views on gold and inflation. They also discussed
South Africa's relationship with the U.S. and the world economy
in the future.

I had been familiar with apartheid, having purchased South
African silver proof sets back in the early 1960s. I certainly did
not share their government's beliefs on racial separation. The
seminar did not change my anti-apartheid beliefs, but it was a
learning experience.

During 1977, as a finance major, I was required to take FIN
485 a 6-credit course which at the time was being taught by just
one professor, Michael P. This professor had previously been a
branch manager of a Merrill Lynch brokerage office. I made the
mistake of letting him know that I was working for a brokerage
firm and was a licensed financial advisor. After the debacle of
my English 102 class at Broward Community College, you would
think I would hesitate to speak out. Instead, I questioned the
professor. I asked why he felt interest rates were going to come
down as U.S. government debt and inflation were skyrocketing.

Judging from the look on his face and his failure to answer, he did not appreciate being questioned in front of his class.

After most of these classes, I noticed a pattern: a couple of young, good-looking female students would cluster around the professor and basically "kiss his ass" with praise. On a few occasions, I overheard him inviting them to his office for "further discussion." As a rule, his classes were lectures and rarely opened to the class for discussion, so perhaps these private visits were the innocent pursuit of knowledge. I can't say for sure, so I'll give it the benefit of the doubt.

Our final grade was based upon completing a 75-page term paper. Students were to select three companies within an industry, then write an analysis of that industry, of the individual companies and provide financial ratios. Professor P. also wanted an economic forecast for the U.S. backed by student analysis. I chose the publishing industry because, at the time, I was working for Dodge Reports, a division of McGraw-Hill. The three companies I reviewed were McGraw-Hill, Prentice-Hall Inc. and Harcourt, Brace, Jovanovich. In order to compile the information, I contacted the companies and got the last ten years of annual reports from their investor relations departments. With my ten years-experience in the stock brokerage industry, doing the analysis would not be difficult. Making time to complete the report would, because momentous things were about to happen.

19

NATHANIEL MARCUS WOLFF IS BORN

My wife Catherine, was pregnant and expecting a boy in mid to late August. Her pregnancy had a few issues, but nothing that appeared too serious. On August 4, 1977 at 3:00 P.M., Nathaniel was born at Broward General Hospital. He was about two weeks premature and weighed about 5.5 pounds so he was placed in an incubator as a precaution. His birth was the happiest day in my life. Catherine was doing well and when I left the hospital at 8:00 P.M. everything seemed great.

All of that was about to change. At midnight a huge thunderstorm hit Plantation, Florida, where we had just purchased and moved into a new townhouse. Outside the windows I saw lightning strikes everywhere. While I was brushing my teeth and preparing for bed, a lightning flash came through the bathroom electrical socket right in front of my face. All the lights in our seven-unit townhouse building and surrounding area had gone out. After an hour, all of my neighbors' lights came back—except mine.

The next morning at around 9:00 A.M., I received a call from the hospital. They told me that a doctor had saved Nathaniel's life at 2:00 A.M. when his blood sugar had dropped to zero. They asked me to drive to the hospital immediately. I spoke to

Catherine and told her I was on my way. A doctor was waiting as I entered her room. We were informed that Nathaniel was severely hypoglycemic and his chances for survival were extremely poor as most children didn't make it past their first few days of being born with this disease. The doctor arranged for Nathaniel to be transported to Jackson Memorial's Children Intensive Care Unit (ICU) in Miami, where he could receive better care. As soon as Catherine was discharged, we drove down to see Nathaniel in Miami. We were both emotional wrecks. I then let her know we had a major electrical problem at home. The lightning strike had burnt out all our copper wiring which would have to be replaced.

Catherine's parents arrived from Los Angeles a few days later. Her father, Charlie, was a retired Los Angeles County School Board electrician. He could not believe his eyes when he checked out the damage in the attic from the lightning strike. It would take an entire crew several days to do the electrical re-wiring of our townhouse.

We were introduced to two pediatric surgeons that worked for the University of Miami medical department and Jackson Memorial's Children Center. Both recommended removing part of Nathaniel's pancreas in an attempt to get better control of his insulin levels. On a daily basis his sugar levels fluctuated wildly. We agreed to the surgery, but not much changed. Catherine worked in North Miami and drove to the hospital daily to spend time with Nathaniel. I had two jobs and was going to Florida Atlantic University at the same time. We both spent every weekend with Nathaniel and his saint-like nurses. Every one of them treated the ICU babies as though they were their own children. I have never met nurses that cared so much and had such warmth in their souls.

Our baby was now a few months old, but hadn't gained a lot of weight. At least we got to hold and kiss him. His insulin level remained a huge problem and once again they performed surgery to remove even more of his pancreas. At that point, about

80 per cent of his pancreas had been removed. We were told that there had been only 50 cases like Nathaniel's on record and almost all had died within a few days of birth. Although Nathaniel was stable, he was not progressing in the hospital. The doctors recommended we take him home and hope the new environment might help him. We gladly agreed, knowing that this may be Nathaniel's only chance of survival, as the prognosis was not good.

Before taking Nathaniel home, a gastrostomy tube was inserted into his belly. Just in case he did not want to take his two formulas orally, we could send the formula fluid directly into his stomach. He had to be fed every three hours without delay. The nurses trained both of us on the feeding process. Being a night person, I always did the midnight and 3:00 A.M. feeding, while Catherine did the 6:00 A.M. All of the other feedings were shared. We used up all our vacation time taking care of him and then brought in an older lady caretaker to watch and feed him when we were at work.

Catherine and I both had excellent health coverage or we would have been bankrupt within a week. Both of us needed to keep our jobs to keep that coverage and other benefits. I usually took him to the pediatrician for his checkups. While sitting in the doctor's waiting room, I told Nathaniel numerous fairytales. Mothers holding their babies would gaze at me in shock as my story telling did not match anything in the books. However, Nathaniel rarely cried in the office, so I guess he liked my plots better.

While our nightmare was going on, I began to get strange calls around 8:00 P.M. from Robert Patterson, the Miami regional manager of Dodge Reports who was responsible for my branch. He said "You called the New York corporate office human resources department and said bad things about me." I told him "I don't know what you are talking about. I've never called anyone in the company regarding you." I also told him my newborn son was very ill. Patterson responded "No, he's not ill. He will be just fine." I was told my boss was an alcoholic. Every few months he would drop by the office and I could always smell the gin on his breath. Others joked about it. If I was out on the road when he made these visits, I'd return and find he had rifled through my desk drawers and tossed my work notes in the garbage. I felt he was paranoid, with a bad temper, yet I didn't dare say anything to him. I simply couldn't afford to risk losing my job and my insurance.

At home Nathaniel gained some weight, but nothing significant. We often had to feed him through the gastrostomy tube during the evening. Although he was stable, his blood sugar levels were not, fluctuating between extremes. I took a week vacation to write my 75-page term paper for professor Michael P. This allowed Catherine to be at work and keep her sanity without worrying about Nathaniel every minute. My economic analysis for the term paper was proved to be accurate within the coming year; however, the paper fell just short of my professor's 75-page requirement. He gave me a C+ grade on the paper and C in the course. There were no comments regarding the paper's content or my economic analysis, which led me to believe he never read the paper and based my grade on the number of pages. I was angry, having spent my vacation writing it when I could have spent more time with Nathaniel.

Catherine's sister, Elizabeth, flew in from Santa Monica, California to see Nathaniel for the first time. We knew that Nathaniel's health could deteriorate at any time, but refused to accept that grim reality and asked his doctors what their thoughts were on taking Nathaniel for two nights to Walt Disney World. They knew that Nathaniel's chances of survival were poor and suggested we go. The four of us spent two nights at the Disney Polynesian resort and used the monorail to get around. Several pictures were taken of Nathaniel smiling as he gazed at Cinderella's

Castle. I know this was a happy place for him, as it will always be for Catherine and me.

After a six and a half-month battle with hypoglycemia, on Feb 19th, 1978, Nathaniel passed away while he was back in the care of Jackson Memorial's Children ICU Center. He fought hard every second of his life and for that we will always be proud to have had him as our son. Nathaniel's surgeon asked permission to do an autopsy. At that time, no other child with the severity of his disease had survived as long as he had. They felt it would help other children in the future, so we agreed. There is hardly a day that goes by that Catherine and I don't think about him. He had the most beautiful smile in the world.

20

SOUTH AMERICA 1978

After the loss of our son, we felt the need for a long getaway and planned to travel around South America on a three-week American Express fully guided tour. Neither of us had ever been to South America and very few Americans were visiting the continent at that time. We both spoke some Spanish and felt it would come in handy as we would be flying to six countries and nine cities.

We continued in our jobs as well as our classes at FAU. Around March or April, my company, Dodge Reports asked employees to submit their annual vacation requests to the Miami Regional office. I had three weeks available and wanted my vacation to come between school terms. Because there were only three reporters in our office, two could not go on vacation at the same time. Seniority determined who got first choice. That seemed fair to me. I was second in line to another reporter, Arthur (Art) Manzino. I told him my vacation plans and asked if I could take those three weeks without interfering with his schedule. Art said "Yes" without hesitation. I let the other office co-workers know of my planned trip and that Art saw no conflict. I believe I even called the Miami office to confirm the policy. After thanking Art, I booked the trip, which was non-refundable.

About two months later while sitting in the office I shared with Art, I opened an intra-office envelope. In it was a denial of the middle week of my 3-week vacation request. The reason given was that Art had reserved that week. Art was sitting there quietly next to me and probably had just received his vacation request moments earlier via our intra-office mail. I immediately went over to his desk and said to him, "I need that week. You ok'd it and knew I had booked a three-week trip around South America. How can you do that to someone who just lost their child? Why do you need that week?" He refused to tell me why, but insisted he had to have it.

This created a very hostile work environment that affected the entire office. I spoke with Dan, our supervisor in the Miami Regional office, and asked him to intervene. He said he would, but never got back to me. Art worked part time as a ticket seller at various racetracks while working for Dodge Reports. I suspected Dan and Robert Patterson knew about his side job, but protected him because he was a good reporter. Over the next several months I only spoke with Art when it was business related.

Catherine and I hoped Art would do the decent, right thing. As the time drew closer for our trip, I even tried talking to him again. One afternoon, I asked Art to join me at a café near our office for a chat. He agreed and followed me over. We ordered coffee and I asked him to let me have that middle week of vacation time as we had previously agreed. He refused. I asked why he needed that specific week and he refused to say why. At that point, I told him I would reveal to Robert Patterson that he was working another job at the racetracks on company time if he didn't give me that week. The next morning Robert Patterson called a meeting and asked if there was a problem in the office. No one spoke. At that point I realized, Art had called Patterson. Who knows what he said to him? I never discussed my vacation with Art again. All I could wonder was, what kind of human being would put a couple through such aggravation just months after losing their only child. Back in Brooklyn, we would have asked "What sewer did he come out of?" Here, no one seemed to care.

So, the specter of knowing I might lose my job was to hang over our three-week trip through South America. Catherine and I decided to go anyway. We needed the getaway badly and no one was going to stop us. We'd used all of our savings to purchase the trip and couldn't afford to lose it.

As it happened, I got sick on the trip and had to see doctors in Lima and Buenos Aires after developing a severe cold. Even if I'd wanted to fly back to Miami after a week and return to work, I couldn't because I developed an ear infection and doctors advised me not to fly. I called the Dodge office from Lima and advised them that I would not be flying back to Miami due to these health reasons.

South America in 1978 was like the wild west. The U.S. Government did not seem to care what was going on down there, so they did not issue travel advisories and there was little coverage in the newspapers. American Express didn't tell us much either. Shame on them all. On the other hand, maybe they would have scared me out of taking a trip that turned out to be a real education.

Our trip started on Avianca, an airline having a slowdown strike. Our delayed Miami flight arrived in Bogota, Colombia in the middle of the night, without our luggage. The guide, who was supposed to meet us, was nowhere in sight. We were told another plane was coming from Miami and our bags "should" be on it. It was very cold in the airport and, during that long wait, I caught a cold. In all, there was a total of 18 people from different states and backgrounds in our American Express "Bossa Nova" tour. Our guide, who materialized hours later, never apologized, though our luggage did arrive with the rest of our tour group.

We visited a magnificent salt mine outside of Bogota. Late in the day, sleezy looking vendors would approach us in the streets outside our hotel, selling fake emeralds they insisted were genuine. They would rub the stone against a store window to show how strong it was. Actually, though, real emeralds lack the hardness of diamonds. With Christmas not too far off, I purchased a small carat, high quality emerald ring for Catherine at a reputable Japanese-owned jeweler.

Next, we flew to Quito, Ecuador on Braniff Airways. When our luggage arrived, there was black oil all over our large leather bag. They tried to clean it, without success. A claim was filed, but I received almost nothing for the damages. While in Ecuador, we toured the Otavalo villages in the Andean Highlands at an elevation of 8,307 feet. The indigenous tribe was well known for their colorful textiles and wood carvings. A group of children serenaded us with their native songs. Before we left, I purchased a wood chess set for $25. Each piece was hand carved and wrapped in newspaper. In Quito, we visited The Church of the Society of Jesus completed in 1765. The wood carvings and gold leaf throughout the church were spectacular. I said to our guide "With the great poverty in Quito, I am surprised the gold leaf has not been stolen." He replied in an angry tone, "No one steals in Ecuador." Later, I heard there was a thieves' market in Quito where you could see those criminals and the harsh punishments that had been inflicted on them.

Lima was our next stop. This time our Avianca flight and luggage arrived at the same time. We stayed a few nights at the Lima Sheraton Hotel. A highlight was our visit to the Cathedral of Lima where a glass casket displaced the mummified remains of conquistador Francisco Pizarro. In a short time, he destroyed the Inca Empire, took control of Peru and made himself wealthy. His greed would eventually lead to his demise. When I studied the conquistadors in elementary school, my teachers rarely told us how violent and corrupt many of them were. They focused instead on their explorations and discoveries. Our tour took us around the University of Lima. Riots broke out shortly after our arrival in the area and our tour guide rushed us back to our bus.

We had to take a one-hour detour back to our hotel to avoid the civil unrest. We were told it involved a worker's strike, but no one outside our group wanted to discuss it.

Cusco and Machu Picchu with their spectacular Incan ruins at altitudes of up to 11,200 feet were our next destinations. Our flight from Lima to Cusco began with a 90-minute delay because the co-pilot had been in a car accident on his way to the airport. Not an auspicious start. When we finally made it to the Savoy Hotel in Cusco, we headed to the restaurant for some coco tea which we were told would help us adjust to the high altitude. After about 3 or 4 cups, we were asked to go to our rooms and lie down for an hour. Following a short nap, our group toured a local alpaca factory, where I purchase a rug. The altitude had no effect on any of us, thanks to the coco tea, and there were a lot of smiling faces. Our guide, who had Incan ancestry, gave us a tour of the ruins around Cusco, where alpacas and llamas roamed in the wild. He was upset with me when I yelled "llamas!" interrupting his scholarly lecture aboard the tour bus. None of us had ever seen llamas before and when I spotted a pack of them running, well, I had to share my excitement.

The following day we took a four-hour train ride to Machu Picchu. As we wound around the mountains, we saw farmers' oxen pulling carts and the Urubamba River flowing below us. The train went very slowly and the ride was scary at times. When we arrived, the sky was overcast with a light drizzle providing us with a mystical feeling. A bus then took us up a mountain and, at the top, rising through the surrounding clouds was Machu Picchu, one of the great Wonders of the World. I thought we were in heaven standing among the clouds.

This magnificent Incan village had been built in the Andes Mountains at an altitude of almost 8,000 feet. Our guide told us the Incas hid their women and children there from the Spaniards, though historians are not sure why the city was built. With the help of indigenous farmers, the remains of Machu

Picchu were discovered around 1911 by Hiram Bingham III, an American explorer who later became a U.S. senator. After walking around the ruins for several hours, we took the train back to Cusco and flew to Lima the next day.

Our next destination was Buenos Aires, with a refueling stopover in Santiago, Chile. When we landed in Santiago, there would be a one-hour layover, so if we wished to stretch our legs in the airport, we were told to "do it now." All 18 of us were leaving the plane when a cleaning crew came on board with huge garbage containers on wheels. Mr. Valdez from our group and I stayed behind to make sure none of our belongings were taken. In September 1973 Chile had a *coup d'etat*, rumored to be supported by the CIA and the country was going through an economic transition to capitalism from socialism. With the guidance of the economist Milton Friedman, Chile became a South American economic powerhouse. However, there was opposition to the military takeover of the government and Chile was not the safest country for Americans to be visiting.

In Buenos Aires, we were shocked to see tanks and army barracks along the streets as hundreds of protesters marched near the government buildings. Many were holding signs that read "Donde estan los ninos?" (Where are the children?). Years later, I learned that Jorge Rafael Videla, an Argentine army commander, had led a *coup d'etat* that became a dictatorship under his rule from 1976–81. During that time 30,000 people became known as the "Disappeared." They were taken by the military and were often raped and tortured before being killed. The brutal dictatorship was accused of killing the parents of newborns and giving the infants to military families to raise as their own. Protests went on for decades. Today DNA is being used to determine who the parents really were.

My bad cold had turned into a severe hearing problem, which lasted for three days. The flight to Buenos Aires was extremely painful and once again I had to get a prescription for an antibiotic. While touring the city, we visited the gravesite of Eva "Evita" Peron. She had been placed in a crypt with her family name, Duarte. We also spent a day at a gaucho ranch where we got to eat some of the best beef in the world. Catherine and I did some horseback riding. The horses were rather small and super slow. I named mine Frustration One and Catherine's Frustration Two.

Argentina, on the other hand, was dealing with hyperinflation (over 1,000% in the mid 1970s). As soon as workers got their paychecks, they headed to shopping districts like Calle Florida and spent their money in the stylish boutiques, glittering restaurants and lively cafes that lined the street. If they waited a few more hours, their pesos would buy less. Citibank was offering 37% interest on six-month Argentinian certificates of deposit with no takers in sight. The United States inflation rate in 1978 was 7.59% and rising rapidly during President Jimmy Carter's term. Could the U.S. become like Argentina? What led to Argentina's hyperinflation? I needed to research how politics had played a role in causing the hyperinflation I was witnessing. I found my answers when I studied Peronism.

In 1946, Juan Peron was elected president of Argentina with help from the General Confederation of Labor, the largest labor union in the country. The union was guaranteed social security benefits in exchange for its support and became part of a major plan for industrial development. Peron's Keynesian style economic policies planned for full employment, progressive income redistribution, industrialization and economic independence.

Peron nationalized the Central Bank so the state now had control over all private bank deposits. In addition, the state controlled all import and export commodity trading and also placed price controls on some commodities.

Within two years, Peron had depleted most of Argentina's gold and silver reserves. Despite warnings from financial experts and conservative bankers, he had used these gold and silver reserves to purchase several foreign-owned properties and businesses in Argentina. They became state controlled and were used as nationalistic propaganda.

During the next 28 years, Peron, as well as successive presidents and military dictatorships, failed in their attempts to improve Argentina's economic stability. What I learned from my study of Peronism, helped me with my clients' investments during my years in the financial industry. While in Argentina I had witnessed inflation, currency meltdowns, international banking, nationalism, protests and dictatorship first hand in a way that no professor or book could have taught me.

We flew to Iguazu Falls, the biggest waterfall in the world and one of South America's great natural wonders. Our hotel was on the Brazilian side. Argentina also borders the falls with Paraguay just a short distance away. Our room was so close to the falls we could feel their vibrations in our bed. A tour was offered to a casino in Paraguay which I chose not to take. I found out the next day that those who had gone and played blackjack lost their money as the dealer dealt himself *two* down cards. Obviously, they were playing their hands in the dark with not very good odds.

Rio was our next stop. Upon arriving at Le Meridien Hotel in Copacabana, our tour group was invited to the rooftop lounge to sample the *caipirinha* cocktail, Brazil's national drink. While most of us were socializing, we heard a woman screaming from the elevator area. I ran in that direction along with a retired air force colonel who was part of our group and we found a member from our tour group had collapsed and was lying between the elevators doors that kept opening and closing. It was his wife we'd heard screaming. The man was 65 years old, a South Carolinian who had recently retired from the stock brokerage industry, and at the moment was apparently suffering a heart attack. We moved him from the doors quickly, removed his tie and opened the top buttons on his shirt to help him breathe, while his wife sought emergency help. Medics arrived shortly after and took him to the hospital where he stayed for the next three days. Our tour guide confirmed he'd had a heart attack, but was stable and expected to be fine. That was good news for all of us, though the couple did not return to the tour.

While in Rio, we visited the incredible Christ the Redeemer statue at Corcovado Mountain and took a cable car to Sugarloaf Mountain. Both tours provided us with spectacular views of Rio. The beaches were crowded with mostly young people enjoying themselves and playing sports.

Regine's nightclub was located below street level in our hotel. The discotheque was a hangout for the rich and famous where celebrities and super models could be seen on the dance floor. Because we were staying at the hotel, we were allowed in the club without being members. At the time I did not have a credit card and paid cash for everything. I ordered a Budweiser beer and it came served in a champagne bucket at the side of our table. When I received the check for $20, I almost fell to the floor as I only had about $22 in my wallet. Thank God Catherine just had a glass of water.

Several of us visited H. Stern's amazing jewelry showroom. The Shah of Iran's emerald-studded crown was on display. Brazil is known for colored gems. If you had the money, 1978 was a great time to purchase them and H. Stern's was the perfect place—especially considering the devaluations of Brazil's currency. I remember walking through the hotel lobby and the doormen would offer me double the official rate for a ten-dollar bill. At the airport our entire group was separated, our passports confiscated and we were individually searched so great were the government concerns about the currency Black Market.

Our last stop before returning to Miami was a day in Caracas, Venezuela. The country was booming at that time with wealth from its oil riches. I was still recovering from my bad cold and the weather was hot and sunny so while Catherine toured the city and a natural forest, I stayed at the pool and enjoyed the sun beating down on me.

The three-week trip was coming to an end and all I could think about was, what was going to happen when I arrived back at the office Monday. Would I still have a job?

21

HIGH NOON AT DODGE REPORTS (MCGRAW-HILL, INC.)

The first day back at the office, I had a message to drive to Miami and meet with Robert Patterson. I knew, that I was about to be fired. I provided two notes from doctors I had seen while in South America, but these were unacceptable to him. He demanded to see airline tickets proving that I intended to return to the U.S. mid vacation. I reminded him that was the week that had been earlier agreed upon between Art Manzino and me, then taken away when he reneged. I had no airline tickets and was fired on the spot. I was driven back to the office. I packed my personal belongings and then was dropped off at my home as Patterson's assistant drove away in the company car.

If their goal was to humiliate me, they failed. Over a period of seven months, I had lost my son, my job, my company car and other benefits. However, if they thought they could take me down, they would soon find out what kind of person I was.

I quickly joined a small family business called Florida Reports. They competed on a local level against Dodge Reports. I was hired to do both reporting and sales. The cost for our service was significantly lower than Dodge. I used all of my previous architectural contacts and government agency connections for my reporting. I went door to door to general contractors, sub-contractors, suppliers and anyone else who I thought could benefit from using Florida Reports. At least 20% of the Dodge customers bought our reports. The problem was, we had priced our reports too low. We still made money because of our low overhead and superior reporting, but not enough to make a good living. I am sure Dodge lost thousands in revenues from cancellations, as our subscriptions took off. People said "I prefer your report better, it's easier to read." I had the satisfaction of knowing Dodge was losing business.

While at Florida Reports, I continued as a financial advisor with Southeast Securities. I was always welcome there. I still had about six courses that needed to be completed at FAU for my bachelor's degree.

My bitterness towards Dodge Reports made me determined to get even. The two phone calls to my home at night by Robert Patterson in which he told me my dying son was not ill had really disturbed me, as did his insistence that I complained about him to the home office when I had never done so. My co-worker Art Manzino's behavior was, I felt, two-faced. It all left me with a need to expose them in a public setting, perhaps a courtroom.

From reading McGraw-Hill's employee handbook, I determined that if I could prove that I wasn't fired for cause, I was entitled to separation pay of one week for each half year of service. I filed a pro se lawsuit demanding a judgement of $1,484.86 plus court costs.

Shortly after, I received a copy of an inter-office memorandum dated November 7, 1978, written by Robert E. Patterson to a McGraw-Hill employee explaining why I was terminated. There were accusations that I had threatened and harassed Art. The implication was that I physically threatened him, which was absolutely not true. Mr. Patterson neglected to mention Art's second job on company time, the job I told Art I would reveal, though it was obvious he already knew. Patterson also neglected to mention that Art had previously ok'd my taking the vacation week in question before I booked the trip. Naturally, Patterson did not mention how he harassed me at home regarding my son's critical health condition. A coverup was in the making. Our trial date of April 24 was cancelled following record rainfall and moved to a July date. When I arrived at the courthouse, McGraw-Hill's attorney was there along with Dan (Patterson's assistant), Art and two other office employees as potential witnesses. None of my former co-workers looked as if they wanted to be there or were prepared to testify against me. They could not even look me in the eye. One was my regular lunch buddy. I know they needed their jobs, but I felt their shame.

Just before the courtroom doors opened their attorney approached me with a settlement offer of $300. I told him where to shove it. He then asked "what are you willing to accept to settle?" I told him I wanted $800 to cover my court costs and meet me halfway on what I felt was owed. He made a phone call and agreed to the $800. We went into the courtroom and he advised the judge of the settlement. High noon with Dodge came to a close with a court victory for me.

In September 1979, I responded to a classified ad by Radio Shack looking for management trainees and was hired after taking their required lie detector test. I resigned my position at Florida Reports, but kept my stock brokerage licenses active through Southeast Securities. The site of my training for Radio Shack was their large store in Plantation's Broward Mall. I learned about stereo systems and numerous tech products. We were guaranteed a minimum wage per hour versus a percentage of sales produced, but Radio Shack was sneaky how they handled your floor time. It seemed whenever you hit a certain point in sales, the manager would switch you off the floor to, say, stock the shelves which limited any chance of reaching a higher percentage level and commissions were based on those production levels. Just before the Christmas rush, I was given the assistant manager's position in a small strip mall location on Davie Blvd in Fort Lauderdale.

I was also about to graduate. Finally, after 11 years of going to college mostly at night, on December 14, 1979, I received a Bachelor of Science degree in Finance from Florida Atlantic University. It was one of my proudest moments as I became the first in my family to obtain a 4-year degree. I also accomplished it without accepting a penny from family or financial aid. It was great to know my life would not be controlled by college debt.

Having had issues with some of my former employers, I knew that in the future I could always be fired from a job, but unlike a company car, they could never take away my education. That left me with a confident attitude.

I was less optimistic about Radio Shack. One night, before closing the store at 9:00 P.M. I was with a customer when three young men in their twenties walked in. They looked like trouble and their actions were immediately suspicious. One strolled into the back storage room. Even though all of our items had price tags, they asked if they could purchase stereos at prices near zero. I remained calm and firmly replied "No, I am sorry but those are fixed prices set by Radio Shack." Realizing the danger, I asked my customer if he would stick around for a few minutes while I made a call. There was a phone under the cashier's counter and I had been told previously by my manager that if I hit one digit, it would summon the police. I went behind the counter, dialed and–nothing, not even a dial tone. I kept my cool because if I didn't, there was no telling what would happen. Shortly after, the three left the store, I thanked my customer for staying, locked up and went home for a few beers. I was considerably shaken.

When I told the manager what happened, he casually dismissed my concerns and did not explain why the phone to the police was disconnected. I had worked 21 days in a row through Christmas without a day off and now it seemed I wouldn't get any days off for another week or so. At that point I told him, "I quit. Good luck." and disconnected with Radio Shack.

The 1980 Census Bureau was hiring workers to help with the count in Broward County. I needed money to help pay our monthly bills, so I applied. I was hired to review the completed questionnaires. The job was temporary and didn't pay much, but it gave me the opportunity to do some serious job hunting. I interviewed with Biscayne Federal Savings & Loan Association and Ryder Systems in Miami for a financial analyst job. Biscayne Federal showed serious interest, but never called me back. They did me a favor by not hiring me, as Biscayne went bankrupt in 1983 along with many other savings & loan associations across the country.

I had a good interview at the Ryder Systems corporate office on a Friday afternoon. They gave me a project to analyze using various financial alternatives. I spent over an hour completing the task and was told I had done "a great job" and they "wanted to hire" me. No money offer had been made, but they asked me to discuss the job with my wife, take the weekend to think it over and get back to them. I told them there was nothing that needed to be discussed and that I wanted the job. It became weird when they insisted that I go home and call back Monday. When I did, no one in Human Resources would talk to me or return my call. A few days later I called and was told the job had been given to an existing employee as a promotion. I was disappointed, but had to keep going.

22

COMMISSION DISCOUNT STOCK BROKERAGE

While at the Census Bureau, I decided to go through the Yellow Pages during lunch and contact all the discount stock brokerages in the area to see if they were hiring. On my very first call I spoke with Robert (Bob) Natiss VP of Commission Discount. Once he heard my credentials, he asked me to come in for an interview after 5:00 at the corporate headquarters in Fort Lauderdale. Commission Discount had at least six branches along the east coast of Florida. Bob was from Long Island and was into playing basketball on a weekly basis. I knew I would be right at home. He offered me a job as an assistant to a much older advisor in their South Miami Beach branch, just one block from the ocean. My starting salary was $10,000 a year with potential bonuses. Without hesitation, I accepted the job and started the following Monday. I informed Ted Kata, Southeast Securities that I was taking the job and, as expected, he and his family wished me the best. I always felt the Katas were an extended family, after all, I had been to three daughters' weddings and they'd attended mine. I also informed the Census Bureau I had found another job and was finished with them.

Although I had never worked for a discount commission brokerage firm before, I felt having grown up in a highly competitive street environment that this type of stock brokerage could be a good fit. On May 1, 1975 the Securities Exchange Commission had deregulated stock commissions. That opened up the gates for the discount brokerages to set up shop. Charles Schwab was one such firm to open for business. Many others joined the crowd.

Catherine was working in North Miami, so often I drove her to work and picked her up on my way home. We saved money not driving two cars and I got to spend more time with her talking about our day. I was backing up an advisor named Len, who was old time Jewish, funny and a schmoozer. Our office had a running stock tape inside a boardroom. Customers could follow the market and have a running commentary. It was sort of like *Cheers* where everyone knows your name. Some of them would spend almost the entire day watching the tape while nursing a cup of coffee from the McDonald's across the street.

Many of our clients were elderly and sometimes you would witness the strangest things right outside our storefront. One day we watched a man try to parallel park his car between two other cars. He went back and forth between the two vehicles, slowly hitting and pushing them further out of the way so he could park his car. After denting both, he walked across the street to McDonalds as if nothing had happened. Then there was the lady with a European accent who would call several times a week and say "Merrill Lynch" over and over again, no matter how often we told her we were Commission Discount. For me it was a great learning experience as it helped me understand and deal with my future clients, particularly the elderly. Patience and understanding would make me a better person and a better financial advisor.

I quickly learned Commission Discount's system and, within three months, Bob Natiss gave me a $2,000 raise to $12,000. He was building a small branch in the Skylake Mall in North Miami and he wanted me to be the branch manager at an additional $2,000 raise. I would have less driving and it was closer to Catherine's office. I was excited about managing my first stock brokerage branch. My job was to help get it open and turn a profit. A stock tape was installed and clients started coming. Their age was somewhat younger than the Miami Beach location and I had to be on the alert for fraudsters and speculators. Both could do serious damage to a start-up branch like ours.

By 1982, the Skylake branch was fairly profitable, even though we were going through a bear market. Fed Chairman Paul Volker had raised the federal funds rate from 11.2% to 20% and inflation was running wild.

The branch manager in our Plantation location left our firm to join one of the large Florida banks. Across the country banks were getting into the stock brokerage business and hiring away branch managers from discount commission brokerages. Our Plantation branch was super busy, sometimes doing over 60 trades a day with just a branch manager and an assistant. Bob Natiss asked me to take over that branch and offered a $4,000 raise to $18,000. I lived in Plantation, so it was an easy decision. Bob felt that with my Wall Street back-office experience and two years of managing a branch, I was ready for bigger and better things. I thanked him for his confidence and did not let him down.

Over the next year or so, all of the major Florida banks were setting up their own discount stock brokerages to compete with the traditional firms like Merrill Lynch, Smith Barney and others who were taking away the bank's money market and CD business. It was a war for assets.

In early 1983, I received a call from Steve Eldredge VP, Southwest Florida Banks Inc., Fort Myers, Florida. They were seeking someone to start up a stock brokerage from scratch. The position was titled Director of Brokerage Services instead of President due to security laws at that time. The SEC regulated the traditional stock brokerages. However, the bank brokerages were regulated by the Controller of the Currency. There were various restrictions on bank brokerages because the banks were subject to the Glass-Steagall Act, authorized by the United States Congress on February 27, 1932, as part of the Banking Act of 1933. This act was designed to avoid the type of failure that 4,000 banks suffered during the Great Depression.

I sent a resume over to Steve and we agreed to a Saturday interview in Fort Myers. Steve was in charge of the municipal bond department for Southwest Florida Banks Inc. and had been given the responsibility of hiring for the stock brokerage. I would report to him. Steve was an extremely bright guy, but had virtually no experience in the stock brokerage field. I was concerned from the start that we could bump heads if he didn't trust me. I told Steve I was willing to relocate to Fort Myers. Two weeks later, he called with an offer of $30,000 a year salary plus bonus. I accepted and told him I would need two to three weeks to relocate. Steve had already hired a cashier from a NYSE-member firm to be our operations manager. Linda was very experienced and confident. I knew she could do the job and would soon find out she was well prepared for the challenge.

23

A START-UP SUCCESS AT SOUTHWEST FLORIDA BANKS, INC.

Relocating across the state meant that Catherine and I were working on two different coasts. While I laid the ground-work for the brokerage, we kept in touch by telephone (no cell phones at that time) and alternated weekend drives across the Everglades. I advised Bob Natiss of my departure from Commission Discount and he allowed me to continue working until I moved to Fort Myers. Bob appreciated the professional manner in which I left and let me know the door was open in case things did not work out.

I was excited. I was beginning a new job with great promise, though I was concerned whether Southwest Florida Banks was fully committed to having a stock brokerage. Were they doing it just because all of the other major banks in Florida had already opened one? They were a conservative old-time bank holding company that had a history of letting a competitor try some-thing new first. Because of this, I knew we were a little late for the show.

Catherine remained in her job, at least until I felt secure in mine. Southwest agreed to provide me with a corporate owned apartment for several months, while I settled into the area. Unlike most bank holding companies, Southwest had sixteen banks, all with different names, comprising the holding company. What name could we use for our stock brokerage that would tie all the banks together? We felt the best name was Money Center Brokerage Services. All sixteen banks used the name Money Center for their ATMs so that name would unify the banks and their branches.

Money Center Brokerage Services (MCBS), a subsidiary of Southwest Florida Banks Inc., signed a contract with National Financial Services (NFS), a wholly-owned subsidiary of Fidelity Investments, to be our clearing broker. As such, they would process trades, dividends, checks, the opening of new accounts, also the receiving and delivering of securities, as well as anything else related to the responsibilities of a clearing broker. At that time, NFS was the clearing broker firm for most bank stock brokerages across the country.

Steve knew all 16 bank presidents and wanted me to meet them. So together with my operations manager, Linda, we were to do a presentation on how Money Center Brokerage could make money for them and what they could do for us. Using some of the forms from NFS and drawing on my past experience in the industry, I put together a 40-page training manual for the bank employees who would be on the front line with our future clients. Every president was also provided with a copy. Our success depended on them.

There was a total of 75 branches making up the sixteen banks in the holding company. Steve came up with the idea of Money Center Brokerage Services being a non-profit subsidiary of the holding company. We would record brokerage revenues, but allocate those revenues to each branch bank. Every branch had its own three-digit number, so when an account was opened, we gave the client an account number with the last three digits representing the branch which opened it. Our costs were fully accounted for and on our books. While we were regulated by the Controller of the Currency, we were not required to be registered with the SEC as long as our trade orders were unsolicited and we did not provide any advice.

Initially, the bank presidents were skeptical of how the system would work, but once their branch started to see the revenues hit *their* books, they were "all in" on the program. The sixteen banks had branches all along the west coast of Florida from Marco Island to Pasco County. Many of them were a two to four-hour drive from Fort Myers. Steve always insisted on driving the three of us, which was ok with by me – until he popped in a cassette tape by the rock group *Air Supply*. There were times I was ready to leap out the car at his taste in music. I said, "Steve, can't you play some soul music like Sly & The Family Stone?" He answered "No." By remarkable coincidence, shortly after this exchange, Sly was arrested on drug charges in Fort Myers. Steve was in my office bright and early to show me the newspaper headlines and joke that my "main man" was in the local jail.

On these trips along the west of Florida, there were nights we didn't get home until midnight. Then we'd have to be at work the next morning. At the same time, we were training a large number of bank employees on how the brokerage business operated in preparation for our grand opening. Most of our staff worked out great. I was delighted with Robbi, who we hired as a receptionist/secretary/assistant cashier. She had past experience with A G Edwards & Sons Inc. However, there was one exception, a financial advisor named Jim, whose limited stock brokerage experience was with Raymond James. I liked her from the start and felt we hired her at a reasonable salary, unlike Jim. Another great addition was Candice (Candi), with ten years banking experience, who transferred over to our department to help us with her bank contacts and assist in branch operations. She was a key addition to our group. She received a raise with her move and was thrilled at the opportunity.

All six of us flew to Boston for our final training at National Financial Services Corp. After a couple days of training, Steve took us out to dinner and celebrated with a couple of bottles of Moet. It was quite a celebration as we were about to enter a new era. After three months of working day and night, we were ready for business. From the first day, the bank employees we had trained were calling us to open new brokerage accounts. Most of our clients had brokerage accounts at full-service firms and were paying high commissions just to place an order. The full-service brokers could provide advice which many of our clients who were senior citizens and financially sophisticated, didn't need or want.

Linda and Candi were working mothers. There would be times when a child was sick and needed them around. I told everyone in our group, "If you need to take time off for something personal, just let me know and as a team we will cover for you. However, if a special situation comes up and I need you to work late or come in on a Saturday, I want to be able to count on you." Everyone agreed and understood our success depended on it. Unfortunately, Jim didn't seem to get the message. Most of the time he seemed to sit by his desk reading golf news as the phone rang unanswered. It was clear he felt he could do a better job than me. Moreover, he was gaining favor with Steve to the point that Steve called me into his office to discuss my job performance and ask if there were problems with Jim. I raised a few concerns I had about Jim, but it would be a few more weeks before Steve realized what a serious problem he posed.

Jim started calling in sick once or twice a week, it seemed to coincide with when he was planning to play golf. On one occasion, Jim called and told Robbi he was going to a golf tournament. He threatened her not to tell anyone and when she got off the phone, she was in tears. That's how we learned what was going on. Jim had also placed about five stock purchase orders in his personal account and not paid for them. We were required by the NYSE to liquidate the positions, which resulted in a $400 unsecured loss in his account. When we called Jim into a meeting with a Human Resources manager, he had nothing to say and we fired him. He did not reimburse us for the loss, so we had a Southwest Florida Bank attorney, named Keith, file suit in small claims. On the court date, Jim didn't appear and we were given summary judgement. We never heard from him again. From that day on, our office ran much smoother. We did not hire anyone to replace Jim, as we felt our team could do the job without adding another salary.

Walking back from the courthouse, Keith asked me if Robbi was single. He'd spotted her on one of his visits to our office. Later, I let her know of his interest and she lit up with a huge smile. Within a year I was dancing at their wedding.

Steve had given me a $25,000 budget for advertising and brochures. Through Catherine's contacts in advertising, I was able to get posters, mailers and brochures printed, below budget. Catherine and I designed the brochure and I wrote it. An artist friend helped with the layout. I felt there wasn't any need to spend hundreds of thousands of dollars for an advertising agency when I had such top talent closer to home. The results showed. Within three months of our grand opening, Money Center was already at break-even.

At this point Catherine and I purchased a homesite lot in Fort Myers and had chosen Maxson Construction General Contractors to build our dream home. Catherine was going to resign from her job once the house was finished and was interviewing for positions in Fort Myers, but our lives were about to change again.

On October 26, 1983, just ten days prior to the closing on our new house, Landmark Banking Corp of Florida announced they were merging with Southwest Florida Banks. Landmark Banking was a 1.7-billion-dollar asset bank holding company based in Fort Lauderdale. Combined, we would become the fifth largest bank in Florida. Steve thought the merger would take at least four to six months. We weren't sure where the corporate headquarters for the combined company would be, but assumed Fort Lauderdale on the East Coast. Steve suggested I complete the closing on my new Ft. Myers house and assured me the bank would purchase it and reimburse me for any losses if I had to be relocated to Fort Lauderdale. He also offered me a choice of flying Catherine to Fort Myers each weekend or paying my mortgage until the merger was completed. It was an easy choice. All flights were out of Miami and the drive to the airport was almost as bad as driving across Alligator Alley. "Pay my mortgage." It turned out the merger wasn't completed until July 1984, roughly eight months following the announcement.

We found out that Landmark's stock brokerage was also using National Financial Services as their clearing broker. That would make it much easier to integrate our systems. My counterpart at Landmark was a woman named Lola. She had worked in Landmark's trust department for several years and was given the responsibility to set up and manage their new brokerage, even though I was told she had never worked in the stock brokerage industry. I remember being told by a Landmark Banking VP named Richard, who would become Steve's counterpart in the merger, that Lola's husband was a registered representative with a major NYSE firm and he was providing her with some assistance. Richard seemed to think that if your spouse works in a specific field, then you assume their expertise. I would soon find out that her lack of stock brokerage experience resulted in significant losses along with policies that were ineffective and dangerous for the bank. Through my contacts at NFS, I learned that Landmark was barely doing 10 trades a day, even though they had started their stock brokerage several months prior to ours.

Meanwhile, Money Center was averaging 50 trades a day and making money. Every month, NFS sent us reports comparing how we were doing versus all of their correspondent bank brokerages with assets similar to ours. At the time, Southwest

Florida Banks was a 1.5-billion-dollar size bank holding company. Our revenues were through the roof compared to the
others. There was not a single bank brokerage in our category
within even striking distance. At Christmas, Steve and I shared
the success by inviting our team and their spouses to spend an
overnight stay at Casa Ybel Beach Resort on the beach at Sani-
bel Island. The room and dinner were covered by Money Center Brokerage Services. If I recall, we went through six bottles of
Moet at dinner. Christmas bonuses had already been received
by my team, which made the celebration even merrier.

Prior to the merger's completion, I was informed that Lola
was going to retire. I would now become Director of Brokerage
Services for both the Fort Myers and Fort Lauderdale locations,
receiving a salary raise to $40,000 a year. After the merger, we
would have 125 bank branches across the entire state. Inevitably,
all of them would go under the Landmark name, which would
help in marketing. Landmark's corporate office in downtown
Fort Lauderdale would become the headquarters for the merged
banks. I became concerned, however, when several of the Southwest executives took "golden parachutes" and left the company,
while others remained in Fort Myers. Most of the Southwest
management and employees were used to a small-town lifestyle
and Fort Lauderdale presented a change they perhaps did not
desire.

At any rate, I became the first person in the merger to start
working in Landmark's downtown Fort Lauderdale corporate
office. Southwest lived up to their agreement and purchased
my just-built home in Fort Myers. I would have liked to keep
the property, but couldn't afford to at the time, so I settled for a
small profit. With all that was happening, we were able to save
some money and pay down the mortgage on our townhouse.

When I reviewed Landmark's stock brokerage financial statement, I was in shock. They had only three employees prior
to Lola retiring, but their salaries when compared to Money

Center Brokerage Services were significantly higher per person even though they had been doing about 75% less in business. Also, they had spent about $200,000 in marketing through an Atlanta ad agency. The four-page brochure was poorly designed and, worse, it outlined policies which virtually guaranteed failure. One of the first things I did was fire the ad agency. Between the past management and an ad agency that did not have a clue about our industry, the result was a complete waste of money. That was about to change.

Landmark had a policy of not opening a stock brokerage account unless they had a prior savings or checking account. They were actually turning new clients away, people walking in with stock certificates in hand! To me, that policy defeated the purpose of the bank's having a stock brokerage. It was only logical that attracting new and existing bank clients to open a stock brokerage account would also help the bank cross sell other products.

I met with Lola a few times before she retired. She left me several fires to put out. For example, there was a lawsuit that never should have happened which occurred when Landmark Brokerage chose to sue a man who reneged on several purchase transactions. When payment was due, Landmark's financial advisor was told by the client on a taped phone call that the client did not have the money to pay for the trades. Instead of liquidating his purchases immediately, the brokerage sent him a letter requesting payment. His stocks continued to drop in price leading to an $8,000 loss. Had his account been sold out at the time of the taped call, the loss would have been $4,000. Richard, Lola's former boss, asked for my opinion what to do about the loss. I had not yet officially started working in the Fort Lauderdale location and it was not my responsibility, so I was a little surprised at his bringing the matter to me. Richard showed me a copy of the client's driver's license. That picture looked like no one I would care to do business with. In fact, he looked dangerous. Then

Richard informed me the client had been jailed for assaulting his wife. I advised him not to pursue the losses.

Richard did not follow my advice. After the client was handed a subpoena, he went to legal aid for help. They turned the case over to a prominent Fort Lauderdale law firm, who had successfully sued Landmark Banking in the past. The client's lawyers countersued, claiming the client was incompetent and held that Landmark Brokerage never should have opened an account. As Director of Brokerage Services, I had to give a deposition explaining what transactions had taken place. Earlier, having heard the taped phone call conversations between the financial advisor and the client, I knew it was inappropriate to have taken orders from him. He seemed incoherent. When it came time for Landmark's attorney to depose the client and I saw him walk into the conference room at the law office, I knew we were in trouble. He took out about 20 pill bottles and lined them up across the table. He could barely answer a question. I wasn't sure he had any idea why he was there.

After the deposition, I again advised Richard to get the case dismissed. He did not listen to me. After that discussion, I never brought up the lawsuit with him. My main focus was to get our revenues up at the Landmark Brokerage side and to at least break even for the year. By the end 1985, Landmark Brokerage finished the year with a net profit of $73,129, while Money Center Brokerage Services had a $186,680 net profit.

Unfortunately, all my hard work was about to be wasted. Citizens & Southern National Bank of Atlanta announced a buyout of Landmark Banking of Florida in 1985. C&S was almost three times Landmark's size. They were also acquiring banks in several other states, as well. C&S National Bank's stock brokerage was based in Atlanta and went under the subsidiary name of First Southeastern Company (FSC). First Southeastern was a broker-dealer and operated under the regulations set forth by the SEC. Their name was later changed to Citizens & Southern

Securities Corporation, which cleared their transactions through Broadcort Capital Corporation, a wholly owned subsidiary of Merrill Lynch.

On July 1, 1985 the SEC Commission adopted Rule 3b-9, which requires banks that conduct discount brokerage and certain other securities related activities, to conduct those activities in a subsidiary that is registered with the SEC as a securities broker/dealer.

In summary, Money Center Brokerage and Landmark Brokerage would no longer be regulated by the Controller of the Currency. This ruling would now require Linda, Candi and Robbi to pass the Series 7 and get registered as agents of a stock brokerage firm. Previously licensed agents would be grandfathered in and would not have to retake any exams. C&S Securities Corp. would at some point require me to pass the Series 24 General Principals exam, which would allow me to run a stock brokerage.

All of my Money Center Brokerage team passed their Series 7 exams. I was very proud, but not surprised. They were smart and also hard workers. I knew they would succeed. The merger of C&S and Landmark Banking was completed in the second half of 1985.

When the merger was first announced I was shown a video of the executive chart and board of directors at C & S. I noticed all of the executives, board of directors and department heads were white males. I did not notice any typical Jewish or Catholic names among them. This was 1985, not 1960, yet no Blacks, Jews, Catholics or women held high positions. I had seen that show before and was afraid I was about to see a re-run.

24

C&S NATIONAL BANK: "YOU'RE JEWISH, AREN'T YOU?"

Following the completed merger of C&S National Bank and Landmark Banking of Florida, I was invited to Atlanta for an introduction to the C&S Securities back office. I had an early flight in and a scheduled 9:00 P.M. departure the same day. My initial impression was negative. To someone who worked on Wall Street for four years in the back offices of major stock brokerage firms, Atlanta's operations seemed chaotic. Also, there seemed to be no clear lines of responsibility.

While I was in Atlanta, branch managers from several C&S Securities locations and I joined them for dinner. Jim Anderson, President of C&S Securities, and Lynn Wood, his Vice President, were both sitting directly across from me. I was seated next to the branch manager from Tennessee. The first words out of his mouth were "You're Jewish, aren't you?" I observed both Jim and Lynn listening carefully to my answer and responded, "Yes, I am. Why do you ask?" He said, "Most people from South Florida are Jewish." I didn't continue any further conversation after his comment. In hindsight, I should have risen from my seat and made a scene over this set up. For set up it was. My last name Wolff, was not definitively Jewish. So, I believe they were determined to find out my ethnic heritage.

My earlier suspicions about C&S being a racist employer with an anti-woman bias would be confirmed by events I witnessed in the months ahead. At the Landmark Banking of Florida corporate headquarters, two of the three attorneys were let go. Both were Jewish. The least experienced attorney, non-Jewish, stayed on. The head of the trust department, also Jewish, was demoted. Two highly educated African American brothers, the Bingers, from the British Virgin Islands would soon undergo the same fate. One had an MBA and held a top position in the bank's mortgage lending department. The other was the branch manager of the main Landmark Banking downtown branch. One was fired and the other demoted. Then there was the female manager in Plantation who had won numerous awards and seemed slated for a major promotion to regional manager. She didn't get the promotion, and many held she was pressured to leave the company shortly after.

With the merger of the two banks complete, the next step was to merge Landmark Brokerage Services and Money Center Brokerage Services into C&S Securities. The process would require our two branches changing clearing brokers from National Financial Services (NFS) to Broadcort. Having seen the back-office system in Atlanta first hand, I knew this was going to be a difficult task.

C&S Brokerage wanted me to get the Series 24, General Securities Principal license immediately. Through their licensing department, they ordered the books I was to study for the exam and set up the test at a local proctoring center. I was given a date for the exam, and had about a month to prepare. Just a few days prior to the test, I was informed by the licensing department that they had forgotten to send in a necessary $50 fee and was not on the schedule to take the test. I almost blew a gasket. The next exam in my area was two months away, However, one was being proctored in Orlando in three weeks. C&S agreed to fly me up for an overnight in Orlando to take the exam there. It was just one example of the disorganization in their operations.

In my entire career, I had never had an employer forget to pay an exam fee. This time I verified with the proctoring center that C&S had paid the $50 fee. When I flew to Orlando, I had a cold and a slight fever, but this was something I had to get done. On Nov 4, 1985, I passed the Series 24, General Securities Principal exam with an 88% score. Shortly after, on January 13, 1986, I passed the Series 4, Registered Options Principal exam with an 86%. Those licenses would set me apart from the Series 7 agents.

With both Principals licenses, 16 years stock brokerage experience and a BS in Finance, I should have felt confident. Instead, I found the Atlanta management and a newly hired regional manager, Mark Williamson, could not be trusted. Indeed, I questioned their competence. In my opinion, they acted as if securities laws and rules did not apply to them.

At this point, to protect myself and my licenses I began documenting most of our conversations as Memos to File. They included marketing issues, operational issues and, most gravely, violations of both banking and securities regulations. One memo shows how management fails to file for an extension from the SEC.

Here are a sample:

Memo to File on December 16, 1985:

Jim Anderson lowers the customer commission schedule for my branches to match Atlanta without any discussion, even though it would have a negative effect on the earnings for both Money Center Brokerage and Landmark Brokerage Servicers. When asked why, Jim replied, with advertising we will gain the active trader."

Jim failed to advertise the lower commission rates, which resulted in lost revenues.

Memo to File on January 2, 1986:

I spoke to Lynn Wood about the SEC 3b9 ruling of require-ments for broker dealers. Lynn worked out a letter with Frank Hagen of National Financial Services to enclose with our trade confirmations. I also requested 100 rubber stamps for Landmark Brokerage and 150 for Money Center Broker-age with the name "Broadcourt" on it to be used by our bank branches when receiving stock certificates from our clients. We also needed new stock certificate receipt forms. Lynn advised me that FSC. did not have its own stock receipt. He thought it would be a good idea to design one after the name change to C&S Securities.

I never heard of a stock brokerage firm not having stock receipt forms. Did management have any clue how a normal stock brokerage is run?

Memo to File on January 10, 1986:

Because Lynn Wood did not file for an extension with the SEC for Landmark and Money Center Brokerages until we converted to Broadcort in February, the following was a list of violations as of January 1, 1986. Landmark had been paying checks to clients from a Landmark account although Landmark was not a broker-dealer.

Robbi had passed her Series 7 in late February. Taking the exam had been delayed because C&S wanted her to help with the conversion. If she had been taking orders from cli-ents prior to passing her exam, Money Center Brokerage would have been in violation of SEC rules.

My comment on memo: During the conversion, Money Cen-ter Brokerage received help from two C& S employees at their location and was allowed to hire an additional financial advisor. The Landmark Stock Brokerage in Fort Lauderdale received zero help. Despite the help Money Center received, they were not coping well with the inferior, though less costly, Broadcort computer system.

Perhaps the memo that best outlines the sheer chaos was the one intended for Mr. Lynn Wood that I got by mistake. By a strange coincidence, this interoffice memorandum, dated February 19, 1986 from Broadcort and intended for Lynn Wood, arrived in my mail. Lynn Wood's name was misspelled as Lin Wood and Ft. Myers was incorrectly spelled, as well. The memo was written by Eileen M. Moritz to another Broadcort employee named Frank J. Salamone. It shows how completely Broadcort and C&S Securities misunderstood how a bank discount brokerage functioned under the regulations at that time. At no time did any of the Broadcort employees discuss these issues with me, yet I was directly responsible for the branch. The memo reads in its entirety as follows:

Subject: C&S Securities-Ft. Meyers branch (47C)
Highlights from memo by Eileen M. Moritz

Due to the situation outlined in this report, I recommend a C&S representative with Broadcort experience remain on-site until the office is trained and able to perform the operations responsibilities.

This matter was discussed with Lin Wood on February 13, 1986. Karen Petersen of Atlanta is being sent to train the staff.

Original trade projections of 40 per day trade seem low-the average trade input numbered around 60. On February 10, we entered an additional 150 Good to Cancel (GTC) orders.

The office will be adding a registered representative and wire operator to their staff. This should help a great deal in handling the volume of telephone calls and in organizing the work flow.

Serious system problems were encountered throughout the week. The change-over of prefixes between this office and the Ft. Lauderdale branch on February 6, 1986 resulted in system problems. All reject messages were crossed between the offices. This hampered entry and name and address input. This should be corrected on February 18th.

Training was hindered due to work volume, understaffed and changes in job assignments. The wire and order were originally scheduled to be handled by Susan, on Wednesday, the job was assigned to Robbi. On Friday, Robbi was out preparing for a Series 7 exam and Lisa assumed the role.

Problems/Concerns

The staffing and organization of the office is a prime concern. The office was functioning in a matter where clearly defined job roles were non-existent. This led to orders being taken from customers by non-registered personnel.

The firm is quite concerned and has hired another registered representative to correct this situation. The operations area is still in a state of flux.

An experienced wire operator was interviewed but to my knowledge no decision was reached to hire this person. Should the person be hired, this will greatly help the office.

The functions are presently assigned as follows

- Susan-Cashiering-not trained; Bookkeeping-not trained.
- Lisa-Trades processing; New accounts-semi trained.
- Robbi-Wire operator-semi trained; Transfers-not trained.

Please note training guides were left to be individually reviewed, along with the procedure manuals.

The cashiering function is still not fully designed. The office pays an average of 20 checks daily and funds are transferred back and forth between the parent bank and the office. This allows customers to have funds automatically transferred from the bank account.

Carlo Franzese and Don Gilbert are working to design a viable system until a bank account is approved for this location.

The supplies still have not arrived and the second printer has been ordered and should be installed the first week of March.

Recommendation:

As previously stated, the office is not able to assume the responsibilities of operations at this time. (End of memo)

After reading the above hatchet job, I wrote the following. Had they followed my original recommendations there would have been no need for such a memo.:

Memo to File by Jerry Wolff on February 22, 1986:

When I was advised by Lynn Wood that both 028 (Fort Lauderdale) and 044 (Money Center) would be converted at the same time, I suggested that the 028 branch go first, because it was ready to comply with 3b9. Branch 044 was not ready and needed to register Candi and Robbi. I was told we would have help from C&S Securities in my office during the conversion. We had none. I requested the hiring of a wire operator two days prior to the conversion, after being shown how orders were entered. I was told by Mark Williamson that Jim Anderson wanted me to wait a couple of weeks before he would consider it. The salaries in my office were once again questioned (particularly Jenny, our cashier). Jenny was one of two employees I managed in the former Landmark Brokerage Services branch, which I had inherited in the Landmark-Southwest Banking of Florida merger. Jenny's salary was significantly higher than the cashier we had hired for Money Center Brokerage Services and she hadn't been cross trained by former management to take on other responsibilities. I agreed Jenny's salary was on the high side for what she did, but left it up to Atlanta to decide what to do about it. About a week later, management agreed I needed to hire a professional wire operator to handle the Broadcort system.

Without any training or additional personnel, my branch was not prepared for the conversion to Broadcort. I pleaded for help, but received none. In most instances, transaction confirms were delayed up to one week. I received several complaints from clients, many refusing to pay for trades until they received a confirmation of purchase. Broadcort confused the 028 and 044 branches so that during our first week any rejections of orders and new accounts went to the wrong branch without the other branch being notified. Also, systematic IRA (Individual Retirement Accounts) dividend payouts failed to be sent out on the Broadcort system. On my own, I discovered yet another serious problem: all client stock option positions converted incorrectly. Confirms on sell trades were printed with incorrect settlement dates, causing 87 delays in payouts to clients.

As of February 22nd, our clients had still not been informed that our clearing broker had changed from National Financial Services Corp. to Broadcort Capital Corp. Only the January monthly client statement mailing had an insert mentioning the change. Furthermore, only a limited number of clients received that insert. This was a violation of SEC law, which required such notice be sent to all clients.

An $18,000 ad budget for the 028 branch was wasted because ads said "call us" yet ran without any phone number. I was told that in ads for the other Florida branches, Landmark's phone number appeared instead of the advertised branch. When I shared this information with Jim Anderson, he didn't appear that alarmed. I felt sabotaged.

After several weeks of dealing with client complaints resulting from the Broadcort conversion, I decided to write a memorandum to Mark Williamson and copy both Jim Anderson and Lynn Wood. I felt either they would accept my input as a learning experience or they would use it as an excuse to fire me. Even though it was likely the repercussions would be great, I felt a need to write it anyway.

Memorandum Written by Jerry A. Wolff to Mark Williamson, CC: James Anderson and Lynn E Wood on March 10, 1986:

It has been four weeks since we converted to Broadcort Capital. I would like to update you on the status of the Fort Lauderdale branch. Also, I want you to be aware of the problems we encountered and the problems that have still not been rectified. With the C&S South Carolina branch conversion due soon, this may be of assistance.

Problems Encountered

1. Lack of training of Landmark personnel on reading stock quotations on the Broadcort system, resulted in numerous errors and time delays (training not complete after four weeks).

2. There was a need for a wire operator as a result of the new system. Wire operator was hired to start March 17th. Orders are often called into Atlanta and Tampa, creating extra workload for them.

3. Because Landmark and Money Center converted at the same time, Broadcort confused the two offices and coded our prefixes 47B and 47C in reverse. For one week, all messages, trade and new account rejections went to each other's wire.

4. Landmark's telephone number appeared on Money Center's confirms. I am not aware if corrected.

5. Option trade commission schedule was erroneous. As of March 7th, still not corrected. We received numerous customer complaints.

6. All joint account name files came over from NFSC not properly coded JT WROS on the Broadcourt System. All

joint stock transfers were rejected. As of March 7th, still not corrected.

7. All stock purchased after January 15, 1986 on NFSC system were not placed into transfer. We are doing manually in response to customer complaints.

8. It takes us an average of 1–2 hours a day to get Broadcort to run our confirms because we have only one printer. I have been advised another printer was ordered two weeks ago.

9. Brinks continues to be erratic on their pickups each day. I often have to remind them to come pick up our stock certificates.

10. Under the Broadcort system, we are unable to book in our securities. We have to spend additional time checking out all buy-in wires each day as a result of the average one-week delay in stocks showing received into client accounts.

11. When the NFSC February client statements were mailed, we received an estimated 50–100 telephone calls from clients asking us what happened to their securities and cash. At least ten were very irate and nasty because we failed to send them the SEC mandatory negative transfer letter, informing them that we were changing clearing brokers and giving client's the opportunity to opt-out. As of March 7th, C&S Securities still have not sent out that letter.

12. Paperwork has increased substantially because of the new account system Broadcort requires.

13. Systematic dividend payouts to third party banks for IRAs and other accounts have not been paid out because Broadcort has not programmed their system for it. As of March 7th, system still not set up.

14. We received over 100 accounts with dividends and small interest credits that would have been paid out February

28th on the NFSC system automatically. They will now have to be sent out manually.

15. The name card catalog file has not been alphabetized. Previously, we could bring up an account on the NFSC system by typing the name in the system. I will be using temporary personnel to get our 3300 accounts in order.

To summarize, because of the additional work load, it has been extremely difficult for my two branches to further develop relationships with our clients. The stress for all of us has been overwhelming. We take tremendous pride in servicing our clients and would appreciate every effort you can take to help us resolve the problems mentioned. Signed Jerry A. Wolff

I received a letter from Jim Anderson dated April 18, 1986 and copied to Mark Williamson. This was the first contact I had from Jim in almost two months. The letter was regarding special products revenue. The letter was a clear message I was about to be fired. It read as follows:

Reviewing your office financials for the first quarter, I'm disappointed in the small amount of special products revenue your office has generated (1.5%) of revenue. All of our other offices have generated 10% to 49% of revenues in special products the first quarter. Our firm goal as you know is 15% of revenues to be generated in special products. These non-discounted products would greatly help the office profitability and offset some of your higher salary costs.

Hopefully, the seminar on April 26 will be educational and Mike Neubeck is always available to assist in selling and executing these products. It will take a greater effort on your part and Katie's to let customers know we have a full line of investment products available.

On April 23, 1986, I responded to Jim's letter regarding special products revenue and copied to Mark Williamson. My letter read as follows:

> For the first quarter of 1986, Katy and I devoted all our time to the conversion. I am happy to report that my staff did a tremendous job in handling the problems resulting from the conversion. I can now say, we are ready to proceed with a major sales effort. Both Katy and I are looking forward to the April 26th seminar. I have no doubt that it will help us increase the special products revenue in the future. With the conversion out of the way, there already has been a marked improvement in special product sales. Despite my positive response to Jim's letter, there was no doubt I was about to be fired. The only question was when?

Katy, a Landmark financial advisor, and I both flew to Atlanta for the special products meeting held on Saturday April 26th. That day was marked by the Chernobyl nuclear power plant disaster. During the entire time of the meetings, I noticed a financial advisor from the Atlanta corporate office was either sleeping or reading a newspaper. Management laughed this disrespectful behavior off, treating him as a "good ole boy." Katy and I had flown up to Atlanta to learn something, not babysit an idiot.

The showdown with C&S Securities was Friday May 2, 1986. When Jim Anderson and Mark Williamson both showed up at my office door, the Door's song *The End* should have been playing in the background.

I was determined to turn whatever the two had to say to me into an exit interview, or rather an exit inquisition. From my Dodge reporting days, I knew how to ask questions. I wanted to walk out of my office with my head held high.

Within the next 24 hours, I wrote my final C&S Securities memo to file on the firing. Just in case a legal matter had risen, I could support myself with the notes.

Memo to File May 2, 1986

Jim Anderson, president, and Mark Williamson, vice president, regional manager, behind closed office doors advised me effective May 2, 1986, a manager change was taking place in my office and that I had resigned. I asked them, "Do you mean I have been fired?" They said "Yes." I asked "Why?" Jim told me he felt my strengths were in operations and he wanted a more "sales-oriented manager." I told him, "That statement is ridiculous." I reminded them that the income statistics of the 1985 earnings for the Fort Myers and Fort Lauderdale branches showed a consolidated $259,000 net profit for the year. The results were ranked number one in revenues when compared to equivalent sized banks of our former clearing broker's clients. Jim and Mark both agreed the statistics were good.

I then asked if this was "a personality problem between them and me?" They denied it was. Finally, Jim stated, "You complained too much about the conversion with Broadcort." He also said "You put too much pressure on Atlanta to get problems resolved." I said "It sounds to me like you want a manager who doesn't care if his branch goes to hell with client complaints." Jim said "that isn't the case." I mentioned we were promised a person from C&S to help out during the conversion and got no one. I also noted lack of response from Atlanta. Lynn Wood and other operations personnel had not returned over ten phone calls. "How would you feel?" I asked. Jim said "I can understand" and nodded his head.

C&S South Carolina was about to convert to Broadcort from NFSC. The South Carolina branch manager asked me to provide any information that would be helpful. I had made a few suggestions. I informed Lynn Wood of the phone call a few weeks later. Now, at this meeting, Jim said "You should have told C&S Atlanta about that phone call immediately." I told Jim "I thought it was common courtesy to help another C&S branch manager when they asked for help." Jim said "No, I didn't mean you shouldn't be courteous, but not advising us immediately could have caused confusion."

I could sense the meeting was turning hostile. Jim continued to rant that all I did was complain about operations and never asked anything about sales. At that point I told Jim "You did not call me or even return a call during the Broadcort conversion to see how we were doing." He then said, "I don't know what you are going to do, whether or not you'll even stay in the business." It was obvious he decided to embellish my firing with an additional insult.

Jim also advised me if I did not cooperate with him, he would "make it hard for me with future references." A moment later, perhaps realizing he had threatened me, he backtracked and said "he would continue to offer his references."

I asked him about my vacation pay (I was entitled to one month's pay). He handed me a letter signed by Richard E. Pfleger VP, employee relations which detailed my remaining benefits. After reading it, I said, "The letter claims that I've talked to Mr. Pfleger regarding resigning, but I haven't discussed anything with him in the last two months. Our only conversation had been on a job applicant." Jim then held up another letter and, keeping it well out of my reach, announced "This is your resignation letter." I could see that my signature had been forged. I said "Do you expect me to sign something?" Jim said "No." I responded "Good, because I don't intend to." They asked me for my office key and gave me some time to remove my personal belongings. During the entire meeting Mark Williamson hardly said a word. Both Jim and Mark stayed in my office until I left.

I felt a little sad, not because I was fired, but because I never got to enjoy the fruits of my successes at Money Center and Landmark Bank Brokerage Services. In fact, I believe the only reason they kept me on as long as they did was to get them through the Broadcort conversion nightmare.

I hired Harry O, Boreth, Esq. and considered filing suit against C&S Securities.

On June 11, 1986, Mr. Boreth sent Mr. Pfleger a three-page letter summarizing several of my memos to file along with notes on my conversations with C&S Securities officers. They included several of my warnings that C&S Securities management was continuously violating SEC laws and showed that they refused to stop such practices or prevent further violations.

A letter dated June 25, 1986 from the law firm of Seyfarth, Shaw, Fairweather & Geraldson to Mr. Boreth contradicted my allegations that C&S had violated relevant SEC regulations and NASD requirements. Their attorney wrote that "C&S takes these obligations seriously and share Mr. Wolff's apparent concern that they be scrupulously honored."

The attorney then wrote: "Moreover, even if all of the "facts" stated in your letter are accurate, Mr. Wolff still has no basis for seeking reinstatement or back pay." The attorney sited several legal rulings in Florida and stated that Florida common law "does not recognize the claim that Mr. Wolff's discharge was wrongful and in violation of public policy."

During that era and for many years to come, Florida, along with several other states, ruled against plaintiffs who were discharged from their jobs for being "whistle-blowers", including those who claimed to be fired because they objected to an employer's illegal activity.

The C&S attorney agreed I was owed bonus money from the net profits earned by the Fort Myers and Fort Lauderdale branches. I received a check for $2,610.95 after taxes. Part of that went to cover legal expenses.

Mr. Boreth and I met with an attorney who was experienced in securities law. Her opinion was if I filed an arbitration case, the NASD (National Association of Securities Dealers) would say "Thank you for bringing this to our attention" and maybe fine C&S Securities $10,000. But I would likely be blackballed from the business. All of us agreed to just let it go.

In the following months, I applied for branch management jobs with several major stock discount brokerage firms. Charles Schwab was expanding and hiring experienced branch managers. My credentials seemed a perfect fit for what they posted in the classified job section of the Sun Sentinel. When I spoke with their Human Resource's manager, he seemed very interested and requested I forward a resume. When I had not heard back from them after a couple of weeks, I called again and could not get anyone to speak with me. That happened to me again with a few other discount brokerage firms. It appeared that Jim Anderson from C&S Securities kept his word when he fired me that if I didn't cooperate with him, he would give me "bad references." I didn't cooperate with him, since I hired a lawyer and threatened a lawsuit that could have exposed C&S Securities SEC and NASD violations. I have little doubt that either Jim or someone else in C&S management told any future employers who contacted them that I was trouble. It's one of those things you knew, but could never confirm.

After not having any success finding a management job, I decided to start my own company: Bank Brokerage Consulting, Inc. I printed out business cards, resumes and a professionally done brochure describing seven services that could help banks make their stock brokerages profitable. After mailing out about 100 brochures to presidents of banks, I followed up with phone calls. To my disappointment, I drew no interest. I suspect if any of the bank presidents discussed my brochure with their brokerage heads, the latter would be reluctant to admit they needed help. No one was willing to admit that, even though most bank brokerages were failing. I had spotted a need and spent about three months to the business before I gave up. However, it was a good learning experience. I realized that just having a superb product (my service) wasn't enough when the leaders of an industry (bank presidents) didn't understand the discount stock brokerage.

25

JW CHARLES SECURITIES: I'M BACK!

I n October 1986, I called Dennis Ferguson, Executive Vice President in Charge of Clearing Services with Alan Bush & Company (soon to become J.W. Charles Securities Inc.) and asked
if he knew of any openings in either management or as a registered representative. When I was at Landmark Bank Brokerage Services, Dennis would stop by my office to see if we might
consider changing our clearing brokers from National Financial
Services Corp to Alan Bush Clearing. We always had great conversations about our industry, learning from each other. Although,
I had no desire to change clearing brokers, I always felt he was
a valuable contact. This proved to be true, as he called me back
the next day and asked if I would be interested in working as an
assistant branch manager and building my own account base
in Alan Bush's corporate Boca Raton branch. I said "absolutely."
After all, I already had two principal licenses which allowed me
to step into the position immediately.

The next day, I interviewed with Robert Anderson, branch
manager of the Boca Raton branch. He was of Irish descent and
reminded me of my former Hayden Stone margin department
supervisor, Bill Nesbitt. Within minutes, I could see I was dealing with a professional. There was instant trust between us and
I was hired on the spot. All Robert asked was that I cover for him
on Fridays and he would pay me $500 a month just for being

his once-a-week backup manager. He golfed almost every Friday and offered his assistance in helping me build my own book of clients. All I had to do was work my butt off and with my background he felt I would be very successful. His door was always open if I needed him.

He made me feel right at home. On my first day on the job, October 23rd, 1986, Robert introduced me to all the registered representatives in his branch. It was great to be back with a NYSE member firm. Conveniently, it was also a self-clearing firm with its operations based in the same Boca Raton building. With my new job in Boca Raton and Catherine's company also having moved their corporate headquarters to Boca, we purchased a single-family home just minutes away from both of our offices.

My timing could not have been any better, as several representatives switched firms. Robert was unlike most branch managers that I had ever met. He was honest and fair with all of his brokers when it came the time to redistribute the accounts of the brokers who had left. Even though I had just started a few weeks earlier, I participated in a pot luck distribution of those accounts. With about 20 brokers in our branch, I watched Robert make piles of account posting sheets and place them by alphabetical order with the name of the receiving broker on top of each pile. I never once saw him look to see which accounts were more active than others. What accounts I got were strictly luck, almost like a lottery. I had been given several accounts with the last names beginning with the letter "C or M".

Now it was up to each individual broker to call those clients and do their best to encourage them to stay with Alan Bush rather than transfer to where their previous brokers had gone.

I spent the following days and evenings calling all of the accounts that had been given to me. About 60% of them chose to stay at Alan Bush and a few of them became treasured clients. It was nice to have a group of clients within a few weeks of joining the firm. Most of them invested in stocks and municipal bonds. I had quite a lot of experience in both fields.

Over time, using the mailing labels I had brought from C&S Securities, I opened about 25 additional new accounts. The majority of these were women and a few became excellent trading accounts. Instead of relying exclusively on stock analysts, I did a tremendous amount of my own research. Often, I found that the information I received from analysts was tainted, because many of them provided research on companies they followed without fully disclosing their interests or personal holdings in a company they were recommending. In fact, it wasn't until the "technology stock crash of 2000–2001" that full disclosure rules went into effect and were regulated by the Securities Exchange Commission.

In 1987 Atlantic Richfield Company (ARCO) sold off 20% of its shares of Arco Chemical, whose name had changed to Lyondell Petrochemical Corporation, which was based in Houston. Shortly after, I began to follow the activity in the stock. I didn't know anything about the chemical industry, but the stock offered a 5% cash dividend and looked attractive. I called the head of investor relations at Lyondell and requested a short meeting in Houston to learn about his company. I flew there, where he spent about 30 minutes with me and explained that Lyondell was a major producer of polyethylene, polypropylene and ethylene and how the cost of a barrel of oil affected their earnings. Once, I understand that, it was easy to figure out how profitable they might be. While I was in Houston I spent a few days with my childhood friend, Lenny, and his family who were living in a suburb outside of Houston. So, I managed to combine business and pleasure.

Alan Bush & Company now had new owners and a new name J.W. Charles Securities Inc. A Canadian businessman was the majority owner. On April 6, 1987, I passed my NYSE Branch Manager series 8 exam with an 87 score. Through the first nine months of 1987 I spent day and night building relationships with my new account base. I discovered Saturday was a great day to contact my younger clients who were hard to reach during the work week. They seemed very appreciative of my phone calls and were anxious to hear my perspective on the stock market and individual stocks.

At one point the Dow Jones average had hit 2,722.42, which turned out to be the 1987 high. The news around the world was bleak and interest rates were quite high at the time. Remembering the 1973–74 stock market collapse and the positive move in the price of gold at the time, I began contacting my clients about a possible stock market selloff in the near future. I recommended putting some money into the Keystone Precious Metals mutual fund. I felt that gold would be a small hedge if the stock market took a hit. About five of my clients bought $5,000 to $10,000 worth.

On October 9th, 1987 the Dow Jones Average stood at 2,516.64. One week later the Dow closed at 2,246.74, down 269.90 points for the week. That drop created margin calls that would have to be dealt with the following week.

Monday, October 19th, 1987, the stock market crashed. The Dow Jones Average dropped 508 points to close at 1,738.99 (a 22.6% decline). On business channels, well-known analysts were predicting the Dow would fall to 1,000. My phone was ringing off the hook all week and I was advising my clients to buy. I recommended high quality stocks like Walt Disney and Johnson & Johnson. I told them they might not get another opportunity like this for a long time and literally begged them to buy. That week my buy transactions ran eleven to one versus the sell side. I worked till 11:00 P.M. for four days, staying late waiting for confirmation of the executed trades. The volume was so heavy, it was almost impossible to get confirmations in a timely matter.

On Friday, October 23rd, at 4:00 P.M. I drove over to the former Holiday Inn on Glades Road and sat for a few hours drinking a couple of beers as I watched the birds hover around the outdoor pool. I was exhausted and needed those moments to reflect on what had just happened. I knew immediately, my earlier concerns about a stock market selloff were correct. However, even though I was right to say that gold would provide some hedge against a market drop, my advice on purchasing the Keystone Precious Metals mutual fund turned out to be wrong. The commodity price of gold bullion went up, but the gold stocks that were held in the Keystone portfolio went sharply lower. I learned a tough lesson from that experience. When margin calls are hitting accounts and speculators don't have the funds to cover them, they will liquidate any or everything they own. It simply doesn't matter.

I remember saying to myself, over the next few months, I would learn whether or not I had done the right thing for my clients by telling them to buy. I felt my stock brokerage career was on the line. December 31, 1987, the Dow closed at 1,938.83, roughly 200 points higher than the October 19th, 1987 crash. The analysts' worst-case predictions never materialized. I knew then that I had a real business that was mine as long as I worked hard and was honest.

As I recall, sometime shortly after being hired, the branch manager, Robert, switched firms which left me as acting branch manager until they hired a replacement. I was new with the firm and building my own business, so I did not expect to get the job nor did I want it at that time. They eventually hired Jim Dolan. an experienced NYSE branch manager who seemed quite capable. I missed Robert and forged a working relationship with Jim.

The stock market volatility was back to a more normal level. Based upon my previous study, I began purchasing Lyondell Petrochemical for a few of my accounts. The correlation between the price of oil and the commodity price of the chemicals Lyondell produced was reflected in their quarterly earnings. I took advantage of a trading pattern that developed when a barrel of oil stayed within an $18.00-$22.00 price range. As a result, in the following years, I bought and sold the stock over 200 times without a loss on a single trade. Often, my clients also picked up an additional 5% dividend return as well. Many traded the stock five to ten times over the years.

Unfortunately, I never had another stock like Lyondell again. In December 2007, Lyondell Petrochemical was acquired by Basell Pololefins at $48.00 a share in an all-cash deal. At any rate I had stopped trading the stock many years earlier following the Middle Eastern wars. Once the price of oil began to fluctuate wildly, all the previous correlations were no longer in play.

In an attempt to broaden my image in the community and do some networking, I got involved with the Florida Atlantic University Alumni Association. In January 1988 I was elected to the FAU Alumni Board. After showing I had leadership skills along with ambitious ideas for the association, I was elected Vice President in 1989 and then President for the 1990–91 period.

FAU was a growing institution, but had become stagnant at times. Often, I felt the alumni association was no more than a social club governed by the FAU Foundation Board liaison. As President, I was determined to change that by declaring our independence, as we were there to support the university and alumni, not be a puppet of the foundation. My goals could be accomplished if, instead of being controlled by them, we would become partners and the winner would be FAU.

An alumnus, an executive with a local cruise line, offered us a great deal for our annual meeting. It would be held on the ship during a day cruise. Everyone paid for themselves and any guests. I was handed the gavel as the new president and immediately took out a $500.00 check. I was starting a FAU Alumni Association scholarship endowment. I had learned that the State of Florida would match by 50% any educational endowment at a minimum of $100,000. Under the state requirements, we would have four years to complete the endowment. Several board members did not know what an endowment was and questioned what would happen if we failed to raise the $100,000. I said "if we didn't reach our goal, we simply would not get the matching 50% and the donated money would still go to scholarships." The endowment did not get approved by the board until our next quarterly meeting.

During my speech to the board, I said "We are going to spend money to make money and we are going to have fun doing it." Board member, Patti Lankford, through her contacts came up with a few ideas on how the Alumni Association could generate revenues through royalty payments. She helped us obtain contracts with a bank, a telephone company and others by offering such services as FAU credit cards. We also began advertising alumni lifetime memberships at a very reasonable cost.

While our board members were adopting these changes, FAU had hired Dr. Anthony J. Catanese as the new President of FAU. Tony formerly had been dean of the College of Architecture at the University of Florida. At his inauguration, I was asked to give a speech as President of the FAU Alumni Association. This meant standing in front of thousands, so I practiced my speech in the auditorium a few days earlier. I learned very quickly the importance of knowing how to use a microphone. On Inauguration Day, I was 30 seconds into my speech, when a two-minute blackout occurred. A blackout was the best thing that could have happened: everyone was laughing which eased any tensions I might have had.

During the year, Tony and I held meetings with alumni in both Palm Beach and Broward Counties. Tony was a soft-spoken individual who held grand plans for making FAU the fastest growing university in the country. He succeeded and had my full respect. I remember an annual alumni board meeting on Key Largo where I sat in a lawn chair discussing with Tony how a football team would bring FAU recognition. The school, which opened in 1964, was known for excellence in academics, but we were ready for more. FAU had to compete for academic talent as well as sports recruits. A football team would get the university noticed, not just by Floridians, but by the rest of the country.

Legendary coach Howard L. Schnellenberger was available and Tony brought him aboard. FAU Football was off and running. Howard started the football program and coached at FAU from 2001–2011 before retiring. In 2007 FAU upset Memphis in the R & L Carriers New Orleans Bowl game, putting FAU on the national map. Catherine, my nephew, Glen, and I were there to witness it first-hand. The game was a thrilling experience and afterward we ran into some of our players celebrating on Bourbon Street. FAU would go on to win three more bowl games.

Catherine had earned a Master of Arts degree from FAU in December 1989. So when my term on the alumni board expired after six years, she was elected as a board member for six years. FAU got the services of two for the price of one. The $100,000 alumni association scholarship endowment I had started was completed in three years and we obtained the $50,000 match from the State of Florida.

One of the annual alumni meetings was held at Dodger Stadium in Vero Beach the old spring training venue for the Dodgers. I spent part of the morning shooting some baskets and when I got through, I joined the rest of the board members. I noticed a copy of the association's balance sheet and observed that there was over $100,000 in available funds. In my basketball shorts, tank top and sneakers I raised my hand and asked if I could make a suggestion. The president said "yes." I said "with over $100,000 sitting in your account and earning 5% from the FAU Foundation, why not do another endowment and obtain a $50,000 match from the state while they still offer it?" I also said, "I am not on the board so I am not going to suggest who or what should be endowed. That is up to you. In fact, I am going to leave the room and you can discuss it. Thank you for allowing me to address you." That afternoon they took a vote and agreed to place $100,000 in a FAU library endowment and obtain the 50% match. Catherine and I added our own donation to it, as we had previously done with the scholarship endowment. Between the two endowments, we contributed at least $4,000.

In Spring 1989, I received approval from the JW Charles compliance department and the firm's top analyst to issue a generic newsletter. It would be one or two pages and include stock market and economic analyses, political commentary, along with financial product discussion. I wasn't allowed to make any specific stock recommendations. I named my newsletter, "The Wolff Financial Newsline" and published it quarterly. It was sent complimentary to my clients and prospects. Many of my clients called me just to find out when they would receive their next copy. Unfortunately, August 15, 1991 would be my last issue. A couple of other registered representatives got wind of what I was doing and started to put out their own reports in which they included specific recommendations of securities. Upon seeing the other brokers' reports, compliance stopped all advisor reports to clients other than those issued by the company itself. I was angered by their decision to shut me down even though I had followed the compliance department's instructions. From a legal standpoint, though, I understood their concerns.

During the first three years at J.W. Charles, I increased my gross commission from $70,000 to over $175,000 while performing branch manager and assistant branch manager functions. Cold calling, referrals and The Wolff Financial Newsline all helped propel my business. In addition, I taught continuing education investment classes at J.C. Mitchell Elementary in the evening and discovered I loved teaching.

On August 2nd 1990, Iraq invaded Kuwait and in two days, Iraq had full control. This assault would lead to the start of the Gulf War (also known as Operation Desert Storm) on Jan 17, 1991. From the time the Gulf War started, the Dow Jones Average was very volatile, but closed at 2,882.18 on February 28th 1991 a couple of hundred points above where it was at the start of the war. Once our country realized that the war would not be long lasting, investors looked ahead. For me this was another learning experience. The stock market always looks ahead.

Over the next few years my production grew to the low $200,000 gross commission area, but I felt as if I had hit a plateau. My pre-tax earnings were around $75,000 a year based on a 35% payout. I wanted to grow my earnings to at least $100,000 a year. I decided I had to look beyond J.W. Charles to do that.

The Dow Jones Average started very well in 1994 and managed to hit an all-time high of 3,978.36. However, inflation concerns crushed the bond market when Federal Reserve Chairman Alan Greenspan raised the Federal fund rate from 3% to 6% followed by six consecutive rate increases. His actions caused the 30-year U.S. Treasury interest rate to hit 8%. That sent mortgage rates through the roof, making it more difficult for homebuyers to purchase a home. Municipalities, corporations and individuals all suffered because of the higher rates. Anyone owning bonds saw their portfolio deteriorate substantially. Insurance companies and banks also took a beating from Greenspan's moves.

Personally, I was never a fan of Alan Greenspan, for all his fancy phrases. Somehow, by the time he finished each speech, I realized I had learned absolutely nothing.

Alan Greenspan had been one of President Nixon's economic advisors during the 1968 presidential election campaign. As I recall, Greenspan made comments in support of price and wage controls. Nixon put them in place by executive order in 1971 and the controls lasted into 1974. The combination of those controls and the Arab oil embargo sent inflation and interest rates much higher and pushed our economy into a deep recession. Throughout my career, it seemed that whenever there was a recession, it seemed Alan Greenspan could be found in a major position of economic influence.

By August 1994, after seven years with J.W. Charles, I began to interview with a few stock-brokerage firms with a plan to change firms over the Labor Day weekend. I interviewed with the branch manager of a Raymond James office in Lighthouse Point because I heard they were moving to a new Boca Raton office building within months. Raymond James stock analysts had a good reputation for picking stocks and that appealed to me. The company flew me up to their corporate offices in St. Petersburg for an interview with top executives. I immediately liked the firm and felt it was a place where I could grow my business.

Catherine and I decided to take a 10-day vacation in Alaska. I gave the Raymond James branch manager the fax number of the Alaskan Hotel in Juneau so he could fax me a copy of the contract if I was hired. When we arrived, a fax was waiting in my room with an abbreviated contract offer from Raymond James. The contract was for three years with an upfront payment and bonus feature based on my production. I was thrilled as I had never received an upfront cash offer before. I felt like a professional ballplayer. I faxed back my acceptance and enjoyed the rest of our Alaskan journey.

Upon returning I called Raymond James and confirmed everything was on target for my Labor Day weekend move. About a week or two prior to the move, I drove to my new temporary office in Lighthouse Point to get a copy of the full contract and the NASD U-4 required registration forms to fill out. When the branch manager provided me with a copy of the full contract, I was in shock. They had changed the terms dramatically. Instead of a three-year contract it had changed to five years. The contract also reduced the amount of upfront money that had previously been agreed upon and instead backloaded the contract with bonuses based on my achieving certain production levels.

I then asked "How is the construction coming on the new Boca Raton offices?' The manager's response was "Oh, the deal fell through. We are not moving there and will be staying in the Lighthouse Point office for quite some time." At that point, I took the contract copy along with the U-4 registration forms and drove back to my J.W. Charles office. After re-reading the contract and realizing that the Raymond James branch manager had not been honest even about the move to Boca Raton, I called him back and I told him, "I don't do business with firms that I can't trust to honor their commitments. Furthermore, when were you going to tell me, you weren't moving to Boca—after I changed jobs?" He had no response. At that point I shredded all the papers relating to Raymond James.

I needed to find another firm immediately because I was determined to make a move over the Labor Day weekend. I knew three former J.W. Charles financial advisors that had gone to A.G. Edwards & Sons Inc. After talking with them, I set up an interview with Rick Harris, who had just taken over as the branch manager of the Boca Raton branch. There were about 20–25 brokers working in the offices and Rick needed an assistant branch manager. Rick was a very conservative, serious manager and the kind of person whose word I felt I could trust. He told me he couldn't pay me any additional salary or bonus, but promised to introduce me to some of his clients he had brought over from his prior firm. As manager, he wasn't allowed to run a book of accounts. What he offered didn't seem much, but over time, I found he always kept his word. Even though A. G. Edwards did not entice new brokers with upfront money, they offered huge benefits, which included a 100% profit sharing plan into all employees' 401K, paid health insurance and a respectable commission payout. They also offered a sterling reputation.

The firm was founded in 1887 and A.G. Edwards had a history going back to the Lincoln Administration. This was a brokerage firm with no debt and stable earnings. Especially attractive to me was their great employee stock purchase plan. Once a year, through payroll contributions, I could purchase shares of the company stock with a guaranteed minimum gain of at least 15%.

Rick offered me the job and the move was made. It was the start of a 22-year sequence that could have been titled, like the movie, *The Good, The Bad and The Ugly*. I survived them all.

26

A.G. EDWARDS & SONS: THE GOOD

On September 6, 1994, I began a new chapter in my stock brokerage career. My U-4 NASD clearance at A.G. Edwards (AGE) came within a couple of days. All my licenses were now valid and I was ready for business. It took about two months to bring over 90% of my accounts from J.W. Charles. I would have been thrilled with just 75–80% coming over with me. It was unheard of to retain such a high percentage of clients when moving to a new firm.

I spent the first three weeks contacting my former J.W. Charles clients by phone, mail or personal visits. I also visited the AGE corporate offices in St Louis. Together with other transfer brokers from around the country, I attended two days of training that stressed the AGE tradition of putting clients first, employees second and shareholders third. One of the main reasons I joined AGE, was because their policy was not to offer proprietary mutual funds or any other "house" products. Such products could present a potential conflict of interest for brokers when advising clients. Often, they generated higher revenues for the firm and commissions for the brokers, creating an incentive for brokers to sell products that may have not been suitable for their clients. In fact, in some firms, the branch manager's bonus was based on his brokers selling a certain percentage of proprietary mutual funds. AGE was unlike most other major stock broker-age firms and a big selling point for me.

During my visit, the transfer brokers were invited to a lun-cheon with Ben Edwards CEO, which was held in the executive dining room. When I left the training auditorium for lunch, I made a stop at the quote machines to check on the market, indexes and some of the stocks I followed. Before I knew it, I was running a few minutes late. I headed towards what I hoped was the executive dining room. Realizing I was lost in the huge office complex, I asked a well-dressed gentleman walking by "How do I get to the executive dining room?" He responded, "Just fol-low me. I'm Ben Edwards," and put out his hand to introduce himself.

Ben was a very special CEO. I never worked in a company so dedicated to living up to its mission statement. Once a month Ben would get on the squawk box with all of the AGE brokers and discuss the growth of the company. If some legislation was of importance, he would welcome discussion by having brokers send in their questions or have us call a specific phone number. His meetings usually lasted 30–60 minutes. If you had a per-sonal question, you could call his office and most of the time, he picked up his own phone.

On one of my visits to Saint Louis, I had a chance to talk with Ben "one on one" in his office. He liked to show off his unique Asian sculptures. As a soon-to-be world traveler, I was fascinated with his very valuable collection. Although our chat was no lon-ger than ten minutes, my respect for him continued to grow. Over time, I noticed that several stock-brokerage CEOs despised him and considered Ben a midwestern outsider and something of a renegade in the industry. Ben did not believe in proprietary products and didn't want brokers to push clients into buying anything. He only cared that a broker did right by his clients, not how much money the firm made. Brokers never had a quota hanging over their head. Just being honest and meeting client objectives were his main concerns. I have no doubt that some major shareholders were not happy with Ben's attitude, but I certainly was.

As a stock broker, I studied and did sector analysis. Once a year, I attended a conference at the home office which focused on sector analysis. Every senior analyst would review their best two or three stock picks in their specific sector. I always took extensive notes. My plan was to provide the brokers in our branch with the analysts' best stock picks along with their printed reports at a branch meeting. I always held those meetings after the market had closed for the day, so I would have time to answer any of their questions.

In 1995, I started teaching at FAU, a two-hour evening course titled "Stock Market Trading Strategies and The Mechanics of The Securities Industry." It was a five-week continuing education course dedicated to personal investing. Students were charged a $55 fee and all payments were payable to the FAU Foundation. I insisted on being a non-paid instructor, as I wanted the funds to go into a continuing education scholarship fund which I helped administer. Since the fee was going towards scholarships it probably was tax deductible for my students. Due to potential liability concerns for FAU, I was instructed not to solicit any students unless they specifically requested a consultation and I always followed those guidelines.

I told Judith Robinson, my FAU continuing education counselor, that my course would be provocative as it was designed to educate my students in how the brokerage industry worked. I wanted them to understand that they were about to be taught the truth about various financial products which their current advisors may never tell them.

On opening night, the first question my students always asked was "Can I record your class?" I always replied "Yes, and if you are from the SEC, NYSE, NASD or you work for s stock brokerage firm, you are also welcome to record me." I have no doubt that many of my students thought I was crazy to be so candid. However, that was the way I taught. Sometimes I had FAU professors taking my course and most of them became my clients. Also, it was not unusual to find a few sales assistants from other brokerage firms taking my course. I often wondered whether they were there to spy on me or to get an education. Either way, it didn't matter to me.

Each term, in my first class, I gave my students a handout of stock brokerage vocabulary with words and phrases that I felt would help them as the course moved along. I also would always go over the stock and bond market history dating back to May 1975. I discussed recent activity and gave my opinion of where I thought the markets were headed. My classes ranged from 12 to 60 students depending on what was happening in the market.

To shake things up and to get an idea of what kind of investors my students were, I liked to bring up limited partnerships, a sore spot to those who had lost money in the markets of the eighties and nineties. In some of the larger firms (i.e. Prudential) there was mass selling of limited partnerships to clients who were promised 10–12% returns annualized over a seven-year period. Most of the limited partnerships involved leasing of real estate, airplanes and other types of equipment. Clients were told they would get their full investment back in seven years. When I was working at J.W. Charles, a wholesaler would come into the firm and do a presentation on why his specific limited partnership was a good deal. We were given a prospectus that was typically 100–200 pages of legalese that even a sophisticated advisor or client would have a hard time understanding. I was curious and tried to understand how these products were going to return 10–12% as well as return a client's original investment in seven years. Generally, the advisors were paid an 8% commission and when I examined the prospectus it seemed that the general partner's expenses to put together the partnership was another 12%. Most of the partnerships used leverage (borrowed money) to obtain the initial 10–12% returns which clients believed they would receive for the next seven years.

To simplify, if you invested $10,000 and an 8% commission was paid to a financial advisor and the general partner's expenses were 12%, it meant that only 80% of that $10,000 was actually available for the general partner to invest. To make things worse, often the limited partnerships had minimal or no liquidity for many years. They did not trade on an exchange or public market. If you wanted to sell them, you were at the mercy of a firm that specialized in limited partnerships. Almost everything about that type of investment looked like fraud, yet the SEC didn't seem to have a problem with them. Fortunately, I did and never sold a single one to my clients.

In summary, I told my students that when real interest rates are 4–6% and someone is offering you 10–12%, run like hell. I said "the problem is threefold: brokerage firm, financial advisor and client greed." After making that statement when I looked out over my class, I usually could read the faces of those who had taken a bath by purchasing a limited partnership.

I have no doubt some of my students had suffered sizeable losses and resented being told that they had been motivated by greed. At the end of the course, I was graded by my students. If I didn't get at least a few bad grades, I assumed I wasn't being provocative enough. I hoped to have my students learn from their mistakes.

The course outline included the following subjects: Product Strategies, Dividend & Interest, Transferring of Securities versus Holding in Street Name, Types of Accounts, Margin Account Strategies, Short selling, Option Account Strategies & Risks and Stock Market Trading (Mechanics). Each category included a detailed breakdown. By the time a student completed my 10-hour course they should have been able to manage their own investments or sit down with a financial advisor and understand any presentation being made.

While teaching my first class of the 1997 term, Hillary Clinton was speaking on the FAU campus. In my lectures, I often brought up how some politicians failed to disclose their personal holdings in corporations to whom they awarded government contracts. Sometimes those interests would leak out through good reporting and I saved newspaper articles as a reference for my classes. When it came to questionable ethics in politics, it didn't seem to matter which party you looked at: Democrat, Republican or Independent.

That night, my talk mentioned Hillary Clinton, a politician who I felt had shown poor ethics in her prior financial dealings. In 1978 she was introduced to a commodity trader named James Blair, an outside counselor to Tyson Foods. Her initial investment of $1,000 at the office of Ray E. Friedman & Co. (Refco) would turn into $100,000 in about ten months. Having worked with a commodity broker in the seventies, I understood commodity margin requirements. It was reported that Hillary Clinton's account did not meet those requirements. She claimed to have rarely looked at the trade confirmations sent to her. In most commodity accounts, discretionary papers are signed by the client giving full trading authorization to the advisor. Even though Hillary probably did not break any laws, I find it hard to believe that she was unaware of the margin requirement violations by her advisor and Refco, the firm handling her account.

Also, I informed my students of another story related to Hillary Clinton. President Bill Clinton selected the First Lady and Ira Magaziner to head the Health Access Initiative. I remember becoming concerned about the initiative because it seemed one's choice of doctors would be based on the county in which one lived. In addition, the initiative proposed price controls, not only on older drugs, but also on new drugs. Such controls, I felt, would destroy the incentive for a pharmaceutical company to invest hundreds of millions of dollars to develop a new drug that may or may not get FDA approval. The financial risk would be massive and price controls would slow down the development of new drugs that were desperately needed. I had invested in stocks like Pfizer, Merck and Bristol Myers. When news broke out about potential price controls, those stocks were hit hard. At the time a rumor came out that the First Lady had invested money in a growth fund that was selling short the pharmaceutical stocks. If she was invested in such a fund and if that fund learned of the administration's health initiative prior to the public announcement, that could have been perceived as insider trading.

Following my comments regarding Hillary Clinton, an older student went to the Continuing Education department and requested her $55.00 fee be returned. She told Judith Robinson that I had solicited her business and had made provocative comments during my lecture. The former comment was not true. A refund was made, but Judith never informed me of the complaint. The first I heard of it was when it came time to register for teaching the following term. When I didn't hear from Judith, I called and she informed me of the complaint. I set up a meeting that afternoon and in it reminded her that my course was designed to be provocative so that students would learn about investing from an insider's perspective. I told Judith "Just follow the news and see how often politicians make money off of the bills they pass." She responded "We love your teaching and want you to continue, just tone it down a little. Thank you and now let's get your course registered for this term."

I toned it down. A year later, I received a letter from the office of B. Ray Holland, FAU Dean of Open University and Continuing Education (OUCE), advising me that I had been selected to receive the 1998 Marilyn F. Federico Continuing Education Award. The letter read "The award is given each year to someone who has demonstrated exceptional friendship and support for learning over a lifetime. Your selection is in recognition of your strong support of OUCE by devoting your time to teach, contributing to the establishment of the Continuing Education

Financial Aid Fund, and serving on the Financial Aid Committee. The first award was given last year to Marilyn F. Federico and named in her honor; therefore, you are the first annual recipient." On December 17, 1998 I was honored at the OUCE faculty holiday reception, held at the Boca Raton Resort & Club.

All my classes were taught 7:00–9:00 P.M. I looked forward to each class no matter what kind of day I had dealing with the markets. I knew from my own experience of taking night classes that enthusiasm was essential if I wanted to keep students from falling asleep. I tried not to be boring and always opened class up to discussion. When I got home after teaching, I was so pumped up, I wouldn't be ready for bed until well after midnight.

Back in 1996 the Dow Jones Average increased to 5,739.63, a 26.01% gain over 1995. In that same year, Fed Chairman Alan Greenspan used the phrase "Irrational Exuberance" to describe what he felt was an overvalued stock market. It was rumored that Greenspan invested only in U.S. Treasuries. If so, I could understand some of his concerns about the markets overheating. After all, the Dow Jones Average had made a substantial percentage move between 1994 and 1996. His prognosis would turn out to be wrong for at least the next four years. The Dow continued to climb and closed year-end 2000 at 10,729.38.

Sadly, around that time, my branch manager became ill. As acting manager, I observed a major change in the types of trades that were being executed in the branch. Nasdaq stocks were hitting all-time highs fueled by the dot-com craze. An initial public offering of a tech stock could be priced by a brokerage syndicate with the offering price at $30 a share and then open up for public trading at over $100 a share. Speculation was rampant. In almost all cases, only institutions and hedge funds were able to obtain shares at the initial offering price. Rarely did the general public have an opportunity to purchase shares at the new issue price. Instead, individual investors were stuck purchasing shares at a much higher price after the stock began trading as a public issue. Many of the dot-com sector companies failed to earn a dime and later went bankrupt or had their stock drop to single digits from being traded as high as $300 a share.

I had a compliance concern. When I reviewed branch transactions, I saw many brokers were moving clients out of conservative stocks and mutual funds into dot-com stocks and tech-related mutual funds. Also, I noticed a huge increase in penny stock trading. Whether the executed orders were solicited or unsolicited didn't matter to me. This had to addressed.

On March 10, 2000, I issued the following letter to all brokers in my office.

> To All Brokers: All of you are aware, we are in a very volatile market. Nasdaq is hitting new highs while the DOW stocks have been depressed.
>
> I have seen a large number of mutual fund switches in the past few months. In most situations, it was for clients desiring more exposure to the technology and biotech sectors, while reducing their holdings in blue chip funds or Dow oriented funds (generally more conservative in nature over a long period of time; i.e. Washington Mutual Fund).
>
> If the changes represent an objective change, I strongly suggest you hand in updated new account cards with the new objectives. This will not guarantee protection should your client get caught on the wrong end of the market again. However, it will show regulators that you were doing your job and the client's objectives had changed.
>
> Also, penny stock trades in this office are hitting new proportions. The client's objectives had better be speculative. This firm hates this type of business, so be careful. Any errors will be your problem.
>
> If you have any doubts whether to take an order, speak with me or compliance. If you are uncomfortable with doing business with a client, you may need to terminate the relationship before it becomes a compliance issue.

Again, thanks for your support and let's have a great year.

Jerry A. Wolff-Assist Branch Manager

On March 10th, 2000 Nasdaq closed at 5,048.62 after hitting an intra-day high of 5,132.52. It had been up 24% year to date. As it turned out, the day I warned my brokers about speculating in technology stocks also marked the peak of Nasdaq. The dot-com craze was over. Investor torture followed with Nasdaq reaching a low of 1,108.49 in October 2002 (a 78.4% decline).

I wasn't invested in dot-com stocks going up. I thought I wasn't in them going down, but several mutual fund companies brought out new technology and communication funds during the dot-com era. A few of the mutual fund wholesalers misrepresented what types of tech or communication stocks the fund managers were purchasing in those funds. One wholesaler had me believing that they were purchasing stocks like AT&T and Verizon in their new communications fund, when in fact they were purchasing dot-com stocks instead. I watched that fund, which was originally priced at $10 a share, fall to $2. A few of my clients and I suffered the consequences from an untruthful mutual fund wholesaler. After that fiasco, I never purchased a mutual fund until I had a chance to view the fund's top ten holdings.

My move to AGE in September 1994 was showing great progress by the end of 1997. My gross commission goal of $300,000 was in reach. From 1999 through 2008 my annual gross commissions were between $300,000 and $380,000. During that period my pretax earnings met my earnings goal of over $100,000 a year. As a transactional broker versus a fee-based broker my earnings were substantially reduced. Despite pressure from the home office, I heavily discounted both stock and bond commissions. My attitude was, I am here for my clients only, not the firm I work for. I rarely lost a client. Having grown up in a poor neighborhood, I never nickeled and dimed my clients and felt the commissions I charged were very fair.

Catherine and I always lived within our means. We never borrowed from our families and when we purchased an item on credit, we always paid the balance in full by the due date. With my earnings stable, we were beginning to enjoy our lives and travel the world.

One of our happy places was Disney World and for many years, we were Disney World annual pass holders. Whenever we went to any of Disney theme parks, we would suffer from second hand smokers while waiting in line to enter a ride or presentation. Prior to 1998, there were virtually no rules regarding smoking on Disney properties. I had seen cigar smokers blow smoke at everyone, including babies, just to get in front of people for a closer view of the parade. As a non-smoker and witness to how cigar smoking ruined my father's health, I had little tolerance for such behavior. When one of those idiots blew cigar smoke in my face at the Magic Kingdom, I lodged a written complaint at the customer services desk, but never got a reply.

In July 1998, AGE held a regional meeting at the Hyatt Regency in Orlando. Later that evening several of us brokers drove over to Disney World's Pleasure Island to have a few drinks and check out the entertainment. As a result of what transpired there and another incident a few days later at a movie theatre, I wrote the following letter dated August 8th, 1998 to Michael D. Eisner, Chairman, The Walt Disney Company.

Dear Mr. Eisner:

As a shareholder, investment broker and patron of your amusement parks, I am sad to report that Disney is a very hypocritical corporation.

You provide great entertainment for adults and children of all ages. Until recently my wife and I have been annual pass holders for your theme parks in Orlando. We did not renew.

Are you aware that on Main Street (Magic Kingdom) the shops are selling cigars? I don't think the children attending Disney need to be exposed to cigar smoke (assisted with your help). Most adults don't appreciate having cigar smoke blown in their faces either. At Epcot English shops, cigars are sold. All over Pleasure Island cigars are sold. I'll assume you sell them at $5 to $6 a cigar. One cigar smoker will chase out ten potential drinking patrons in the show lounges. I watched a young woman smoking a cigar while on a rotating dance floor. She must have caused at least 30 patrons to leave. Subtract your profit on one cigar from the losses of numerous drinks at $3 to $4 a piece. That is poor business all around, not to mention the irritation the cigars cause everyone.

At the theatre recently, I noted Buena Vista Productions is a main supporter of the Will Rogers Institute. Please explain how Disney can support an institute which spends millions of theater patrons' donations on lung diseases when Disney promotes the sale of cigars throughout its parks. What is wrong here?

I filed a written complaint regarding sales of cigars once before at the Magic Kingdom, however I never received a response.

My clients and I own over 34,000 shares of Disney. Disney is a great company. Don't forget your roots. The few dollars Disney is making from cigars cannot compete with the lost revenues from unhappy ticketholders. Most people will not write a letter like this, they just will stop attending the parks. If you have a sincere concern for the health of Disney customers, please stop selling cigars. I welcome your response.

Sincerely,

Jerry A. Wolff

Within a week, I followed up the letter with a call to Eisner's office in Burbank and to my surprise I got his secretary, who confirmed receipt of the letter and said I would receive a response within a month. I received a letter dated September 10, 1998 from Jephrey Cox, Walt Disney World Manager Guest Communications. He addressed some of my concerns and let me know he had forwarded the letter to their Safety and Merchandise divisions. I left a few phone messages, but never heard back.

A year later Catherine and I visited Epcot. When we got to the World Showcase, we stopped for a pint of Bass Ale at The Rose & Crown Pub. As we sat down at the bar, I said to Catherine "Something is different." A sign read "No smoking allowed." I asked the bartender about it. He told me that a new policy had gone into effect about six months earlier. With the exception of a few designated smoking areas, the theme parks and hotels were now all non-smoking and they were no longer selling cigars at the British shops in Epcot or on Main Street in the Magic Kingdom. When I heard that, I was thrilled to know that my letter may have made a big difference. I felt like dancing on top of the bar, but settled for a jig outside the pub instead.

In a letter dated September 25, 1999, I congratulated Eisner and thanked him for placing the health of his Disney patrons first. I also renewed our annual passes to the Disney theme parks.

Following my best earnings year in 2000, my confidence as a portfolio manager was at a high point. I felt I could assist any company if the corporate executives were willing to listen. I knew my business and understood what I could do for theirs. However, I faced one major problem: I was not connected. I didn't have college friends, family or anyone else in high places. My clients were all retail. Some were wealthy retirees. None were connected to corporations. I had no institutional accounts. I tried to get involved with the FAU Foundation, but for some unknown reason, was unsuccessful. As a past president of the FAU Alumni Association, I was automatically given a one-year seat on the foundation board in 1990–91, but when I tried to continue as a Foundation board member, I was rebuffed. Why? Who knows? There were other financial advisors on the board and perhaps some considered me competition. Their loss. Then, too, I can be outspoken.

Since I'd successfully contacted Michael Eisner, I asked myself why not seek some of Disney's business? What do I have to lose? I sent a letter offering my financial services to Winifred Markus Webb, SR. VP Investor Relations and Shareholder Services along with my resume and some of my prior correspondence with Disney. Mr. Webb responded with a letter dated February 28, 2001, advising me he had notified the appropriate personnel of my extensive experience and background.

Shortly after, a DVD of Beauty and The Beast arrived at my home as a gift from Disney, followed by an email advising me that I have been placed on their investor information list which included updates on corporate news, earnings and other events. Sometime after September 2004, I was invited to a Disney two-night analyst meeting at Disney's Yacht Club. All of the top executives were there along with over 75 stock analysts. I was probably the only non-analyst invited to the event. Catherine joined me, but did not attend any of the business meetings. I paid for my suite, while the analysts had their expenses covered by the companies they worked for (including the AGE analyst who I ran into at the meetings). After listening and taking notes for two days, I had no doubt that Disney was going to be a great growth company. Anytime the stock market took a big drop, I used that as an opportunity to buy Disney shares.

A highlight of this visit was a behind-the-scenes tour of the Walt Disney World underground. I got to see the various costumes and go through a secret door used by Disney characters to make their appearance at street level. We were also shown where and how Disney prepares their topiaries. While I was in the meetings, Catherine spent the two days at the theme parks. In the evenings, we attended several corporate events for some light fun. Before we headed home, we even enjoyed spa treatments compliments of Disney. The experience was great and I will always be thankful for the opportunity to learn so much from a first-class company.

27

WORLD CRUISING: JUMPING INTO THE DEEP END

The stock market was hitting new highs, my Disney anti-smoking campaign in 1998 had seen success and now a world of adventure was about to begin. Catherine was working as a copywriter for Orient Cruise Lines in Fort Lauderdale. They owned just one ship, but a great ship, the *Marco Polo*. Catherine wrote the copy for the ship's cruises and excursions. Debbie Nathanson, President of Orient Cruise Lines had hired her. Debbie was an extremely bright and thoughtful leader. I knew that she was the kind of person Catherine could enjoy working with. We both had profound respect for Debbie.

The best part of Catherine's job, aside from working with great people, was that we would get to cruise once a year as a business trip. Instead of getting my feet wet on a mini-cruise, I literally jumped off into the "deep end" for some remarkable adventures. Our first cruise for example, combined a safari in Kenya with a cruise to the Seychelles. It was very memorable, but it almost didn't happen.

On August 7, 1998, Al-Qaeda set off car bombs next to the U.S. embassies in Dar es Salaam, Tanzania and Nairobi, Kenya. There were 224 deaths in total with (213 in Nairobi and 11 in Dar es Salaam). More than 4,000 were injured. We weren't aware that

Al-Qaeda was responsible for the bombings until after the U.S. retaliated on August 20th by launching cruise missiles against Osama bin Laden's terrorist training camps in Afghanistan.

We were scheduled to fly to Nairobi in early November to begin a three-night tour of the Masai Mara, followed by a two-week cruise starting from Mombasa, Kenya. When word got out that Al-Qaeda was responsible for the embassy bombings, about 70% of the Americans who booked the trip canceled. Orient Lines, through its London office, offered a 2-for-1 cruise to fill the cancelled spots and a large number of Brits were happy to snap up the offer. Many of them had experienced the London bombings in World War II and they seemed fearless. Our family members and friends often asked "Are you going to cancel your trip? My answer was "Not a chance."

After flying 18 hours with a stopover in Frankfurt, we arrived in Nairobi. We did a city tour the next day and our bus driver took us past the U.S. Embassy building that was the bomb target. Part of the embassy was severely damaged, but still standing. The building next to it was where most of the deaths and injuries took place. As our tour bus continued through the city, you could see windows blown out for several blocks from the blast. Later that afternoon, Catherine and I went for a mile walk from our hotel. At that point we knew very little about Al-Qaeda. If we had known more, most likely we would have stayed in our hotel until the next day for our five-hour drive to the Masai Mara. At some point in our walk it hit us: we were the only white people anywhere in the streets. Having grown up in Brownsville, that didn't concern me. A young man from Sudan tagged along with us for a while. He seemed very curious and wanted to learn about education in America. At all times, he was a gentleman and never hit us up for anything. On occasion, we received some stares, but at no time did I feel threatened, only fascinated.

That night we joined our tour group and ate dinner at The Carnivore Restaurant. The specialty of the house was game meat served on spits, skewers and platters brought tableside. There was everything from wildebeest, hartebeest and zebra for the adventurer (Catherine), as well as ribs and chicken for me. The meats were well cooked and for the most part had a gamey taste. Catherine sampled almost everything they presented. She also ate a fair amount of salad and what she said was "the sweetest pineapple in the world." The next day on our way to the Masai we saw monkeys, giraffes and at a rest stop, I purchased a couple of African masks.

After arriving at the Mara Sopa Lodge, we were given a welcome drink and prepared for a 4:00 P.M. game drive. We were in one of two open vehicles, each carrying six people. Our drive took us past zebras, elephants, giraffes, gazelles and a pair of dik-diks. As darkness approached, our vehicle came upon three lionesses high fiving each other as they prepared for their nightly hunt. It almost seemed as if this was their happy hour. Just to the left of us about 1,000 Cape buffalo were grazing in the grass and not showing any fear of the lionesses just a short distance away. Once happy hour was over, though, the lionesses would "put on their game face" as they lined up behind each other ready to begin their assault.

It was at this moment that Catherine chose to announce "I am very sick and am getting out of the van." She had lost control of her bodily functions. I yelled at her "you are not leaving the van with three lionesses 20 feet from us!" Catherine and I sat in the back, with three women and the driver in front of us. The other vehicle was a few miles away from us. Panic doesn't begin to describe what was going on in ours. One of the passengers, Linda, offered two Imodium pills in a blister pack. I got out the first pill with no problem. The second one was sealed tightly and, when I couldn't open it, Linda loaned me her Swiss Army Knife. If the knife had scissors, I didn't see them. As I tried to open the Imodium packet, the knife blade slid off the foil and sliced through the top of my left index finger to the bone, hitting an artery. Now I was gushing blood all over my white shorts and camera. While yelling and cursing at the world, I used a hand-kerchief to make a tourniquet hoping to stop the bleeding. It didn't work.

Our driver radioed that we were heading back to the lodge, but when he tried to start the vehicle, it made a noise that sounded like the transmission was gone. It took a few minutes, but he somehow got the van started for the 40-minute drive back to lodge. I held my hand up in the air through the pop-top as two vultures followed us for over 20 minutes. I assume they could smell blood and were viewing me as a potential dinner. I couldn't imagine there would be a doctor available to treat my wound. At this point all I could think about was that my trip was over and we were a five-hour drive back to Nairobi. It was too dark to have a helicopter come. Would I survive the night?

Our van barely made it back to the lodge and just before we got there, our driver stopped and knocked on a door. A man who looked like a young Sidney Poitier invited me in. Catherine, along with the others continued on to the lodge. The man (Patrick M. Mukotli) informed me he was the local doctor and would be treating me. The room was dark and about the size of a large walk-in closet. He did not have an anesthetic to give me, but was able to clean the wound while my finger continued bleeding. The doctor used sutures to reattach part of my finger. My toes curled from the pain as each stitch was made. After the third suture, I asked, "How many more, doctor?" He said in his musical Kenyan accent "Maybe one or two more." Finally, after the fifth suture the bleeding stopped, but I was still in a lot of pain and all I had was a bottle of Bayer Aspirin. I asked the doctor "What do I owe you?' He responded "You don't worry about the money. Go have dinner and I will come see you later in your suite."

I went back to my room to change out of my blood-drenched white shorts and take a few aspirins. After getting cleaned up I went to dinner and found Catherine finishing up her dinner with the three women from our van. Catherine was no longer ill and sipping a Hippo's Blush. She thought the delicious pineapples she ate the night before and again during breakfast may have caused her illness. The water the restaurants used to wash the fruits and salads could also have been the culprit. I drank three bottles of Tusker Beer with my dinner, hoping that would take the place of pain killers. It didn't.

Shortly after dinner, the doctor showed up at my suite and reexamined my finger to make sure the bleeding had stopped. Once again, I asked "What do I owe you?" He responded "You don't worry about the money. Just go on your safari tomorrow morning and I will check on you around 3:30." We went on safaris the next two days, during which we spotted over 25 lions, thousands of Cape buffalo, herds of zebras, antelopes, giraffes, elephants and much more. Every day the doctor showed up at 3:30 to check my finger. On the final morning, he handed me a bill for 1,500 Kenyan shillings (at the time about $30) and asked us if we had extra shoes or books for him. I couldn't give him my shoes and we didn't have any books, so I gave him additional money and thanked this wonderful man for everything he had done.

From the Masai Mara we boarded a small plane to Kenya's port of Mombasa. There we boarded the Marco Polo, and I headed straight to the ship's doctor. I explained what had happened as two giggling Philippine nurses listened in. The doctor, originally from Australia, examined my finger and said "Good job, but I have never seen sutures as thick as these in my life." I explained that the Masai Mara doctor's job is to stitch up Masai warriors when they are attacked by lions. It seems the tribe has a lot of cattle and if a lion attacks them, they use spears, circling the lion. Often the lion will bite a leg or thigh before he is killed. The doctor patches up these large wounds with very thick sutures and the wounded are transported to Nairobi for further care. Aboard ship I became known as the Lion King during our two-week cruise. The good news was I did not have any infection and after 10 days, the sutures were removed. The doctor thought the torn ligaments would heal and be back to normal in a year. That did not happen completely, as I have very little feeling in the top of the finger and occasionally drop small items. Still, my left-handed basketball hook shot remains as good as ever— maybe better.

After a spectacular cruise, I mailed over a hundred pounds of books (some for his two young children) to Patrick M. Mukotli at the Mara Sopa Lodge. I will forever be thankful for his care.

Even though my African safari didn't go as planned, world cruising was now part of my DNA. Every opportunity to experience the world was not to be missed and happily the Marco Polo cruised to all seven continents, including Antarctica. Catherine and I felt that there was no better education than exploring the world and its various cultures.

Our next trip was to the Greek Isles and Italy on August 13, 1999, starting in Istanbul. Having toured the city's incredible Blue Mosque and the Grand Bazaar in the prior days, we were headed for the ancient ruins at Ephesus via the port of Kusadasi, Turkey. Our guide was a young Sephardic Jew, who gave us an insightful tour. The site had a theatre renowned for its acoustics and it was easy to imagine a time when gladiators fought lions to the death within its walls.

On our cruise we visited Santorini, Delos and Mykonos, Greece. On Santorini, a tour took us to a winery carved in caves overlooking magnificent views of the Aegean Sea. We had lunch in the main town of Thira spread across steep cliffs and the chance to ride a donkey or a cable car back to the port below. We decided the cable car looked like a safer way to go. Delos was a sacred isle of 6th and 7th century BC beauty. Apollo and Aphrodite are said to have been born there. Walking around the spiritual ruins I could feel the sense of Greek history at every turn. When we arrived in Mykonos, our plan to explore one of their nude beaches was put on hold. Due to the Feast of the Annunciation holiday the day before, the buses were not running and lines for taxis to the beaches were very long. While Catherine and I were waiting for a taxi, two well-tanned, gorgeous, Bulgarian girls asked me if I'd like to share a taxi to one of the nude beaches. With Catherine trudging uphill a few feet behind me and hopefully not paying any attention, I promptly said "Yes!" After all, we were in the land of Greek goddesses. Alas, when a taxi pulled up, there was room for just two passengers so the beauties jumped in and that was the last I saw of them. By now, like in the good old days at Ephesus, Catherine was ready to turn me into a gladiator and feed me to the lions. We finally got a taxi to a typical Greek beach, though not the naturist one I had hoped for, which I enjoyed with Catherine, my American goddess.

August 17th was a sea day to be remembered. While watching the BBC news, a 7.6 magnitude earthquake hit northwestern Turkey. The city of Izmit was the epicenter. Istanbul was also heavily damaged as many buildings had collapsed. The death toll was over 20,000. We were sailing to Rhodes, Greece, but changed course due to tsunami fears and continued to Malta. Having just left Istanbul on August 13th, we realized how lucky we were. I hate to imagine what could have happened if the passengers had still been in Istanbul when the quake hit. With some relief, we concluded our voyage in Rome.

Going through customs in Miami, I declared a carpet that I had bought in Istanbul for $600. This, together with other clothing and shoe purchases in Italy, put us over the duty limit at that time. I remembered that the salesman stated that Turkey had a special trade treaty with the U.S. and that the carpet would be excluded from the limit. When I mentioned this to the customs officer, she said "Where is Istanbul?" Considering that the earthquake had been in the news every day, Catherine and I wondered how she could not know. I told her Istanbul was in Turkey. She proceeded to open up a very large book that had details of U.S.

custom taxes. She turned the pages to Turkey and after ten minutes of frantic searching, gave up and simply said "Go." I hoped the other agents had better geography skills.

Our next Marco Polo cruise left from Copenhagen July 17, 2000 and started with two wonderful days traveling around the city. We got to enjoy the Copenhagen Jazz Festival which was held at night in the Tivoli Gardens, so full of bright lights that fireworks were not needed. The Danish restaurants were delightful. A train ride to the Louisiana Museum outside the city gave us a feel of how the Danes live and a peek at the works of Alberto Giacometti and Andy Warhol (including a famous Campbell Tomato Soup Can painting).

From Denmark, we sailed past Sweden towards the Norwegian fjords at Hellesylt-Geiranger where we toured a beautiful countryside with sod roofed cottages, sheep, rivers and waterfalls. In an open market at the next port, Bergen, I saw a spectacular display of fresh salmon laid out on tables ready for sale. The Bergen Art Museum featured an exhibit of Erro's political paintings which some have characterized as pornographic. A few days later we arrived in the remote Faroe Islands and explored their cliff-lined beauty on an afternoon tour.

I had great expectations that exploring Iceland would be the highlight of our cruise. We arrived on July 24, 2000 at Reykjavik, the capital. There we joined a full day tour to the Langjokull Glacier which included rides on the glacier itself, both a snowmobile ride and also a two-kilometer drive on a Ski-Doo. There were 36 people on the tour, all from our ship. Catherine and I had previous experience with glaciers in Alaska where we had hiked around Mendenhall Glacier outside of Juneau and been on a helicopter tour to that glacier's top where we witnessed Mendenhall's glacial blue ice and moulins. Walking the glacier's surface, we were warned about the danger of crevasses and cautioned not to deviate from following our guide.

That Alaskan experience may have saved our lives. Catherine and I have a taste for adventure, but I know my limitations and try to avoid trouble. Now, in Iceland, on a glacial excursion, Catherine sat behind me on the Ski-Doo. Bikes always made me nervous and I'd never traveled on a Ski-Doo before, so I was driving 5–10 miles an hour, while everyone else flew by at what seemed 50–60 miles an hour. The trailing guide decided to put Catherine on his bike thinking it would speed me up. That was not about to happen, as I was scared of falling into a hidden crevasse. Slowly, I finished the two kilometers and I was ready to celebrate having avoided injury.

At the top we traded helmets and Ski-Doos with the other half of our tour group and boarded a van-like Snowmobile for what we thought would be a relaxing ride back to the lodge. From our open-air vehicle we could observe the second set of Ski-Doos. Some were veering up to 200 feet off the lead guide's path. Within minutes, we heard panicked yelling from behind us. I remember seeing a bike lying on its side with a crowd standing around. Our driver turned around and headed back to see if our larger vehicle could help. As we got close, we could hear a man from inside the glacier screaming. At that point we knew at least one person had fallen into a crevasse, which can go the depth of three football fields. The Islandic guides went into rescue mode, securing a rope to our Snowmobile and tying it around one of the guides. This brave young guide climbed down into the crevasse and within 20 minutes brought up a tall Dutch man in his sixties with a deep gash on his forehead. They asked the man three times, "Was a second person on your bike?" and each time he answered "No." One person thought a woman, known for her unusual hats, was part of our group. If so, she was missing. After a count was done, we suspected that she'd been on the back of the bike and had also fallen into the crevasse.

The same rescue guide descended into the glacier's crevasse. Then we heard a loud scream. When he climbed back up, he was drenched in ice water and needed to get out of his clothes immediately. We were about the same height, so I gave him my jacket and boots. I had additional clothes under my jacket, but I did not have gear to keep my feet warm and the temperature was around 20 degrees Fahrenheit on the glacier. At this point over half the group had been rushed back to the lodge, including the Dutch man, who was taken to a hospital and never made it back to the ship. Initially, we were told that the woman had been found, but that they would need a helicopter from Reykjavik to get her out. We assumed she was dead, but it was not confirmed until we got back to the ship. I was still on the glacier and my right foot began to freeze up so I knew I couldn't wait any longer. When the vehicle arrived, the last of our tour group hopped in and Catherine and I just managed to get the last seats in the back. Just as the driver started back, the man in front of me yelled "Stop! I can't find my baseball cap." I said "We need to go now. I have a frozen foot and I'll buy you another hat." After hearing this, the driver proceeded to the lodge where I was able to thaw my feet. It turned out the baseball cap was lying on the floor of the vehicle.

When we arrived back at the *Marco Polo*, we had a meeting with Captain Eric, who had never lost a passenger in his long career and was sick over what happened. He advised all of us that the woman had died and a service would be held aboard ship. She was a 65-year-old retired Los Angeles school principal.

Early next morning, we sailed into Akureyri, Iceland and got a great view of the Eyjafjordur fjord. After our horrific experience the day before, we needed to come out of our shock. We could see Iceland was special, but it was not Disney World: there were no fences, no guard rails and few caution signs. A mistake could cost you your life. Common sense was your guide in this super natural setting.

Catherine and I spent the day on a whaling tour from Husavik, a fishing village on the north coast. Minke whales swam close to our boat often showing off their dance moves as they slowly turned in the water. We went by an island where thousands of puffins lived. Later we disembarked for a buffet lunch offering the best smoked salmon I had ever tasted, along with an excellent Icelandic lager.

In Scotland's Shetland Islands we had a day to explore the capital, Lerwick. Although it was rainy, we managed to roam the flagstone streets doing a little shopping and having a pint in a pub. A short tour took us through the countryside to Viking and Medieval settlements built on grassy cliffs overlooking the sea.

Our cruise ended in Oslo, Norway with a visit by ferry to the awesome Kon-Tiki Museum where we saw the balsa raft Thor Heyerdahl used to sail from South America to Polynesia in 1947. From there, it was a short walk to the FRAM museum exhibiting the boat that Norwegian Roald Amundsen, together with a crew of four countrymen, used on the first expedition to the South Pole in 1911.

Just three months later we were traveling again, this time from Bali to Hong Kong on the *Radisson Seven Seas Navigator*. Through a connection with the cruise line, we had been offered a reduced rate, and we couldn't resist the opportunity. It was our first time in Southeast Asia.

We arrived in Hong Kong on October 24, 2000. Even though we were exhausted from our flights, once we saw the spectacular city lights from the panoramic Sky Lounge in the Kowloon Sheraton, we simply had to step out and take a midnight stroll around the city. After two flights and over 21 hours of fly time, I chose to have a two-hour massage and got back to our hotel after 2:00 A.M. The next morning, we flew to Bali, where most inhabitants are of Hindu heritage.

I had booked five nights at the Ritz Carlton located in Jimbaran Bay for just $150 a night. Both of us had several massages during our time on Bali. After a session with a petite Balinese masseuse, I wondered if any bones in my body hadn't been broken. Following that massage, a flower bath helped soothe the pain. Within a couple of hours, though, it felt as if I had been reincarnated with a new body. That's how good a Balinese massage can be.

The Ritz Carlton was set on a bluff in southwest Bali. The 173-acre property was incredible. Every morning we had fresh fruit and flowers in our suite. Every day around 5:00 P.M. two men would play the Gamelan just down the hall from our room. The best way to get around Bali was to hire a driver. We visited several temples and learned about Hindu customs. We ate lunch overlooking Lake Batur and the smoking Gunung Batur Volcano. Our driver also took us to a Balinese batik store offering beautiful silk sarongs in patterns fit for a princess. When Catherine tried on a two-piece blue and gold sarong, I had to buy it for her. Any time she wore it on the ship, she got stares from everyone, no doubt wondering what royalty she was.

One day we took a bus to Kuta beach, where we both enjoyed blissful two-hour massages for $22 each. Kuta was a popular resort with Australian surfers. It was a place to have cheap drinks and relax on the beach. By the end of our time on Bali, the one Hindu custom both Catherine and I were ready to adopt was that of bowing instead of shaking hands. It demonstrated respect and had a special grace. I can't remember a time in my life when I was more relaxed.

On October 31, 2000, we left Bali's Benoa harbor and cruised to Surabaya and Semerang, ports in Java. During our visits, we witnessed an insane bull race with pre-teen male jockeys. The bulls pranced under umbrellas, all dressed up with velvet stars and sheathes on their horns. Eight pairs of bulls competed in 200-yard dashes that were completed in a matter of seconds. Our tour group watched the races from behind a flimsy "fence" woven of banana leaves. Locals watched from across the way sometimes without any fence at all. One set of bulls headed right at them, but luckily no one was hurt.

Our next adventure was a visit to the world's largest stupa, Borobudur. The construction of this UNESCO World Heritage shrine started around 750 AD and contains over two million cubic feet of stone. Over time it had been hidden under jungle growth and volcanic ash. Catherine and I climbed to the top and following tradition, touched the knee of the Buddha, thus assuring ourselves that all our wishes would be granted. After climbing down the stone terraces, we were treated to a puppet show depicting the war between good and evil, accompanied by strange music.

On November 2, 2000, we sailed into the former British Colony of Singapore. When I was a child in New York, my mother worked with Harry Alter, an import/export company, and would bring home cancelled stamps from Asian countries. They made me want to learn more about those countries. When I looked at those stamps, Singapore always seemed very modern in comparison to the others and one day I hoped to see it for myself. Now, after several visits, Singapore is my favorite destination.

Our first time in Singapore we took a city tour which took us to Mt. Faber for a panoramic view and then to a gem factory. It was there that I learned that the large beautiful shells I had purchased from beach vendors in Bali for just a dollar were genuine mother of pearl. For the first time I saw lavender jade, some of it was very expensive, and realized jade is not always green. We also toured the Merlion Fountain, Raffles and Government House. We learned about the planning of Sentosa Island with its man-made beaches. Sentosa was built in 2010 and houses a Universal Studios theme park, hotels, an aquarium, a casino and other attractions. Singapore was planned for future growth. The city was clean with no garbage on the streets and no graffiti on the metro trains. Gum chewing or drinking anything on a train could lead to a fine. Illicit drugs were not tolerated. This was not Brooklyn. I prefer to live in a clean city rather than one that looks like a garbage dump and am willing to accept a few personal restrictions for that privilege.

During the rest of our time in Singapore, we visited the scenic Botanical Park, home to an amazing orchid collection, then spent a few hours exploring Chinatown and its temples. We also hailed a cab to the exclusive shops on Orchard Street. There I discovered my favorite leather shop, Kwanpen, known for the finest crocodile accessories in Singapore. I purchased a wallet and business card holder for myself. I wanted to get Catherine a gorgeous navy crocodile handbag. She wouldn't let me spend the money and I regret that I missed the buy of the day.

Three days later, we sailed into Ho Chi Minh City (Saigon). Upon arrival, I felt anxiety, wondering how we would be treated as Americans. The Vietnam War had ended 25 years earlier. I hadn't served in the military, but given my age the Vietnamese could perceive me as a former enemy. Back home I had a co-worker at AGE named Len who was servicing my clients while I traveled. Len had been an MP during the war. I let him know that I was going to Vietnam and intended to tour the Cu Chi tunnels and visit China Beach. He asked me to bring back a bag of dirt from the tunnels and a bag of sand from the beach. I said "ok" without giving it much thought.

On our first day in Vietnam, we toured the Cu Chi tunnels. About 40 guests from the ship joined the two-hour drive to Cu Chi. Most were over age 60 and didn't seem very nimble. We were taken to an area where during the war a B-52 had dropped a bomb and left a massive crater. Nearby was the entrance to the tunnels. Three months earlier I'd had surgery for a torn meniscus in my left knee, so I was wearing a knee brace as I went down a ladder into the tunnels. Only a few people from our tour group joined us and we were told to follow the arrows to find the exit. The tunnels were carved three to four stories into the earth and extended for miles, even going under a former American base where Bob Hope had entertained the troops. Due to our physical size, we were only allowed to go down one story as the lower tunnels had not been modified for our American-sized bodies.

As soon as we got down the ladder, we heard machine gun fire. I remember saying to Catherine "What the hell is going on?" The firing had stopped and we continued through three settings that recreated a command headquarters, an underground hospital and a munitions storage facility. We crawled through the tunnels on the dirt floor and when we neared the end, I pulled out a Ziploc bag and filled it with dirt. As we exited the tunnel, we saw a Japanese tourist nursing a severely bleeding hand. I was told there was an AK47 shooting range nearby and the tourist almost blew his hand off. Apparently, that was the machine gun fire we had heard earlier.

We had a full day visit to Da Nang where we were enticed to do a treacherous trishaw tour of the city. The traffic was massive and it was amazing we weren't killed. A highlight was our visit to the Cham Museum where our guide, a former teacher, would ask questions about each exhibit and reward the correct answer with a piece of candy. By the end of the tour, I finally proved to Catherine that I was a better listener: I had far more candies than her. I think the guide was in shock at my accomplishment. As always it was fun competing.

Later that day, we visited a small country village where young children had just finished classes. Our tour was being hosted by a local leader and the students came by his home to get a feel of what we were like. One little boy had on a Los Angeles Lakers jersey and another a New York Yankees cap. Some of the boys began jumping on my back, while the girls laughed at their efforts. I stand 6 ft. 2" and they were curious how high they could jump. These children showed me that no matter what part of the world you are in, given the chance, kids will be kids. I enjoyed them as much as they enjoyed me.

From there we stopped at China Beach where I put sand in a Ziploc bag. Realizing Vietnam was a communist country, I hoped I was not violating any laws, but now my mission for Len was complete. When I got back to work and handed Len both the Cu Chi bag of dirt and the China Beach bag of sand, Len told me for Christmas he was sending them out in small packets to Vietnam Veterans and thanked me for my effort.

Our cruise continued along magnificent Ha Long Bay on November 8, 2000. The scenery was awesome, but many of the passengers seemed more focused on the presidential election between Al Gore and George W. Bush. They were watching the results on a huge screen in the ship's show lounge and U.S. passengers were split 50/50 Democrats and Republicans. You could feel the tension. As results were reported, one group would cheer and the other stayed silent. A press release announced that Al Gore had won Florida, Michigan and Pennsylvania. This followed an earlier press release that George W. Bush had won Florida. By the end of the day, no one knew who was going to be our next president.

At 5:00 a.m. tour groups gathered in the Navigator's hallway as we prepared for a long drive from Hong Gai to Hanoi. While waiting to disembark a fight broke out between two men in their late sixties over the election. Their wives failed to control them so passengers intervened. I could just imagine what the long drive from the coast to Hanoi would be like. On the way I observed men and women working with outdated equipment trying to prepare the roads for paving. It was 6:00 A.M. when we left for Hanoi and when we returned that night at 8:00 P.M., we witnessed the same people still at work.

Temperatures were hot in Hanoi, so hot we were told we could not go inside the Ho Chi Minh Mausoleum. However, we did get to visit Ho Chi Minh's stilt house. We had a buffet lunch at a local hotel, where I ate mostly chicken and rice, while Catherine tried everything from dandelion greens to mango pudding. After lunch we visited the Vietnam Military History Museum. Upon entering I noticed a man around my age dressed in military fatigues eyeing me up. He seemed to follow me around the museum which made me somewhat nervous. On display outside the museum were remnants of a U.S. plane and helicopter that had been shot down. The display was disturbing and I felt better when we left the museum.

What surprised me the most in Hanoi were the street vendors hawking their goods and running small businesses. Most of them spoke excellent English and were very polite. I purchased a few inexpensive clothing items to help the vendors continue their new capitalistic ways.

While in Vietnam, I received a fax from my sales assistant, Denise, that my branch manager, Rick Harris had passed away. She informed me that Jim, the branch manager from the Boynton Beach branch, was given the job as the new branch manager. Had it been offered to me, I would not have taken the position, because I would have been required to surrender my clients. Still, I felt it was disrespectful not to have been given a chance to interview for the job. After all, I had successfully run the 40-broker Boca Raton branch for over 18 months while Rick was ill. I believe the regional manager could have waited a few more days till I got back.

Hong Kong was our final stop, where we spent two nights at the J.W. Marriott Hotel. After a walk around a local park, we visited the Hong Kong Museum of Art. Later in the day we took a ferry over to Kowloon to do some last-minute shopping and visit a local landmark, the Peninsula Hotel. With our 25th wedding anniversary just two months away, I wanted to give Catherine a pearl strand necklace. When you walk around Kowloon there are pearl shops all over and I had no idea who was legitimate. In the Peninsula Hotel we discovered a pearl shop named Vogue. Once we walked into the store, I knew Catherine would soon have a beautiful gift of pearls. I told the salesman what we were looking for and he immediately showed us two strands of pearls. Both were the same size and cost. However, some pearls in each strand looked better than others. After hearing that this gift was to celebrate our 25th anniversary, he said "I am going to take the best pearls from each strand and combine into one, just come back in a few hours." With two hours to kill, we window shopped several stores and listened to the orchestra serenading the afternoon tea in the hotel lobby. The Peninsula Hotel was known for its fleet of pink Rolls-Royces, and featured in the James Bond movie, *The Man with the Golden Gun*.

Later I had the pleasure of watching Catherine model her pearl necklace. She was gorgeous wearing it and I was pleased that the salesman had done a great job getting it ready for her. You could say the Buddha made me do it, because throughout the sales process a small shrine with incense on the floor cast its spell. It all made our 25th anniversary even more special. Now it was time to fly home.

28

A.G. EDWARDS & SONS: THE BAD

Following my return from Asia, I met with Jim, my new branch manager. From our first meeting, I had concerns about the future of the branch, which had just had its two best years of production under Rick Harris and myself. Jim gave me the impression that the effort I had put into managing while Rick was seriously ill would not be recognized. He said "I will keep you on as assistant branch manager for the time being." I did not feel reassured. I mentioned that I had a B.S. in Finance from FAU, had taught a continuing education course at the university and was a past president of FAU's Alumni association. At the time I recall him responding that he, too, had graduated from FAU. Years later, at a restaurant, I overheard a co-worker ask Jim what university he'd attended and this time Jim said "The School of Hard Knocks."

In that first meeting Jim described his hiring strategy. "I hire unlicensed trainees and every one of them will become a $300,000 gross commission producer within the first two years." I suggested, "But why not take a broker currently producing $200,000 and turn them into a $300,000 producer?" There wasn't any risk doing it that way. However, he dismissed the idea and it seemed to disturb him that I even offered my opinion. It seemed to me that all he wanted was a "yes" man to bull shit with him every day in his office. That was not me.

Several months later in our weekly Tuesday morning meeting, a financial advisor named Tom walked up to the front of the conference room and congratulated five of us, including myself, who were all having a very good commission month. If anyone was to hand out congratulations, it should have been Jim or me. So after the meeting I promptly went into Jim's office and asked him why Tom gave the speech and what was going on. Jim said "That's the way it is and when I say the sky is yellow, you will back me up. Also, I want you to spend more time in my office." Without a further word, I walked out of his office.

During our Tuesday morning branch meeting on September 11th, 2001, we received information that a plane had just crashed into the World Trade Center North Tower. Fifteen minutes later at 9:03 a second plane hit the South Tower. All of us were in shock as we now realized this wasn't an accident, but a terrorist act. The stock market did not open for trading that day and stayed closed until September 17, 2001. I stayed in the office for a few hours as reports came through of two more airplane crashes in the U.S. I recall going home with tears in my eyes wondering who could have committed such atrocities and why. It wasn't long before Osama bin Laden and his Al Qaeda terrorist organization were held responsible for over 3,000 deaths. It was the same group that had attacked our embassies in Africa three years earlier. Feeling I had to do something, I drove to our local blood bank in Boca Raton and waited in line for two hours to give blood. Unfortunately, there were no survivors from the crashes to receive the blood.

During the first week of trading after September 11th, the S & P Index dropped more than 14% following panic selling. All planes were grounded. Memorials for New York police officers and fireman who had died in rescue attempts at the WTC were ongoing. Our country had shut down and was full of anger. We felt war was imminent and were driven to hunt down the mass murderers. President George W. Bush made his intentions clear in a speech to Americans stating that terrorists anywhere in the world were no longer safe.

During 2001 and 2002, Catherine and I took three more cruises. We were determined not to allow the terrorists control our lives. In July 2001 we visited Italy and Spain aboard the *Crown Odyssey*. Two months later we took a Windjammer cruise from Tortola to several beautiful white sand beaches of the British Virgin Islands before returning home. We slept in bunk beds and went around in bathing suits during the six-day cruise. It was a lot of fun, very informal, and we looked forward to a future Windjammer cruise in the Grenadines.

It was three months since the September 11th attack, when Catherine was offered a last-minute opportunity to cruise to Antarctica departing from Buenos Aires on New Year's Eve, December 31st 2001 aboard the *Marco Polo*. Orient Cruise Lines had her on a waitlist and apparently there were some cancellations due to 9/11, as well as violence on the streets of Buenos Aires. Argentina was having an economic crisis and there was a run on its banks. People could not get their money out, so they started to riot. The police were using rubber bullets in an attempt to control the riots. When my family and friends heard we were going there they said "Are you crazy?" I responded "Don't worry, the police have run out of rubber bullets." We arrived around 10:00 A.M. at Calle Florida, the famous shopping street of Buenos Aires. A few days earlier Citibank, along with several local banks, had its windows shot out. While shopping we heard someone yelling on a megaphone and a group of young people banging on pots and pans. I told Catherine "Let's get back to the hotel and our luggage." It was a shaky start to a dream vacation. Our two-week cruise to Antarctica was magnificent and well worth the risk of riots in Buenos Aires.

We toured the Falkland Islands, also known as Las Malvinas by Argentina. The citizens living in the Falklands are primarily of British heritage. However, in 1982, Argentina claimed sovereignty when their military forces invaded the Falklands. After ten weeks of fighting, Argentine forces were handily defeated by the British. We toured a fenced area where over 25,000 land mines had been laid by Argentinian forces. Most of them remain as they are, too dangerous to remove.

On the way to Deception Island, we cruised through the notorious Drake Passage. The Drake is known to have taken ships down to the bottom of the sea, but was calm for our southern journey. We arrived in a Zodiac at Deception Island on Jan 6th, 2002. At a black sand beach, we were greeted by a giant elephant seal lounging next to a leopard seal. Deception Island is the caldera of an active volcano. We were told that steam-heated water would keep us warm if we decided to take a dip. At that point Catherine and I stripped down to our bathing suits and went swimming in Antarctica. The water was very cold, but about every 90 seconds, I could feel a warm surge wash over my body. Unfortunately, the heat only lasted for a few seconds. After a couple of doses of the thermal-heated water, I made a mad dash back to the beach where I had left my clothes, only to find spectating passengers occupying the bench making it impossible for me to change into warm clothes. I was freezing and had to yell at them to get off the bench and let me sit down. After a few desperate words, they got the message.

We continued to Port Lockroy (a British Antarctic Territory) where two penguin rookeries were waiting for us. At their post office, I purchased some colorful stamps and a first day cover dated November 25, 1996 which pictured a whale breach.

The next day, we visited the Chilean station at Paradise Harbor. Inside, they still had a Christmas tree display and a small souvenir shop, where I purchased four Chilean-made leather coasters with the Antarctic insignia. It was here that Paige, a fellow passenger who was also a maestro for the Denver Symphony Orchestra put on her tuxedo and, with a tape of the orchestra playing in the background, waved her conductor's wand in front of the Chinstrap penguin rookery while a guide recorded the "concert." It was absolutely spectacular as the penguins appeared to be listening to the music – I guess they like classical—and posed in place dramatically. Later that day, while Catherine was blow-drying her hair for dinner, a humpback whale leapt out of the ocean a few feet from our window, perhaps to say good bye. We saw several more whales as we headed back to the Drake Passage.

This time going through the Drake was not so easy. A 30-foot rogue wave hit the port side of the ship and everything not nailed down went flying. Fortunately, no one got hurt. Catherine was having afternoon tea when the cups and saucers were tossed in the air. I was walking through a cocktail lounge when a display wall of guests' photos tipped over and narrowly missed hitting me. On board with us was a famous sculptor, Scott Hanson, whose work can be seen in Wyland Galleries. Scott was a guest lecturer known for his whale and marine life sculptures. Several were on display and, fortunately, they were firmly anchored to escape damage from our wave-tossed passage.

Marco Polo had assigned dinner tables. Catherine and I were very fortunate each night to be with Scott Hanson, also Maestro Paige and a great group of individuals that made our table the most coveted on the ship. The crew were mostly Filipino and accepted donations for a Filipino orphanage. Scott decided to donate the proceeds from an onboard live auction of one of his sculptures entitled "Tail of The Whale" to this charity. I got into a bidding war with two other individuals. Scott stopped the bidding at $2,500 and donated three sculptures instead of one. Each of us would get a sculpture at $2,500 and, as a result, $7,500 went to the orphanage. I still look at my sculpture every day and can't wait to return to Antarctica. It was the most exciting place I had ever seen. The glaciers and wildlife were incredible. However, I needed to get back to reality as September 11th, was taking a heavy toll on our lives and the economy. A new year had begun and I had some anxiety not knowing what would be waiting upon my return.

Back at work, I observed Jim and Tom going to lunch together almost daily. I later heard a rumor that Tom was studying for the branch manager's license. Even before Tom passed his exam, it was clear Jim wanted me out of the branch, because he offered me the branch manager's position in the Lake Worth office. I declined the position, though it was obvious that Tom was being groomed to take my place as assistant branch manager.

I had a verbal agreement with Jim on how my assistant manager's annual bonus would be paid. AGE was on a February fiscal year, so bonuses were paid in late April. On April 26th 2002, Jim came to my office and told me that I was resigning my assistant manager's position. Ironically, his reason for removing me was that I had not spent enough time training the new trainees. He previously had bragged to me how his training would make them instant $300,000 producers. Now, it turned out that after hiring over 35 trainees during his reign, all their commissions *combined* barely managed to hit $300,000. Moreover, because I cared about a few of the trainees, I tried to help them coordinate seminars and get ahead. When Tom found out that I had assisted a trainee, I was told he went ballistic and told the trainee "If you ever get involved with Jerry helping you again, I guarantee that you will fail." In the end, I agreed to resign only if the firm would maintain all of my supervisory registrations. At Jim's request, the regional manager, Alex Bigelow, agreed to this condition and the firm honored that agreement until I retired.

Although I was upset about losing my assistant branch manager's position, I had already learned that life had its ups and downs and it was more important to never surrender your principles. In just a few hours later that same day I was drinking champagne with my fellow FAU members of the Parliament of Owls as we celebrated the Alumni Plaza dedication. I was thrilled to see my name engraved in granite along with the other members of this select group of FAU Owls, which included all past Presidents of the FAU National Alumni Association, past Presidents of FAU, Hall of Fame recipients, Student Government leaders, and other alumni who had provided special contributions to FAU.

From my first meeting with Jim, I was suspicious of his intentions for the branch. He indicated he was going to change the way things were run. Almost every email or letter he sent to the brokers included a threat about unsatisfactory production, branch expenses or not showing up at his Tuesday morning meetings. Jim was determined to cut office expenses by "nickeling and diming" his brokers. I noticed that, in addition to Tom, two or three other brokers were spending a lot of time in Jim's office laughing at his jokes. It became obvious who were his "ass kissers" and who was on his shit list.

I had a conversation with a financial advisor who had been invited to a house party that included Jim, Tom and a handful of other brokers. At that party, he heard Jim tell attendees that he was going to get rid of the lower producers and give most of their accounts to Tom. Jim had already fired two brokers. Both were Jewish and were experienced low to mid-range producers, yet they were not the lowest producers in the office. What they had were valuable client accounts which were turned over to Tom. I heard from other advisors that Jim bragged how he was going to make Tom a million-dollar producer.

In the stock brokerage business, a common branch practice is to give brokers at least one floor day per month, based on the number of brokers in the office. Under this system, the receptionist would forward walk-ins or phone calls from individuals seeking to open an account to the broker of the day. Prior to Jim's becoming branch manager, I would occasionally get an excellent client from a call-in or walk-in on my floor day. Under Jim, on my floor days, I would only receive call-ins for quotes and walk-ins that needed assistance with paperwork. I heard other brokers also complaining about the lack of prospects on their floor days. I found out that on one broker's floor day, a call had come into Carolyn, our receptionist, seeking to transfer a large municipal bond account from another AGE branch to our office. The call was forwarded to Jim and then to Tom. Tom got the multi-million-dollar account, although the jilted floor broker let Jim and Tom know how he felt. I later asked Carolyn why she transferred the call to Jim instead of the broker of the day. She said "I didn't have a choice. Jim had instructed me that any call-ins from clients looking to transfer their accounts to our branch were to be forwarded to him or to Tom." Naturally, I began to wonder how many prospects on my floor days wound up with Tom.

In 2002, Jim began deducting a monthly cost for our sales assistants and charging the advisors for their annual state registrations. The costs were based on the broker's production for the previous year. My costs were reduced based on my membership in the Crest Club. Most advisors already gave bonuses to their sales assistants, so Jim's new charges were an additional cost per month for the brokers. I had a terrific, loyal sales assistant named Denise. I shared her with two other advisors, and, based upon my production, was allocated 50% of her time. Often Denise was asked to help trainees, which took time away from me. However, Denise was great and I would not have traded her for anyone else in that office. I felt that, together with Rick, we built the branch and it had its two best years before he passed on. Despite this, Jim showed no recognition to me or Denise.

Just prior to Jim forcing me to resign as assistant branch manager, he fired a trainee who had a $5 million-dollar hedge fund account that was opened around 2001-2. Jim gave that account to Tom. One of my responsibilities was to review trade runs every day. Before Tom took over my position as assistant branch manager, I had noticed large commissions being generated in Tom's name that did not relate to our branch. I suspected something irregular was going on and I began to hear rumors that the same hedge fund had opened $5 million accounts in several other AGE branches from which Tom was being paid trail commissions. As it turned out, that hedge fund account would eventually lead to both Jim and Tom being suspended from the industry and fined by the SEC for market timing of mutual fund trades as well as other violations.

According to the SEC filing, Tom had executed 1,352 trades representing $1.126 billion between September 2001 and September 2003, on behalf of certain companies owned and controlled by one individual. Between January 2002 and September 2003, at least twenty-three different mutual fund companies sent Tom approximately 135 Restriction Notices. In summary, the hedge fund accounts were restricted from any more trading with those twenty-three mutual fund companies. To avoid being caught, Tom set up three new accounts in the Lake Worth branch office and another one in the Boca Raton branch to avoid further restrictions. At one point there were a total of at least sixteen different accounts controlled by one individual. It is estimated that Tom's market-timing trades caused losses of approximately $0.9 million to other shareholders of the affected mutual funds.

The evidence showed that Jim was aware of and helped facilitate Tom's use of deceptive practices. It now made sense why Jim removed me from the assistant manager position and promoted Tom. If I had seen the Restriction Notices, I would have shut down Tom. I don't know if Jim ever benefited financially from helping Tom, or if he just needed someone's friendship. I do know their actions hurt me financially and doomed the Boca Raton branch. Once the news of the SEC investigation hit *The Wall Street Journal* and the local *Sun Sentinel*, it put an end to any possibility of hiring good producers and destroyed my chance of bringing in new clients. As more news came out, I found my earnings declining by at least 15%. Brokers were receiving phones calls from clients wondering what the hell was going on in our branch. Each time a news-related item regarding the SEC investigation appeared in local newspapers our credibility as brokers was diminished.

Shamefully, even after the SEC had completed its investigation and filed charges, AGE continued to allow Jim to manage the branch with Tom as his assistant. This was not the AGE I had signed on with in 1994. Benjamin Edwards, our former CEO died April 20, 2009 at age 77 from prostate cancer. Management had changed years earlier and, sadly, not for the best.

My long-time assistant, Denise, went on long term disability following a serious injury in our office building parking lot. Then, in the summer of 2003, I hired an intern named Irina. She was finishing her Bachelor's degree in Finance at the University of Florida in Gainesville. She was extremely bright and I offered her a job as my sales assistant upon graduation in December. I told her I would get her licensed, trained and we would become a team. I was willing to pay 50% of her salary and bonus, provided the branch picked up the other 50%. Based on my prior 12 month's production and membership in the Crest Club, I was entitled to that arrangement and Jim approved. Irina was supposed to work only with me and help out with office issues as needed.

I wanted Irina to study for and pass her Series 7 exam so she could begin to execute orders for clients. For several months Jim delayed Irina from taking the exam in order to help Tom's new sales assistant with her exam.

Ironically, Jim sent me an email dated September 22, 2004, subject: Irina, which said "I need to know what campaigns she has run for you. I don't see her doing anything that a normal sales assistant couldn't be doing for you, but I am sure I don't see everything. I thought the idea would be moving towards helping you automate your business and working on getting my ROA (Return on Assets) improved. Like any investment I make, I re-evaluate and make business decisions on the success or failure of the investment. Do you have specific campaigns to do just this that she is working on? Let's sit down early next week and discuss. Thanks. Jim."

Again, I was being harassed. I was the one who made the investment in Irina, not Jim. Furthermore, because Jim delayed Irina taking the Series 7 exam, she was not able to solicit clients and my business suffered. When Irina finally did take her exam, she scored higher than any of the trainee brokers Jim had projected to become $300,000 producers.

Around the same time, AGE rolled out a new computer system as part of a Beta conversion. The new system was not properly tested for a firm as large as AGE and had several problems. The Bond One portion of the new system, for example, was a complete disaster. For weeks brokers weren't able to view any of the municipal bonds, corporate bonds, U.S. government bonds or CDs that were available for sale in AGE inventory. Since 35% of my business was municipal bonds, the conversion cost me serious dollars, for which I would not be reimbursed. In a May 20, 2005 e-mail to Jim and other branch managers, Alex Bigelow, the regional manager, bragged how the conversion would help "the infrastructure of AGE." The fact that the Bond One system had crashed, didn't seem to bother him at all. Instead, Alex was upset that some managers anonymously aired their frustrations with the new system over the squawk box. In fact, Alex was so upset that he threatened anyone again voicing such complaints on the squawk box would be "unemployed."

On June 9th, 2005, I had a meeting at 5:00 P.M. with two new clients at Century Village in West Palm Beach. The husband and wife opened several accounts and signed the required documents to transfer their brokerage accounts to AGE from their former broker. Upon leaving their apartment I was planning to drop off the paperwork at the office, but I was getting tired so I called Catherine to meet me at the Longhorn Steakhouse for dinner in Delray. That decision to have dinner instead of driving back to the office may have saved me from getting injured or killed.

I found out the next morning that the night before Ray, a fellow broker, and his wife were mugged in the office building parking lot just as they were exiting the lower-level elevator at 6:45 P.M. If I had driven to the office instead of meeting Catherine for dinner, it was likely I would have arrived at the time of the mugging. Jim sent out an email to everyone advising us of what had happened and requested a Boca Raton Police officer to come by and inform us how to better protect ourselves. Jim continued to praise the building management for their handling of security. While Ray was being tackled outside the elevator and his Rolex watch stolen, his wife's purse was also taken. The camera outside the elevator was not functioning and looked as if it had not been examined in years. There were no security personnel. Yet here was Jim sending out an e-mail praising the building's security. In a fury, Ray went to the Boca Raton police department to learn the real story. He obtained a list of 29 incidents from January 11, 2001 to June 10, 2005 all reported for the building at 1900 Glades Road, Boca Raton Florida. That was a record that should alarm – not please – any manager. A few weeks later I noticed a purple car in our lower parking lot that fit Ray's description of the getaway car. I called the Boca Raton Police and told them I had seen a car fitting the description that was used in the mugging. Also, I provided them with the direction the vehicle was headed, but I never heard anything more about it. Eventually, the building installed a traffic control gate with card access, which helped cut down on crime.

On April 30th, 2006, I was shocked to see Jim featured in a story on late night news Channel 5. He was being filmed outside the AGE Lake Worth branch office, the one I'd been offered to manage three years earlier, but had turned down. Apparently, the office was being closed and a broker had failed to shred sensitive documents that may have included clients' statements and

social security numbers. Documents were found scattered outside the building by a garbage dumpster. This was not the kind
of news any broker or client would want to see on television. I
can't blame Jim for that screw up as the Lake Worth branch was
not directly managed by Jim, but he still had some supervisory
responsibilities for that branch. The next day Jim forwarded an
email from Alex Bigelow to all the employees of the Boca Raton
branch, advising everyone to take responsibility for shredding
sensitive documents.

It was a bit of a catastrophe for me. On the same day, the Channel 5 news story ran, Irina and I had set up a display booth at a
Florida Atlantic University charitable event as part of an effort
to introduce ourselves and AGE to the public. We had a drawing for a $50 gift card, then called back the 25 individuals who
had provided names and phone numbers, but not a single one
of them would discuss their investment strategies further with
us. A few mentioned they had seen the Lake Worth incident on
the news. Any leads we might have gotten from our effort went
up in flames.

On May 12th, 2006 I received a 12-question Manager Survey
email from Tad Fryer in the home office. I called Tad Fryer, who
I thought was in Human Resources, to express my concerns
regarding the survey's confidentiality. It turned out he wasn't in
Human Resources and it was never made clear what department
he worked in or if he was from an outside entity. He insisted,
though, that the survey would remain confidential. I said "How
can it be confidential when my survey response will contain
my computer identification number? He assured me Jim would
never see my survey answers and comments, but I didn't believe
him. Still, I completed the survey and it contained mostly negative comments and poor ratings.

Shortly after, Jim held a broker meeting to discuss his "report
card." In the meeting three of us, including myself, made comments when he opened the meeting to discussion. Within days

all three of us suffered repercussions involving unwarranted actions Jim took against some clients.

In my case, without any warning, on May 30, 2006, Jim phoned one of my Hispanic clients, who I will call Mr. L, and harassed him at work. My client was an engineer and worked in an open space so anyone could hear the highly insulting conversation. My client called me immediately to let me know he was furious. He said Jim had questioned him about his personal account and asked an insulting question: "Are you doing casino gambling and why do you constantly remove money out of your account?" This client had a margin account that was heavily concentrated in IBM stock. The equity in the account was above margin requirements and he did not have a margin call. He had been a great client since 1987 and always met any margin calls when a margin call existed. Mr. L and his wife also had sizeable IRA accounts with our firm, which Jim never bothered to look at prior to making his phone call. My client held real estate investments as well as a sizeable number of shares of IBM in a 401K account. His debit balance was not from trading stocks, but rather from paying expenses. Jim had no business calling him. My client also told me that Jim said he'd have to transfer his account to another firm if he did not reduce his margin balance, even though this was not an AGE requirement at the time.

Moments after speaking with my client, I received an email from Jim regarding his conversation with Mr. L. It said, "I would like for you to call him and discuss a strategy to sell stock, reduce his margin balance and diversify him. If he refuses to commit to any of these, we need to ask him to transfer his account to another firm." In short, his account contradicts my client who said he did tell him he'd have to transfer his account. After reading Jim's email, I ran into his office and informed him of Mr. L's financial situation and I told him "If you have a problem with one of my accounts, you come to me first before calling any of my clients." Neither my client nor I received an apology from Jim—no surprise.

Jim also made phone calls to clients of Robert V., one of the other two brokers who had spoken out during the branch meeting. Robert had clients who sometimes traded penny and low-priced stocks. Without discussing the related accounts with Robert V., Jim called his clients and suggested that they stop doing those types of trades even though those trades were not in violation of AGE policy.

On May 31, 2006, Jim sent an email to all Boca Raton employees, regarding the Manager's Survey. The following is excerpts from it.

> *"It's okay to Tell the Emperor he has no Clothes." If you feel that a decision is not consistent with the policies set in place or that there should be an exception to a decision, or that a decision is flat out wrong I need to hear this from you. I don't think it's healthy for a member of a branch or any family for that matter to not speak up. If an explanation for a decision is needed, I need to know. This is part of "Understanding your Role." Nothing creates more trust and loyalty than honest sincere feedback, (good or bad), with solutions or ideas. If you know of a decision that is somehow unfair or disadvantageous to one or a few in the branch, then be a friend and speak to me or encourage the individual to speak with me.*

If Jim had been sincere in this May 31 email, he would not have harassed my client or Robert V.'s clients as repercussion for our speaking out. Everyone knew if you challenged Jim, you may as well start packing your personal items.

Ben Edwards' philosophy had been to always do the right thing for your clients, whether you were acting in a fiduciary capacity (fee-based advisory) or as a transactional (commission-based) broker. Things were changing. On July 19th, 2006,

I received an email from Jim inviting all local branch advisors that had 50 million dollars in assets on their books to attend the Let's Rock Workshop in Sarasota on August 12th. The subject was: Converting to Fee Based Business and it was noted as High Importance. It seemed to me that AGE was getting pressure from shareholders to increase their earnings. A good way to do that would be to have brokers convert as many clients as possible to fee-based advisory accounts and guide them away from the traditional commission-based accounts. The firm and brokers would make more money, but what about the clients?

Most firms had already pushed their brokers in that direction, but AGE had been slow to adopt that strategy. On average, depending on the value of the client's assets, the fee-based account would generate 1–2% in annual fees. The client had to sign several papers giving the recommended money manager full trading discretion. Therefore, neither the money manager nor the broker would have to call a client for permission to do a transaction. In essence, the client trusts the broker's selection of the money manager, who is assumed to be talented and skilled in managing a specific type of portfolio (growth, value, taxable income, tax-free municipal income bonds, foreign securities and precious metals, to mention a few).

Over a two-year period, I had been given three small advisory fee-based accounts from brokers who had either been fired or had left the firm. When I first received them, I saw that all these fee-based accounts had performed poorly and lost over 30% of their value. One of them was performing so badly, the money manager shut it down. After I reviewed the positions in that account with the client, we liquidated numerous stocks and added the proceeds to some stocks that I felt had potential. A few years later, my client had gained back all the money that had been lost. My client was not charged a management fee, but instead paid discounted transactional commissions. Over the years, she became a great client.

I understand why brokerage firms want their brokers doing fee-based advisory business instead of recommending individual stocks. After all, a high percentage of brokers do not have business or financial degrees. Many couldn't analyze a financial statement if their life depended on it, nor would they care to. Brokerages want salesmen not analysts. With fee-based business, the firms have a steady residual of revenues whether the stock market goes up or down. That is how brokerage firms and brokers make money. To encourage brokers to change their business to fee-based, the firms raised commissions on stock trades and lowered the payouts on transactional commission-based business. I was not persuaded. In fact, I felt that I could outperform most money managers, so why should I change a business model that was working quite well? I had integrity and was determined to do what I felt was in the best interests of my clients. I had assets over 100 million-dollars on the books and if I had converted just 60% to fee-based, I would have tripled my income and never had to work as hard as I did. In addition, I was constantly pressured by management to change my business model, but I quietly refused. My business was primarily a mix of mutual funds, tax-free municipal bonds and stocks. I enjoyed what I did, my special relationships with my clients and seeing their accounts grow. Some of my older female clients would say to me, "Treat me like you would treat your mother", and I did.

On August 8th, 2006, A.G. Edwards was fined $400,000 by the NYSE for charging excessive account fees and making unsuitable trades for customers. The case involved an AGE internal fee-based program called Client Choice. Customers were charged excessive fees based upon the clients' assets. The accounts were traded infrequently and, had they been traded on a transactional basis, the total fees would have been significantly lower. The firm didn't have systems in place to ensure that brokers alerted customers about the fees, which could be more than 20 times higher for investors who traded infrequently, according to the NYSE disciplinary panel. The case involved the Augusta, Georgia branch where AGE had already paid $25 million dollars in restitution to customers and $550,000 in fines to the state of Georgia. In one instance a household made no trades in over a four-year period, yet paid $12,180 in fees. That case was a perfect example of why I avoided fee-based accounts. Obviously, the NYSE didn't feel AG Edwards held the clients' best interests in mind when setting up those Augusta, GA fee-based Client Choice accounts.

Still, whenever I attended a regional or home office meeting, it was a normal practice to have a successful fee-based broker conduct a class on how to convert your business to fee based from transactional. Those producers often bragged about much more money they were earning while working less hours. You would never hear about how well the clients were doing. Unfortunately, that was the direction the industry leaders had taken.

On May 2, 2007, A.G. Edwards reached an agreement with the SEC over charges that the firm failed to supervise brokers who engaged in illegal market timing. AGE wound up paying 3.86 million dollars in penalties and was also censured. The case involved Jim and Tom along with two other employees who worked in the Back Bay, Massachusetts branch office. Jim and Tom contested the charges. Articles appeared in the Sun-Sentinel, Palm Beach Post, Investment News along with other financial news outlets mentioning the charges and settlements related to the Boca Raton branch. The next day, I received several client calls asking me if their accounts had been subject to fraud? Once again, my credibility was being questioned. The case involved trading that took place from 2001–2003. While all this was going on, Jim and Tom remained in their jobs and continued to boast to brokers that they were going to win their case.

I recall Alex Bigelow holding a branch meeting the day after the 3.86-million-dollar AGE settlement was announced. I was sitting in the front row in our conference room and said to Alex

"The executives must have been celebrating last night with champagne." Alex said "Why would they be celebrating?' I responded, "Consider what some of the other major brokerage firms wound up paying the SEC for doing the same type of illegal activity." Alex looked at me with what I felt were daggers in his eyes. No doubt he didn't appreciate my comments.

29

WACHOVIA SECURITIES: WORST MERGER

On the morning of May 31, 2007, I said "Good morning" to Irina, my sales assistant and she replied "You don't know." I said "What do you mean?" She said "Wachovia is buying us out." I had a one-word response: "Shit." Then I walked into my office and closed the door. Wachovia's reputation sucked. I didn't want to believe what was happening. A few months earlier I had attended a meeting at the AGE corporate headquarters in St Louis. I remember being with thousands of brokers in the main auditorium when our CEO Bob Bagby told us "We will remain independent." Everyone stood up and applauded. Almost everyone. I did not. I had major concerns about AGE under Bagby's leadership. Almost every letter I received from him prior to his becoming CEO, led me to believe that, unlike Ben Edwards, he stressed production only. I could sense changes were coming.

One of my observations was that AGE had started to advertise on television, something the company had never done before. Over the years, I had noticed a few companies, such as Tropicana Orange Juice and Quaker Oats advertise their companies aggressively, followed by a takeover. A.G. Edwards & Sons was not a household name, but such advertising might bring them attention. Apparently, it did.

Over the next 30 days after the Wachovia announcement, I was bombarded with phone calls from recruiters, brokerage firm branch managers and former brokers with whom I had previously worked, all inviting me to join their firms. I had some very promising offers, which I turned down because I didn't want to put my clients through the headaches of moving their accounts to a new firm. Despite warnings by brokers, who had previous experience with Wachovia's back office and policies and told me Wachovia was a "disaster," I stayed with the merged company. It turned out to be the worst move of my 48-year stock brokerage career. True, it worked out for most of my clients, but not for me. On July 3, 2007, I sent a letter to Bob Bagby asking him six questions regarding the merger, I wrote asking him to "convince me why I should stay." His disappointing response did not answer any of my questions. I should have left immediately.

Bob Bagby had pissed off thousands of brokers who had trusted his pledge to remain independent and it was rumored that he had received several threats and that his BMW had been vandalized. Bagby retired on May 1, 2008. According to an article in Investment News dated May 16, 2008, Bagby received a "lump sum payment of 1.2 million, two times his salary, plus a bonus of 4.5 million." The article also states that he received 7.5 million in Wachovia stock which vested upon his retirement, as well as other benefits. I had heard from an AGE corporate employee that his departure package was worth over $22 million. Perhaps, Bagby got a chance to look at the real financials of Wachovia and decided to get out before the shit really hit the fan.

The Sub-Prime Loan nightmare on Wall Street would change the financial world in 2008. Following a very good stock market in 2007, stock valuations were beginning to look lofty. I was nervous, but the only action I personally took was to go to 100% cash in my 401K. That turned out to be a great move, though I was still exposed to the market in my other investments.

My clients were the best and our relationships sometimes made great stories. Like the day, at around noon, Irina rushed into my office and said Ann, one of my favorite clients, was on the phone and thought she was having a heart attack. I immediately got on the phone and Ann said "I think I am having a heart attack." I told her to "Call 911." She said "I don't want to do that because the paramedics will take me to Delray Medical Hospital and I don't like that hospital. I want you to take me to Boca Raton Regional Hospital." I didn't know what to say other than "Ok, I'll be there in 15–20 minutes." She said "Don't rush, I need to have my lunch and wash my hair. Could you come at 3:00?" I said "Yes." I drove over and she was waiting for me at the entrance of her retirement center. We drove to the emergency center at Boca Regional Hospital and I stayed until she was discharged at 11:00 P.M. grabbing a sandwich from a vending machine. Ann had shoulder and back pains, but no heart attack. So, I drove her home. That was one crazy experience, however she amended her trust to have me execute all stock transactions after her passing.

Justice was served on March 10th, 2008, when the SEC disclosed an initial decision release of the administrative proceeding file #3-12626 (in the matter of Jim and Tom). Both were both found guilty of violating the Securities Exchange Act of 1934. Tom was suspended from association with a broker or dealer for a period of one year and was ordered to pay a civil money penalty in the amount of $250,000. Also, the SEC ruled he was required to pay a disgorgement of $39,808.53, plus prejudgment interest, because a person should not benefit from antifraud violations. Jim was suspended from association with a broker dealer for a period of thirty days and barred from association with a broker or dealer in a supervisory capacity. He was also required to pay a civil money penalty in the amount of $250,000.

Jeffrey (Jeff) Kanter was the branch manager in the local Boca Raton Wachovia Securities, located nearby, and he was expected to also manage the AGE brokers once the merger was completed.

Jeff held a meeting with the AGE brokers the day after the SEC decision came down on Jim and Tom. He informed us that the prior evening he had met with both of them to officially tell them that they had been fired. He said "They manned up when they heard the news." After hearing that, I could only wonder what kind of branch manager Jeff was going to be. Had I been the manager, I would have apologized to the brokers for suffering through several years while an SEC investigation hung over the branch. Instead, he praised those two as "stand up guys."

Soon after, the remaining 15 AGE brokers were asked to move into the Wachovia Boca Raton branch which Jeff managed. Generally, I type with my left hand due to basketball-related injuries to my right thumb, so I requested an office designed for a left-handed employee. Even though I was promised that type of office, when I arrived, I found I had been assigned an office geared towards the right-handed. They ran a cable across the carpet and rearranged my desk so I could type left-handed, but the cable represented a hazard to visiting clients. I asked Jeff to come into my office while he was roaming the halls. I advised him that there were over ten cables and wires sprouting out of my walls and they represented an electrical hazard and should be addressed. He said "I will not spend the money to have them removed." I also told him that when I was placing items in my desk, I cut my hand on three thin nails positioned in the drawer in an apparent attempt to stab anyone placing their hand inside. He laughed. I heard that several Wachovia Boca Raton employees had been let go to make room for our group. It didn't take long for me to realize we weren't welcome. In our weekly branch meeting, I noticed that whenever any of the former AGE brokers asked a question, a hostile response from a Wachovia broker would be sure to follow.

On September 15, 2008, Lehman Brothers filed Chapter 11. The financial world was about to collapse. One after another, the following financial companies were either filing Chapter 11 or were about to: AIG, Merrill Lynch, Washington Mutual Inc., Bear Stearns, Countrywide Financial Corporation, Fannie Mae, Freddie Mac, to mention a few. Also, later that evening on TV's "Mad Money Show," Jim Cramer hosted Robert Steel, CEO of Wachovia Bank and Former Under Secretary Treasurer, as a guest. Cramer recommended buying Wachovia stock on weakness. After interviewing Mr. Steel, Cramer based his recommendation on Steel's positive comments about Wachovia Bank. Steel also stated how important it was to have transparency as to the nature of the bank's mortgage loans. In two emails from Mr. Steel to all Wachovia Colleagues dated July 15, and July 22, 2008, he stated "I remind you that Wachovia is a strong and stable company on sound footing. We have a strong liquidity position, with more than $150 billion in liquid funding capability. We also reported our capital and liquidity levels remain very strong." The latter statement was based on Wachovia's second quarter June 30, 2008 financial results.

Catherine and I had just arrived at my timeshare in Palm Desert, California for a week's vacation when all hell broke out. The stock market was crashing. I planned to visit with clients from Redondo Beach and Mission Viejo. Naturally, they were very concerned about the financial crash and during the week I was able to take them to lunch and calm their nerves. My clients were investors, not speculators, so they understood the ups and downs of the market; but this was much worse. There had not been anything like this since the crash of 1929. Mostly, I spent the entire week on the phone "holding hands" with clients, hoping to avoid panic selling. Happily, I succeeded.

Just a few weeks later, Catherine and I were in St Kitts hoping for a more peaceful vacation. Unfortunately, that was not in the cards. On September 29th, 2008, CNBC breaking news announced that Citibank was buying out Wachovia's banking operations for $1 a share in stock in a U.S. government-brokered deal. Wachovia Securities/ Evergreen Mutual Funds owned by Wachovia and other nonbanking related operations would remain as a publicly traded company under the Wachovia name. The FDIC claimed Wachovia did not fail and that the Deposit Insurance Fund would not be affected. In shock, I watched as Wachovia's stock price collapsed. Although I didn't personally own any shares of Wachovia, I knew the ramifications were sure to be nasty.

Obviously, Robert Steel's previous emails to employees and his TV interview with Cramer were meaningless hot air. In just two weeks, how did Wachovia go from having "strong capital" and "liquidity" to near bankruptcy? The FDIC must have had a look at the full exposure to sub-prime loans that were on Wachovia's books. Also, on that same day the Dow Jones Industrial Average fell 777.68, the largest drop in history. In addition to Wachovia's announcement, the U.S. House of Representatives failed to pass the Bush Administration's $700 billion bailout plan, further contributing to the historic selloff.

Following the announced Wachovia takeover of AGE, my sales assistant, Irina, decided to leave the business and obtain a PhD in Psychology. I wondered if she was tired of dealing with the gender bias that was too often on display in the AGE Boca Raton branch. Given Irina's three years-experience in the stock brokerage field, and her skill in handling clients, I knew she would do well. She continued her studies, earned her doctorate and, as much as I missed having her as my assistant, I was proud of her accomplishment, knowing that she was doing something she truly enjoyed.

My vacation week in St. Kitts continued to be a disaster when I received a phone call from my new sales assistant, Karen, who had replaced Irina. The announcement of Citibank acquiring Wachovia's banking assets for $1 a share had, unknown to me, started a run on some banks which included Wachovia Banks. One of my biggest clients allegedly had over $600,000 in CDs and money markets with a Wachovia Bank branch and had requested to withdraw all the funds in cash. She did not want funds to be wired and refused to accept a cashiers' check. I was told by Karen that the bank had advised my client they did not keep that kind of cash in the bank and it would take time to have it delivered to their branch. My client was around 80 years old and her husband was close to 90. The Wachovia Bank manager wanted me to call my client from St. Kitts and explain to her the dangers of withdrawing in cash. After all, Wachovia would not provide security for her, so once she left the bank with the money, that would be her responsibility. At this point I did not know a run on at Wachovia Banks was taking place. My client, I knew, could be a charming, loveable person, but had her stubborn, irrational moments. Her husband was far more financially astute. I had done business with both of them for about 25 years. I told Karen that I was very uncomfortable calling my client as this was a banking problem and should be handled at the bank and I might be running the risk of losing all their brokerage accounts with such a call. I asked Karen to check with Jeff and if he insisted that I call her, I would. Karen responded that Jeff was not available, but the assistant manager insisted I make the call.

When I called my client, she told me to call her back in an hour, she was eating lunch. I called her again and verified her banking withdrawal intentions. I stressed my safety concerns of taking out $600,000 in cash and asked what were her intentions? She responded "That is not anyone's business as to why I am taking it out. Furthermore, that is pocket change to me." She also stated "that there were several people in the bank withdrawing cash." Shortly after, I called Karen and told her to let the bank know that my client was not deviating from her earlier request.

On Monday, upon my return from St. Kitts, I received a call from that client who was outraged. Wachovia, she said "requested that a Florida State Health Department employee come to my home to see if I was crazy." She asked if I knew anything about it. I said "No." She then told me that she and her husband were transferring all their brokerage accounts (totaling over $10 million) to another firm. Within three weeks, all of their accounts transferred out. After my clients' phone call, I called the branch manager at the Wachovia Bank to find out if they had indeed called a Florida State health official to check on my client's sanity and the manager replied "Yes." I also asked, if my client took out any of the $600,000 and the manager said "I can't tell you that." I then advised the manager that the bank had just caused me to lose over $10 million in account assets. I received no apology. They simply did not care. When the accounts transferred out, I informed Jeff, and he treated it as a joke. I billed my branch office $100 for reimbursement on the phone calls between St. Kitts to my client and Karen, since the calls were made at the insistence of the branch. In reality, had Wachovia Banking declared bankruptcy, my client would have been covered by FDIC insurance for far less than the $600,000 she was trying to withdraw from Wachovia. FDIC insurance was only $100,000 per account. Perhaps, my client had been the sane one, after all.

On October 3, 2008, Wells Fargo outbid Citibank's $1 a share offer for Wachovia's banking operations. The bid was for $5 equivalent in Wells Fargo stock and they would buy the entire company, including Wachovia Securities. Wells Fargo had a good reputation at the time. At least the firm wouldn't be bankrupt. Wells Fargo completed the Wachovia acquisition on December 31, 2008.

My business continued to suffer from the Wachovia fallout. My wealthiest client was a fine, older gentlemen, who sadly had been going through kidney dialysis for several years. He had a $13 million portfolio of mostly conservative stocks and insured tax-free municipal bonds. Unfortunately, he also owned 2000 shares of Wachovia Banking and had seen Cramer's "Mad Money Show" when Robert Steel CEO of Wachovia told the world that Wachovia was a financially strong bank. After the Wachovia buyout announcement, he called and told me "You should have known Robert Steel was lying on Cramer's program," so therefore he was going to transfer his accounts to another firm." I was speechless and could sense his anger. Rather than argue, I just told him "I am sorry to lose your accounts and I only wish you all the best." He passed away about four months after transferring his accounts. After a successful and trusting relationship that spanned ten years, I was greatly saddened by his death, as I considered him a friend not just a client. I offered my condolences to his son (successor trustee) and, although I no longer had the accounts, I offered him any historical financial information he might need to help settle the estate.

While Jim Cramer added Robert Steel to the "Mad Money Wall of Shame", his interview probably cost me at least $50,000 in lost revenues. If Cramer ever reads ths book, I just want him to know I do not blame him. I blame Robert Steel for either lying or being too stupid to understand the risk that Wachovia had taken on with sub-prime loans. I have to wonder if he got a golden-parachute deal when Wells Fargo completed the buyout.

Why Didn't Anyone Go to Jail?
A Brief Look at Sarbanes-Oxley

In my opinion, the 2008–09 stock and bond market crash resulted from greed, fraud and falsified accounting, as well as intentional incompetence directly related to the financial industry. On July 30th, 2002, the U.S. Congress passed the Sarbanes-Oxley Act of 2002. The co-sponsors were Senator Paul S. Sarbanes (D-Md.) and Representative Michael G. Oxley (R-Ohio). The law was to protect investors from fraudulent financial reporting by corporations and it imposed tough new penalties on lawbreakers. The Sarbanes-Oxley Act of 2002 followed the fraud committed by Enron, Tyco International and WorldCom. All three companies had previously been involved in issuing fraudulent corporate financial statements at the shareholders' expense.

It was my understanding that Sarbanes-Oxley required the top executives from the S & P 500 companies to sign off on the accuracy of their financial statements, stating that, to the best of their knowledge, the financial statements were correct. During the 2008 financial crisis, though, the CEOs of several financial companies found a way to blame accounting procedures and a variety of other reasons for their financial reports to be inexcusably inaccurate.

For example, in 2008 Martin J. Sullivan, former CEO of AIG, gave congressional testimony blaming accounting require-ments that forced market to market pricing of AIG's secu-rity holdings as the market crashed. Lack of liquidity and sub-prime loan issues forced AIG's security values to drop substantially.

If I had composed a letter, I would have written the following.

Dear Mr. Sullivan,

When I sold my shares in AIG, I received the market price, not what you may have thought your company was worth. I walked away with a large loss. Also, I don't recall you ever say-ing AIG was overvalued before the crash. Having been in the stock brokerage field for over 40 years, I always marked my securities to the market, not to a value that I think it should be worth. That is the real world. When you left AIG in 2008, you received a severance package worth $47 million. During a congressional panel inquiry on October 11, 2008, Cali-fornian Congresswoman Jackie Speier said "Shame on you, Mr. Sullivan." after it was disclosed how millions of dollars in bonuses were paid to employees for arranging insurance on what turned out to be sub-prime loans instead of AAA rated mortgages. As I watched this play out on television all I could wonder was: where is the SEC enforcement team and why aren't they there to handcuff you, Mr. Sullivan, and charge you and others with violations of Sarbanes-Oxley? I recall in 2007, Mr. Sullivan, that you mentioned that AIG only had one billion dollars exposure to sub-prime loans. We would find out in 2008, AIG had one trillion dollars exposure. By the way, Mr. Sullivan, I totally agreed with Congresswoman Speier, "Shame on you."

Sincerely, Jerry A. Wolff

The following is a sample list of CEOs who departed from their companies at the time of the 2008 financial meltdown and are said to have received severance pay, pensions or other benefits valued in the millions.

- Bank of America-CEO Kenneth Lewis
- Citigroup-Charles Prince
- Countrywide Financial-Angelo Mozilo
- Fannie Mae-Daniel Mudd
- Freddie Mac-Richard F. Syron
- Merrill Lynch-Stanley O' Neal
- Wachovia Corp-Kenneth Thompson

I recall several companies received TARP (Troubled Asset Relief Program) monies from the U.S. Department of the Treasury or were taken over by another financial company. The SEC filed civil security fraud charges against executives who had worked for Fannie Mae and Freddie Mac over the issuance of sub-prime loans. However, the SEC settled the cases for under $500,000, a mere slap on the wrist. Most of the TARP loans were repaid with interest over time.

I owned shares of Citibank and Bank of America during the 2008 crisis. When I reviewed the annual reports and 10Ks', there was no indication of how bad the sub-prime loans were on their books. After the 2008 fiasco, I never again purchased a financial company in my personal accounts.

So, why didn't any of the CEOs go to jail? In my opinion they all violated Sarbanes-Oxley and probably numerous SEC violations as well. I believe the relationships Senator Christopher J Dodd, Representative Barney Frank, Fed Chairman Alan Greenspan and other politicians had with several financial companies may have played a role. Senator Dodd had ties to Countrywide Financial. Rep. Barney Frank was said to have put pressure on Fannie Mae to buy up risky mortgages. Although Fed Chairman Alan Greenspan was no longer chairman in 2008, he had previously failed to regulate sub-prime loans. Lacking proper regulation, greed ran rampant.

My brother, Larry, a real estate agent, told me he was buying a condo in Orlando with a $25,000 down payment. The development hadn't even started, although maybe the land had been cleared. He planned to "flip it" and make a quick $25,000-$50,000. Knowing my brother's income wasn't very much, I asked him "How are you getting approved for the loan?" He responded "The mortgage company didn't care what my earnings were. All I had to do was fill out a one-page application." I told him "If anything goes wrong and you can't flip it, you'll be a landlord and in trouble." He said "Don't worry, that won't happen." Naturally, the real estate market crashed and delayed the development being built for over a year. Larry was unable to flip it and became a landlord until he passed away several years later. The same scenario was being enacted throughout the country.

30

WELLS FARGO: THE NIGHTMARE CONTINUES

F ollowing the takeover of Wachovia by Wells Fargo, I found myself in a conflict I wanted no part of. One of my active stock trading clients called and requested I help him with a Wells Fargo Bank problem his parents were having. If I didn't get it taken care of, he threatened to transfer his brokerage account to another firm. Having lost two of my biggest accounts because of Wachovia's financial disaster, I didn't want to lose an active trader and I thought the matter deserved a closer look. My client claimed a local Wells Fargo Bank was stealing $4,000 in interest owed on his parents' CD. Although I had no direct relationship with the Wells Fargo Bank branch, I was now held responsible for getting the problem fixed.

Throughout my life I have always been a 'take charge' person. My attitude is, when I want something done, go right to the top of the corporation. With that mindset, I called the office of John G. Stumpf CEO & Chairman of Wells Fargo and asked to speak with him. His secretary replied "He won't speak with you." I asked "Can I speak with any executive or I will lose a valuable client?" She replied, "No executives will speak with you" and offered no alternative. Before I lost my temper and said something I would regret, I hung up. I cooled down and called back ten minutes later. This time, a different secretary answered and after I explained the situation, she took down my information. I received a call from the regional manager responsible for the Wells Fargo Bank where my client's parents had their CD and within 24 hours the problem was solved. The bank employee had misrepresented the features of a product and the parents' account was recredited the $4,000. I kept my client.

On January 20th, 2009, after eight years of President George W. Bush, two wars, a disastrous economy and crashing stock market, Barack H. Obama was sworn in as the 44th President of the United States. Shortly after he took office the Dow Jones average dropped to 6,469.55 on March 6, 2009. After two terms under President Obama, at the close of January 19, 2017, the Dow was at 19,732.40. During my lifetime, the Dow Jones recorded the three best gains under Presidents William J. Clinton (+228.9%), Barack H Obama (+148.3%) and Ronald W. Reagan (+147.3%). The three worst presidents for losses were Richard M. Nixon (-28.3%), George W. Bush (-26.5% and James (Jimmy) E. Carter, (-.7%). At least since 1949, when you examine the numbers and ignore the political rhetoric, it became apparent that the stock market had performed much better under Democratic presidents than Republican presidents. Still, when it comes to politics, people believe what they want to believe.

To be competitive with other bank and brokerage firms who were also being acquired during the 2008 financial meltdown, the top executives at Wells Fargo Advisors promised brokers sizeable retention bonuses to stay with the firm. After six months, management reneged on their promises. Now, in order to receive any kind of retention bonus, brokers would be required to put together an Envision report (a financial plan) for each client with over $250,000 in net household assets in their brokerage accounts. None of the former A.G. Edwards brokers had been trained on the Envision system prior to the so-called retention bonus being announced. Yet, without any training, they were expected to complete at least 50 reports within two weeks. Each report required that the broker call eligible clients and complete an Envision report for them. Jeff was kept on as branch manager after the Wells Fargo takeover of Wachovia and stopped by my office to insist that I do the Envision reports to obtain the bonus monies. He asked me to join a training class along with a woman broker. She worked down the hall from me, and when I arrived at her office for training, she asked "What are you doing here?" I explained that Jeff had asked me to join her. In front of the trainer, she announced "I don't want you in my office." I left and almost gave up, but the trainer followed me out and set up a short 45-minute session for 6:30 P.M. in my office Although I took substantial notes, I didn't feel prepared.

With Karen helping and working weekends, I completed 66 Envision reports, or so I thought. At stake was a potential $168,000 pre-tax retention payout. Part of the program was a contract that would also lock me into Wells Fargo Advisors for at least nine more years. If I left the firm earlier, I would owe a substantial amount back.

Having completed my task by June 30th, I expected a check for the Envision Report retention bonus. I was informed around September 1st, Jeff had approved just 11 of my 66 reports, so I would receive no payout for at least another quarter. When I first submitted the reports neither Jeff nor the home office questioned any of them. Now, Jeff informed me that he had declined almost all, because, he didn't like the fact that 80% of my clients had already met their financial objectives. During a heated argument, I asked him to show me what, on each rejected report, was unacceptable. This he refused to do.

Michael Chavez, the branch liaison from the corporate office was supposed to help us with any Envision questions. He joined in a conference call with Jeff, Karen and myself to help clarify what needed to be done to get my Envision reports approved. The next day, I emailed Michael Chavez to confirm our conversation.

The email read was as follows:

> From: Jerry Wolff
>
> Sent: Wednesday, September 02, 2009 11:52 A.M.
>
> To: Michael Chavez
>
> Subject: Sep 1, 2009 conference call on 4 Front Program
>
> Per our conversation with Jeff Kanter, Karen and myself, regarding what adjustments or fine tuning the 66 Envision reports, I would like an email confirming my understanding of what is needed to meet the Envision team's criteria for approval.
>
> The following is my understanding of what was stated.
>
> 1. Again, contact the 66 clients and review their reports
> 2. Adjust and fine tune no more than 3 accounts per day
> 3. Add in any banking relationships not previously disclosed
> 4. Review social security payments and adjust as needed
> 5. As stated, 64 out of 77 accounts are retired and comfortable with their income. Thirty-three of them were born prior to 1930 and seven prior to 1935. These clients are satisfied and pleased with their portfolio performance and income being generated. It would be inappropriate to suggest changes to their objectives or portfolios by adding more risk. After forty-two years in this industry including running a bank brokerage and being in management for over 25 years, I understand compliance. I have never paid out a client in all those years. I do not intend to suggest changes to my successful retired clients for the purpose of generating commissions and run the risk of suitability issues or churning. I hope that is understood. For the record in my 15 years with this company, I generated $4.5 million in commissions for this firm and have been in management.
> 6. I was trained on Envision June 23, 2009. I followed my trainer's guidelines which included making the reports

available to my clients online. That was a choice. I was previously informed at the end of June that my reports were ok by you and I was congratulated by Jeff Kanter for the job I had done. Since that time, there were numerous opportunities to correct any issues with my reports. Up to now, no one was willing to explain to me in detail what the problems were, despite several requests by me.

7. Most important, I will do as asked, provided you will confirm by email that the items mentioned that need to be adjusted or reviewed are done as requested will be accepted by the envision team. If there is anything else missing, I ask that you provide that information to me, so that I will not be delayed any further in being paid for my work.

Thank you very much for your immediate response. Jerry A Wolff

Jeff Kanter responded to my email instead of Michael Chavez. The following email, including grammatical errors, is exactly how it was written.

Jerry. "There will be no email from Chavez regarding what we discussed. I think its pretty clear what we have to do to get you paid on the Sept. 15 cycle. Lets just do them. If you think some are fine, just re submit how they are." JK

Jeff and the Envision crew only approved 47 of my reports, forcing me to wait another three months before I could receive what was owed. Each delay extended my contract with Wells Fargo Advisors by three months. I got into a screaming match with Jeff over the failure to get approval for the 50 reports needed for a full payout. I was sick and tired of all the bullshit and took it up the regional manager, Tony Saponaro, on January 3, 2010. I finally got paid by the end of April, 2010.

After talking with former A.G. Edwards brokers, I learned I was not the only one whose Envision reports failed to be approved by

Jeff and the Envision liaison employees. On the other hand, the former Wachovia brokers had their reports approved immediately for payout, though in many cases they hadn't even called their clients for the necessary information. For whatever reason, the hostility formerly shown by Wachovia employees towards former AGE brokers in that office continued well into the Wells Fargo Advisor era.

Contrary to what management might think, I was a team player throughout my career. For example, while working on my 2009 taxes, I discovered a discrepancy on my 1099's municipal bond interest received and adjusted cost basis on bond redemptions. I spent hours trying to figure out why they did not match and concluded that Wells Fargo Advisors had a major systems problem. After speaking with John Kalinowski of Wells Fargo Advisors Direct Financial Solutions, I agreed to allow him to use my 1099s to find out why the transactions didn't match. Initially, John was doubtful about my discovery. However, he called me back a few weeks later to tell me I was right. There was a big problem throughout the firm.

John followed up with an email dated March 9, 2010 to Tony Saponaro, Jeff Kanter and me.

It read as follows:

> Subject: Jerry Wolff's Assistance
>
> Dear Sirs,
>
> I just wanted to take a moment to call your attention to some very significant assistance both myself and this firm received from Mr. Jerry Wolff. Jerry called me to report a problem he was experiencing with the Turbo Tax download, there was much to this issue, but in short, downloaded data was not matching 1099 reported data. Jerry's insight and familiarity with this issue and his ability to explain what he was seeing were instrumental in getting several very serious issues resolved. 1099-INT Tax Exempt Interest (Box 8) and Special

Private Activity Bond (Subject to AMT) (Box 9) were not coming over in the download. Also, on the Schedule D, original cost basis was being used rather than the adjusted cost basis. All of these significant issues could potentially cause problems for our clients when downloading. It was Jerry's follow-up that helped me to gauge the possible impacts of this problem and get upper management working on it right away. We identified over 5,000 clients who were impacted by incorrect downloads. Letters and communications were sent to these clients, some may have to amend their 2009 Tax Returns, but needless to say it would have been much worse had Jerry not reported and explained the issue. Jerry was also very gracious to allow us to use his personal accounts in testing to help us come to a resolution. Perhaps most importantly, while all of these issues were going on and I was in constant contact with Jerry, he was always nothing more than a true gentleman ready to help. Jerry quipped that "he outta write a book," I know I for one would certainly read it and learn from it!

Sincerely,

John Kalinowski

Often, when I called John, he would answer while working in another corporate department. John reminded me of myself when I was troubleshooting problems in several departments on Wall Street. Very few people get to learn the brokerage operations by gaining experience in several different departments. I hope his knowledge was appreciated.

I never received a phone call or comment from Tony or Jeff regarding John's email, but wasn't surprised. Quite frankly, I never asked management to like me, but I always wanted and expected them to respect me.

To celebrate my long-awaited payout from Wells Fargo, I booked a seven-day trip starting April 17, 2010 to Antiqua, Guatemala. We stayed at the Hotel Soleil La Antigua and explored this colorful Colonial city with its parks, music, bars, cantinas and jade shops. The people were friendly and welcoming. Everywhere you walked, there was something to see and enjoy.

On a clear day, you could see the peaks of volcanos in the distance. Catherine and I were going to book a tour to one of them, but were forced to cancel when two people died a few days earlier while visiting the Pacaya volcano. Personally, I was relieved. Instead, we chose to do a two-day adventure around remote Lake Atitlan located in Guatemala's southwestern highlands.

After a 3-hour bumpy bus ride we arrived at the lake, located on a volcanic crater. The huge body of water stretched out for over seven miles in length and over 50 miles in area. Mayan villages surrounded the lake and the people were identified by their clothing color and their different Mayan dialects. After checking in at the Hotel del Mundo, we were met by our personal Mayan guide who would take us for a boat ride to the lake's villages. We ate dinner at the hotel's Italian restaurant and, although my Spaghetti Bolognese tasted fine, I couldn't finish it. At the time, I didn't think anything about it.

The next day, our guide took us out on a boat around Lake Atitlan. We visited several Mayan villages where we roamed the streets and mingled with the locals. During our travels, we witnessed fishermen catching crabs, women weaving clothing out of colorful wool and even savored Guatemala highlands coffee. Together with our guide we ate the local black bass at a typical restaurant. I continued to lose my appetite and began to have stomach disorder. I tried taking Lomotil which helped some. but my condition was a concern. What was missing from the highlands was a quality medical center, though I had witnessed a shaman at a church shaking a can and chanting blessings to anyone near him. Our tour veered even further off the beaten path when we visited a shrine to Maximo in a small town called Santiago on the southern shore of Lake Atitlan. (The tale has it that Maximo was never a man, but a wooden figure created by shamans to defend the village from witches). There were many other legends. Maximo was often shown with a Stetson hat and a cigar in his mouth. At the tiny shrine we visited, a family prayed for help for an ailing family member and made a donation. Being superstitious at times, I also made a small donation to Maximo in hope that he might cure my stomach disorder.

On Friday afternoon, we took the tour van back to Antiqua. The three-hour drive was pure torture. My stomach was getting worse and I felt quite sick. It was essential for us to make it back to Antiqua for our return flight to Miami Saturday evening. I barely made it and was quite relieved to be back in Miami where I could receive proper health care if needed.

Sunday morning, I received a phone call from Jay, who I shared Miami Heat season tickets with. He informed me that I had the Heat-Celtic playoff game that afternoon, so Catherine and I went, hoping the Lomotil would calm my stomach disorder. I had no desire to eat anything and drank one soda at the game. After the Heat won, we stopped at Nestor's Deli after the game. It took me an hour to finish a bowl of matzo ball noodle soup.

I called my new sales assistant to let her know I wasn't feeling well and would stay home Monday, but would see her on Tuesday. That was not about to happen. On Tuesday, I woke up at 6:30 A.M. with a high fever. I told Catherine "Drive me to Boca Regional Hospital emergency center." Sometime after 7:00 A.M., I was seen by an emergency room doctor where I was told my temperature was 102. The doctor pressed down on the right side of my stomach, but I felt no pain. After tests, the doctor told me that my appendix had ruptured and I had a severe case of peritonitis which required immediate surgery. I told him the stomach disorder started about six days earlier in Guatemala. He said "With the poisons you have in your system, I don't understand how you survived after two days." I told him "I was an athlete my whole life, am still playing serious basketball and have never smoked." He replied "That is probably the only reason you are still alive." He added "You need to have emergency surgery or you won't last another 24 hours." He recommended Dr. Andrew Ross M.D. who was immediately available. I asked him what could he tell me about Dr. Ross. He told me he'd worked on his wife a year earlier. That was good enough for me.

Shortly after, Dr. Ross examined me and said "I was full of poisons and, depending how much they had spread, it may require additional surgeries." He, too, was shocked that I was still alive after six days with a ruptured appendix. I was very scared and couldn't believe this was happening to me. The operation took place around 5:00 P.M. Following the surgery, I had to have an extremely painful urinary catheterization. Within a couple of days, a Picc line was inserted into my shoulder, instead of having four lines sprouting out of my veins. Although I did not feel pain from the ruptured appendix prior to the surgery, I had massive pain after. I was given various narcotics, which provided relief for only 15–20 minutes. After several days in the hospital, I told the nurses, I didn't want the pain killers any longer. It just wasn't worth the risk of getting addicted. Normally, I hate taking pills unless absolutely necessary.

At one point, Dr. Ross prescribed a pill which was supposed to help speed the healing process. However, for two nights in a row, I had the same two scary hallucinatory dreams. In one, four-story walls were closing in on my Intracoastal Waterway townhouse with no way to escape as darkness surrounded me. The other dream placed me in a hellish setting. There was a large underground room with beautiful naked tanned women dancing to music on a platform with fire all around. No one was attempting to leave the room, nor was anyone being burned. After two nights of having these identical scary dreams, I told Dr. Ross to take me off the drug, which he did. I never had any of those dreams again. When, I described the two dreams to Dr.

Ross and my GP, I got the feeling they wondered why I would want the naked girl dream to end.

Each day my nurses pressured me to walk the hallways while pushing the IV pole attached to my Picc line. If Catherine was with me or a nurse was available, I would try. Every time I began that walk, though, I was in massive pain and often bleeding. I found myself getting depressed and frustrated. During my first 10 days, I had several CAT scans to make sure that the poisons had not spread to other organs. Often, I was given a drink called Contrast prior to the CAT scan and the taste was disgusting. Up until day ten, I did not think I was going to get out of the hospital alive. I remember saying to myself, "I am an athlete. I am a basketball player. If they want me to walk the halls twice a day, I will do it. If I fall, they will have to pick me up and if I bleed, they will have to clean it up. But I will do it." With excruciating pain, I started to walk the halls twice a day by myself. I could tell the nurses appreciated my effort. By the 19th day, I was walking the halls eight times a day and the doctors felt I was ready to be discharged, so did I. I couldn't wait to have a real meal and gain back the eleven pounds I'd lost. I had been fed through IVs the first 16 days, but when they finally served up solid food, it tasted awful.

After five weeks out on short term disability, I went back to work on June 10, 2010. I discovered my new sales assistant had tossed away some mail containing important marketing information. In addition, she had ignored time-sensitive home office wires regarding tender offers and other items. Because they had expired, I could no longer act on them for my clients. Although my assistant had 16 years-experience in the stock brokerage field, her lack of knowledge in the business created a lot of headaches for me. I blame her previous brokerage firms for her lack of training. It was an industry-wide problem. Banks and brokerage firms had stopped doing hands-on training since the eighties. Instead, they used outside trainers and online courses.

Operation managers were more concerned about protecting their own jobs, so they did not bother to share their knowledge. In my opinion the best way to learn is through mentors, not computers.

It took almost a month to get caught up with my paperwork and to let all my clients know that I was back and healthy. On weekends I headed to the basketball courts. Initially I was so weak, I could not hit the basketball rim from the foul line. It would take several more weeks before I had my strength and 3-point shot back to normal.

New issues with Jeff and Wells Fargo Advisors were just around the corner. One day at the office, I went to the closest men's bathroom and discovered water all over the floor. I left and immediately let Jeff's assistant know what was going on so she could let building management know. Shortly after, the bathroom was put on lockdown and a note on the door advised us to use another bathroom on another floor. One day I spotted two guys in hazmat suits walking into the bathroom. No one was telling us what was going on. Several individuals were developing coughs. I developed breathing issues, had seen my doctor and, for the first time in my life, was put on inhalers for a period of six weeks. The hazmat suit fellows weren't talking, so I ran my own investigation and found out that the urinals had been leaking into the walls. In short, we were breathing poisons through our office air vents. I called the head of Wells Fargo Human Resources, explained what was going on and requested they investigate.

I was told they would have it taken care of "immediately". Instead, I received a hostile call from my manager, Jeff, and he said "Are you the one who called Human Resources?" I replied "You're damn right I was the one." He hung up. After a few more weeks of nothing being done, I called Human Resources again and they pretended to be surprised that no action had been taken. I asked them to hire an environmentalist to check the air in the bathroom and my office vents. Once again, I was told they would "take care of it". The owners of the building were taking their time fixing the problems, as they hoped they could solve the problem without having to gut the entire bathroom. They were wrong. It took over two months before we were able to use the bathroom again. An environmentalist, hired by the building owners, showed up *after* the construction was completed and reported no violations in the bathroom. He also checked my office air vents and found that they had not been cleaned for over 10 years and the air was considered borderline safe. Only then were they cleaned.

Jeff departed from Wells Fargo Advisors and a new era began with Alex, my former AGE regional manager, now my branch manager. Due to past experiences, Alex and I both knew it was best to keep a distance from each other. Sometime in March 2011, my disastrous sales assistant gave notice she was going to another firm. That was a happy day for me as well as the other brokers she serviced. I sent an email to Alex asking him to not hire another sales assistant until we had an opportunity to interview several candidates.

Bank takeovers of stock brokerage firms can be a disaster, especially when they already have their own brokers working in a branch. I was told on several occasions the bank brokers were not allowed to solicit my clients and if any of them did, there would be major repercussions. What I found was that bank employees could see my clients' cash balances and total value of their portfolios if they banked with Wells Fargo, but I could not see their bank balances. This uneven balance of information exposed my clients to being solicited by Wells Fargo Bank branch brokers, even though it was against stated corporate policy. On several occasions, Wells Fargo bank brokers attempted to steal accounts and a few even succeeded. When I protested to my branch manager and other higher ups, I was ignored.

On March 4, 2013. I received a call from an upset client who had been solicited twice by a Private Banker at a Wells Fargo Bank in Boca Raton. My client of 20 years, along with her niece, requested I do something about the undesired solicitations. She told me he had insisted it was important that he visit her and evaluate her brokerage account, even after he was told that I was her long-time broker. She was not interested in such a meeting and asked him to stop calling her. I treasured my client and our relationship had been excellent. I was so angry after hearing her distress, that my sales assistant, Gary, had to calm me down. Gary knew I had grown up in the tough streets of Brownsville and would not tolerate another Wells Fargo employee stealing one of my accounts. When I told Gary, I was going to drive over to the bank where this broker worked and have a discussion with him, Gary asked me to calm down because he felt I might wind up being arrested or fired. On my behalf, Gary wrote an email detailing the incident and sent it to Jodi, an assistant to the branch manager. He requested she look into the solicitations and mentioned that this was the fifth time my clients had been solicited by the banking side without any consequences. Neither Gary nor I ever heard back from anyone. I told Gary "If this SOB calls my client one more time, nothing will stop me from paying him a visit."

It took about four years for me to realize that Wells Fargo was unlike any financial institution I had ever worked for. They had a great PR department–and they needed it. John G. Stumpf was the CEO of Wells Fargo and any time I heard him speak, I felt skeptical. He reminded me of those politicians who expect their audience to applaud at anything they say, regardless of the truth. On a few occasions, brokers were invited to join in a "town hall meeting" in which Stumpf was the featured speaker. Some brokers and bankers were even invited to attend in person and often gave him standing ovations. I never attended in person, but when I heard him address such meetings around the country in video conference calls, I usually cut off from the "rah rah" atmosphere of the call within minutes. As far as I was concerned the benefits and the company he was describing didn't exist, at least for me.

In my opinion Wells Fargo was a company that only cared about their bank executives' bonuses and bottom-line earnings. Stumpf never showed any interest in the Wells Fargo Advisors subsidiary, other than its profitability. In lieu of a Christmas bonus, Wells Fargo would send out an email describing our compensation package for the new year. Every year they cut our net payouts on transactions, as they thanked us for the great job we were doing. That was the festive Wells Fargo way of recouping the Envision retention monies they had used to lock us in with the firm for 9–10 years. I had never worked for a company that handed out bonuses or other compensation and then cut pay year after year to recoup what they had previously given.

In July 2013, my new branch manager, Michael Origlia, emailed us that we were about to change our Nasdaq market data quote system on August 16th. The firm called this action the NASDAQ MIGRATION. Wells Fargo had found a new way to cut costs, this time with a cheaper quote system. We were told that traditional quote services were increasingly expensive and difficult to manage, moreover other major brokerage firms were said to be using the new system which would provide the Nasdaq basic service augmented with the NYSE exchange feed. Here's what happened when we went live with the MIGRATION. The new system was so inferior to the old, I thought I was back in the Bunker Ramo dinosaur days of the sixties. Previously, the system had shown fluctuations in pre-market and after-market Nasdaq quotes as trades took place, but I saw nothing on the new system. If an earnings report or other news was reported pre-market or after-market, I would not see the action taking place on my monitor. Instead, I would have to click the individual stock symbol for a snap quote to see the activity. The problem was how would I know what was going on, unless I kept clicking individual stock symbols.

It was also a physical nightmare due to my prior torn and detached retinas in both eyes (related to basketball injuries). Now things were about to get worse. The new quote system had the letter D in front of my Over the Counter (OTC) bulletin board stocks and all open-end mutual funds on my monitor. The big D stood for delayed quotes. I didn't need to be told what D meant. Furthermore, it was a shock to my eyes every time I looked at the monitor. Also, the D replaced an uptick or downtick on various stocks I monitored. For an active stock trader like myself, that was important. Now, I couldn't get bid-ask on Nasdaq stocks, although management promised that would be available on the new system. They took all the good features away and left us with a shell.

On Saturday August 17th, I was over 40 minutes on the phone with three Wells Fargo technicians, including their supervisor. Not one had ever heard of the NASDAQ MIGRATION. I sent an email to Mike Origlia outlining my problems with the new system. He forwarded my email to Todd C. Wichmann, Gulf Coast regional operations manager, who informed me nothing could be done. I asked Mike if I could be put back on the old system. He asked me to get a note from my ophthalmologist explaining what my eye problems were. Mike felt I might be able to get a disability exception, but I knew from past experience with Wells Fargo's Human Resource's department that my chances of getting such an exception were poor.

On Thursday, August 22nd, at 1:01 P.M., everyone in the firm that had gone through the Nasdaq Migration received an email from Todd Wichmann informing us that our new Nasdaq system was down, all stock trading through our new system was halted and brokers were asked not to duplicate any trade orders. As usual, management left us in the blind. We were a 50-broker branch and, along with a few other branches, were being used as guinea pigs for the company's newly purchased Nasdaq system. There's a popular expression "You get what you pay for." This was a perfect example. I continued my efforts, calling our IT department, hoping to find someone who understood the new system and could help clear up my problems.

I provided my doctor's note to Mike on Oct 1st and cut down my time at work, so my eyes would not be too irritated and informed Mike of my reduced work hours. I had a week vacation in St Kitts and when I returned on October 23rd, Mike informed me that my doctor's note had been submitted and he was waiting to hear back. It was now nine weeks since we changed our Nasdaq system and nothing had been done to help me. I wasn't surprised. One day I was dealing with our technology department on a different issue and speaking with a lady from a specialized area. When I explained to her the problems, I was having with the new Nasdaq system, she offered her help and I authorized her to sign on to my system. Within two minutes, she was able to remove the big D in front of my quotes and eliminate my screen view issues. I was delighted with her accomplishment and sent her a Starbucks gift card as a thank you. She is the type of employee that the stock brokerage and banking industry has been missing for years. I let Mike know my problem was solved and I wouldn't need the exception. However, it didn't change the fact that the new, cheaper system was still vastly inferior to the one it replaced.

31

WELLS FARGO:
AN ARROGANT LEADERSHIP

Wells Fargo Advisor's management finally found a way to push me into retirement. On February 4, 2014, 9:57 A.M. both Michael Origlia and Alex Bigelow received an email from Judy Escobar of Barnett Associates, a third-party company used by Wells Fargo for Human Resource issues. It read as follows:

Subject: Wolff, Jerry A Due By 2014-02-18

Request for Information-No Separation Information on File

Please reply to this email answering all questions in the questionnaire below as soon as possible as data is time sensitive.

As you may know, Barnett Associates has been authorized by Wells Fargo to handle all unemployment claims and hearings. For further assistance or guidance, you can click on the following link.

Name: Wolff, Jerry A

Last Four Digits of ss#: XXX-XX-(actual 4 digits listed)

Location: 0000036903

Termination Reason:

Hire Date: 9/8/1994

Last Day Worked:

Claim Due Date: 2/18/2014

Barnett Associates has received an unemployment claim for the above employee.

We do not have separation information regarding this claimant. Please select the appropriate option below and provide the requested details. Your response must be received by 2/18/2014 at 2 pm (EST) to meet the state's due date.

Do not provide confidential personal customer information

( ) Voluntary Termination reason code. Fax the Voluntary Termination form and /or Resignation letter.

( ) Involuntary Termination: Provide Termination reason code and the description of the final incident that led to Termination. Fax Involuntary Termination form and Counseling/Corrective Action documents as well as any supporting documentation pertaining to the final incident.

( ) Involuntary Displacement/Layoff (no further information required)

( ) Still Working: Has the Employer had to reduce work force/hours? Is there an expected return to work date? Has the claimant changed their availability, requested a reduction in hours or refused hours offered? Was the claimant hired as a full-time or part-time employee?

( ) Other: Please explain.

Name of first-hand witnesses:

Name, job title and telephone/email of the supervisor with knowledge of the reasons for the employee's separation from the company (e.g., the supervisor who terminated the claimant, if applicable)

Thank you,

Judy Escobar

Client Service Representative

P: 516-750-7044
F: 516-750-7144

The same day, at 11:25 A.M. Michael Origlia responded with this e-mail:

> "To my knowledge no answer options are accurate. Jerry is in the office working hours as he has done for years. Please explain."

When Michael J. Origlia and Alex Bigelow (both with considerable branch and/or regional managerial experience) received the email from Judy Escobar, it should have been a red flag that identity fraud had been committed. They should have contacted me immediately. The email indicated my social security number had been used to file a fraudulent Florida State unemployment claim. Such use is a definition of identity fraud. Yet, neither Mike nor Alex bothered to call, walk into my office or share a copy of Judy Escobar's email. It seems they decided to keep me in the dark regarding the identity fraud (perhaps due to their personal dislike or because they were totally clueless).

Over my career, I worked for racist, anti-women and alcoholic branch managers, as well as those who had no problems with violating SEC security laws, so it shouldn't be a surprise that I often had conflicts. Now I had a new grievance: a management who seemed unaware of identity fraud – and it was my identity being compromised.

Two weeks later on February 18, 2014, my stock brokerage career was about to enter a tumultuous period with Wells Fargo Advisors, when Michael Origlia forwarded a second email from Judy Escobar. This somewhat incoherent memo (I have left the grammar intact) reads: "It seems that there is a unemployment claim filed for Mr. Wolff. Since he is still working for you please have him the state of Florida to let them know his currently still working for Wells Fargo. Here is the number 1-800-342-9909."

Michael emailed me both the February 4th and 18th emails from Judy Escobar along with his responses and nothing else. After reading them, I called him and asked "What the hell is going on and when were you going to tell me?" He brushed me off and said "Just call the State of Florida phone number listed in the email to let them know you are still working here." He then hung up without answering my questions.

During the next two days, instead of doing business, I spent hours on phone calls with the Florida State Unemployment Department, Internal Revenue Service (IRS), Federal Trade Commission (FTC) and other agencies trying to stop the identity fraud. It was an attempt that would be unsuccessful. On February 18th, I was told by a FL State Unemployment employee that Florida had paid out $275.00 to the criminal. After my call informing them that I was still employed at Wells Fargo Advisors, the state still paid out another $275.00. I then spent two hours waiting to speak with someone from the IRS fraud division. I told them that I was going through identity fraud and had mailed them my 2013 tax return on the same day that I was informed of the fraud. I was told by the IRS, there had been three attempts online to file a tax return in my name. For various reasons my personal information did not match, so no payment had been made. The IRS agent told me he was red flagging my account, "not to worry" and requested I file fraudulent claim forms. I sent them immediately. I also informed them that I never file tax returns online, so if there were any further attempts to file online, they could assume it was fraud. I spent more hours contacting the FTC regarding potential Social Security fraud. They noted my information and asked me to set up an appointment with the Social Security Administration to set up passwords in person to avoid identity fraud, which both Catherine and I did.

Catherine and I were planning our first visit to the Middle East on a Seabourn cruise departing March 31, 2014 from Dubai. I was expecting a tax refund and I looked forward to the extra spending money for our trip. On my third call to the IRS to make sure they had received my fraudulent claim papers and to check on the progress of my refund I was informed they had paid out an online tax filing on February 18th, the very day I first made them aware of the identity fraud. The agent apologized and then revealed I probably wouldn't see my refund for 9–12 months. I was outraged. "How come you paid out a criminal when my account had been flagged?" She replied, "It took an extra day from your call to get the information into the system." I asked "Is there anything I can do to expedite my tax return, being that the IRS had messed up?" "No, I'm sorry." Of course, if I had been told earlier by my managers about the situation, none of this would have been an issue.

After sending a polite letter to the IRS fraud division, I received my refund check on March 23rd, 2014. I was pleased that the IRS honored their mistakes and did the right thing in my case. However, nothing had changed in the attitude problems between Mike and myself. I insisted on getting an answer as to why Mike didn't let me know about the Florida unemployment claim when he first received notice. He avoided me whenever he saw me and never returned messages.

One night I was invited to the Capital Grille for a private dinner seminar with a mutual fund wholesaler. When I arrived at the restaurant, I spotted Mike sitting at the bar. He seemed shaken to see me. As other brokers were arriving, Mike said "Do you want to discuss your identity fraud now?" I told him, "This is not the proper place for such a discussion. Can we get together tomorrow morning?" We met the next day and again I asked why didn't he let me know someone had used my social security number to file an unemployment claim. He said "I thought it was a mistake and there was no need to mention it to you." I responded "What if it wasn't?" He answered "Are you blaming me?" I told him how, by withholding information, he had cost me time and money. I left his office in disgust.

Foolishly, I contacted Vonda R. Hess, in charge of Wells Fargo Human Resources. I left a message for her to call me back. Instead, I received a call from Tanya M. Douglas, Executive Assistant to Vonda Huss. Per Tanya's request, during the next week, I followed up the phone call with a few emails explaining the identity fraud that had taken place. Also, I advised her of the problems caused by the failure of Mike to follow Wells Fargo procedures when identity fraud was suspected. Mike also violated Wells Fargo Confidential Information Policy by exchanging emails with Barnett & Associates using the last four digits of my Social Security number without any encryption. On several occasions, Barnett & Associates lied to me as they attempted to conceal or coverup for their failure in handling my identity fraud problem.

So great was my anger with management, I was becoming concerned about my health. After consulting with Catherine and my good friend and co-worker, Rany Janover, I signed a succession agreement with Wells Fargo Advisors allowing Rany to become the receiving financial advisor upon my retirement. Rany would become my partner for a minimum of one year ending February 28, 2015 (subject to change by either Rany or myself). Previously, several brokers in the branch had approached me seeking to become partners and buy my book of business should I retire. I trusted Rany to service my clients the way I did. Rany was honest and I knew he would continue to discount commissions, as I had done. He wasn't money hungry like some of the brokers who were anxious to take over my accounts. I knew he would recommend suitable products for my clients and do his best to follow in my footsteps. Although Rany did not have the same experience I had, I felt he had his own strengths, as well as the life experience and ethics that would make him a great partner. Some of the brokers who sought to partner with me had dealt with serious compliance issues and various complaints. I never would have entrusted my clients to them.

Catherine and I went on our Middle Eastern cruise on March 23, 2014 aboard the *Seabourn Legend*, a 225-passenger ship. I had a last-minute opportunity to upgrade to one of the ship's four luxury suites. After leaving Dubai, we headed to the Gulf of Aden, calling first at the Port of Salalah in Oman. This was the same port from which Captain Phillips and his Maersk cargo ship *Alabama* had sailed in April 2009, only to be kidnapped by Somali pirates and later rescued by Navy Seals. I expected security to be present on such a cruise, and it was. After dinner, we found a note on our cabin door reminding us of potential dangers during our five-night journey through the Gulf of Aden with Yemen to the southwest and Somalia to the southeast. We were advised to keep our drapes closed, stay off the balcony and avoid walking out on the decks for the next five evenings. The following morning all of us learned that six ex-British military had joined us. We never saw any weapons, but I felt well protected.

Our first stop after cruising the Gulf of Aden was Jordan, where we visited the ancient ruins of Petra, one of the 7 New Wonders of the World. In the movie *Indiana Jones and The Last Crusade,* Petra was the site where the hero finds the Holy Grail. A building known as The Treasury, carved out of sandstone rock, was a magnificent highlight.

From Petra, we cruised through the Suez Canal, where we noticed several docked flat boats that the Egyptians used in the 1967 war with Israel. We did not stop at any Egyptian ports on our way to Ashdod, Israel. Upon arrival, we went on a full day tour of Jerusalem. In a conversation I had with our tour guide, regarding anti-Semitic racism in the United States, I vowed to never again conceal the fact that I am a Jew. I explained to the guide that because of physical attacks and racist comments I had experienced over the years, I had rarely let people know my religion. From that moment I said "Never again." It felt good to be a proud Jewish man and I have honored that vow ever since. My brother, Larry, had recently passed away and I placed a note for him in the Western Wall (Wailing Wall). I became very emotional and had to be alone for several moments as I observed the praying going on. Later, Catherine also placed a note into the wall for a client and friend, Sandra Rosen, who also had passed on.

Our next port, Haifa, included a full-day tour featuring a boat ride on the Sea of Galilee. The fisherman demonstrated how to catch Tilapia by casting a net into the lake. We could only imagine it being done the same way thousands of years ago. After our boat ride on the lake, we visited Bethsaida, believed to be the hometown of Peter and walked around the ruins of what our guide said was his home. We completed the tour with a drive through Nazareth. A few days later we departed the ship in Athens and spent a day hiking around the Parthenon, a great way to end a vacation.

Unfortunately, I caught a bad cold during the trip, which slowed me down some. I have no doubt that the stress and lost sleep from the identity fraud had weakened my resistance. My blood pressure was running high as the aggravation took its toll. However, the cultural and educational experiences we had were priceless. I can't wait to go back.

Upon returning from the Middle East, I was still feeling hostility from Mike. I was very upset that no one from Wells Fargo Advisors or the Human Resources department was willing to acknowledge that identity fraud had even been committed or apologize for their role in allowing the fraud to perpetrate. May 11th, 2014, I emailed Tanya in HR (copied Vonda Huss) an outline of all that Wells Fargo incompetence had cost me in damages. I probably should not have sent the email. I knew my email would likely cause repercussions, but if I did nothing, my health stood to be damaged. The next six weeks would confirm what a ruthless, heartless and arrogant firm Wells Fargo had become.

In summary, I outlined over 20 phone calls to government agencies and visits to various police departments in Miami along with the time I spent with each. I asked for a few thousand dollars to cover what I lost in commissions, expenses and time.

On Thursday, May 15, 2014, I received the following email.

> Hello Mr. Wolff: Tanya Douglas has forwarded your recent communications to me. I will review your concerns and respond to you by the end of next week. I am your point of contact on this matter, so please direct any further communications only to my attention.
>
> Sincerely,
> Bruce J. Berrol
> Employee Relations Manager
> Wells Fargo Wealth Brokerage & Retirement
> WBR Human Resources, 550 California Street, Sacramento Tower, 3rd floor, San Francisco, CA 94104

After some research, I found out that Mr. Berrol was a San Francisco attorney who reported to Vonda Huss. The following is a summary of Mr. Berrol's email response to me on May 22, 2014.

Berrol determined that there was no basis to grant my request for compensation. He stated "Your manager was not provided with nor had any information on which to reasonably conclude that you were a victim of identity fraud." This was typical attorney language for a denial of claim. In my view, when someone uses another person's social security number for gain, that is the ultimate definition of identity fraud.

During the following week, I called Mr. Berrol to contest his denial. I also advised him that Mike was retaliating against me and I was being harassed. I told him I wanted to file a new claim. He told me to call HR and provided the same phone number for Tanya Douglas. I left a phone call and an email message for Tanya to get back to me, as she was the only one, I had prior contact with aside from Mr. Berrol.

While my identity fraud complaint against Mike Origlia was being handled by Mr. Berrol, Mike sent an email to all the brokers in the branch describing production income, revenue and assets under management. He listed the names of 12 brokers with assets under management over $100 million. However, for the second straight time he left me off the list even though I met the criteria. Previously, when a number of brokers were spotlighted for bringing in new business, I was also left off the list, even though I did receive a bonus for the additional business. When I brought it to his attention, he said "Why didn't you tell me?" Naturally, after telling him, he did not bother to send out a corrected email. In my opinion, Mike was leaving me off the list on spite.

Instead of hearing from Tanya, on May 30, 2014, I received a threatening email from Berrol.

The following paragraph of Mr. Berrol's email read as follows:

"Finally, Ms. Douglas is not 'HR'-she is an administrative assistant for a WBR Executive. Your repeated e-mails and phone calls to team members whom you have been told are not appropriate points of contact are unproductive and interfere with the conduct of business. I recognize you disagree with the decision regarding compensation and that it is upsetting having to take steps to protect your identity. But I also need you to understand that your conduct in sending unnecessary and disruptive e-mails and phone calls is unprofessional. Should you continue to engage in this type of unprofessional conduct, you may be subject to corrective action."

Mr. Berrol also informed me that regarding retaliation and harassment by your manager, someone on the Employee Relations team will contact you within 48 business hours to discuss this further.

A few days later, I received a phone call from Ken Tolson; Employee Relations Consultant to discuss my retaliation and harassment claims. Although he was extremely polite, I knew he would take the corporate position in defending Mike Origlia. Although he agreed with me that Wells Fargo identity fraud procedures should be updated, he felt the way Mike treated me after the identity fraud was not retaliation. When I said to him, "the use of someone else's social security number for personal gain is the definition of identity fraud. He disagreed, no surprise. I had no reason to expect any other outcome. After all, this was Wells Fargo 2014, not the Wells Fargo that began with a six-horse stagecoach in 1852.

Less than two months passed, when suddenly, Mike Origlia changed my sales assistant without telling me. I found out from one of the other sales assistants and immediately called Mike to ask that he reconsider his action. I also let him know that, as the person directly affected, I would appreciate being told of such changes before hearing of them from a sales assistant. I reminded him that even though I could retire after March 1, 2015 with full benefits, my intent was to continue through September 30, 2016. After our discussion, he agreed not to change my sales assistant.

Mike continued his irrational emails on November 6, 2014, which named me and seven other advisors as potentially committing fraud against Wells Fargo. The company had been a sponsor to some professional sports teams and because of this, sometimes I was able to procure four tickets to a Miami Marlins baseball game. The seats were great. The only stipulation was that they be given to quality clients and that I attend with them. Anytime I received tickets, I always attended the games with my clients and found it a good way to build on our relationship. However, some advisors did not attend the games with their clients and, worse, sold the tickets on Stub Hub.

If tickets were sold on Stub Hub, Wells Fargo Advisors would have known who had sold those tickets. I played by the rules each and every time, so I was outraged that my name was mentioned in an accusatory memo. I advised Mike that I did not appreciate being mentioned as a person who might have partic-ipated in fraud. After hearing that I was insulted by the email, Mike agreed that he should have handled it differently. At the time, I thought perhaps he had finally learned how to respond to a problem. It wouldn't take long, though, before Mike once again showed his true colors.

Throughout my career, even after computers recorded all our clients' trades, I always posted every transaction on account cards that I had designed and paid to have printed. I was a rare breed, still posting trades, and often called "a dinosaur" by my co-workers. However, when our computer systems failed, I was the only advisor who could see the existing positions on clients' accounts. This was a tremendous help if my client needed to place a sell order.

Through my career, I purchased billions of dollars of fed-eral tax-free municipal bonds for clients. When I posted the purchase to an account page, I also indicated the maturity date and when the issuer could call the bond in (known as the call date). On a rare occasion, as I posted a redemption on my cli-ent's account page, I discovered that a bond had been redeemed prior to the call date or, worse yet, at a price of 100 instead of 101. In one instance, after realizing my client had received a price of 100 instead of 101 on January 2, 2015, I waited until January 8, 2015 to see if the error would be corrected. When that didn't happen, I called Kevin Seay at the bond redemption department to draw attention to the discrepancy. Kevin asked me to submit an "Excellence First" form. (This program by Wells Fargo was for employees to make suggestions or note when problems arise that need investigation).

It turned out that even though my client owned only a $5,000 bond, the firm had $2.2 million being held at the time of the redemption. That meant the firm's clients had been shorted a total of $22,000, not to mention that the tax reporting for all of those clients would have been incorrect for tax year 2015.

Because of my hand posting, I was able to pick up on the error and all the firm's accounts received the correct payout because I made the error known. Kevin Seay followed up with an email to eleven key employees including my branch manager, Mike Origlia, his boss, Alex Bigelow, and Tony Saponaro, the regional manager. In the email he recognized "exceptional internal client service that Jerry Wolff provided." None of my three bosses ever mentioned the memo.

Once again, my immediate Wells Fargo management displayed their personal weakness by failing to acknowledge my contribution to Wells Fargo Advisors. No matter how many times I went out of my way to help by writing an "Excellence First" form, not once did I ever receive a compliment or "thank you" from management. Corporate department managers appreciated what I did for the firm and respected my knowledge. For me, that had to be enough.

On March 10, 2015, I received an email from the Wells Fargo Teamworks department. It was just 13 months after Mr. Berrol from Human Resources had stated that when my social security number was used to file a Florida State unemployment claim, "that my branch manager had no reason to believe that there was fraud." Worse, he had threatened if I continued to pursue the matter.

Now, the March 10th corporate notice was saying the very thing I'd said earlier: "Identity theft is fraud committed or attempted using the identifying information of another person without authority. Examples of identifying information are names, Social Security numbers, dates of birth, driver's license information, and so on. As an example of tax identity theft is when a fraudster uses a stolen Social Security number to file a fraudulent tax return to claim a refund." The email went into greater detail on the use of a Social Security number and other potential fraud. Obviously, Mr. Berrol never discussed my case with the fraud division nor the person who crafted the corporate notice.

Every year Wells Fargo Advisors required all financial advisors and most of its employees to take between 10 and 20 continuing education courses on a Wells Fargo internal system. The courses covered rules and regulations related to financial products, but also included banking products that were not part of my business as a financial advisor. I always conscientiously completed the courses, although I felt many of them were a waste of time as they had nothing to do with my business. Several of them covered bank fraud, money laundering and banking regulations.

Curiously, executive Wells Fargo Bank management and their bank employees did not have to complete the continuing education courses required for financial advisors. That's a pity, because what followed would destroy the great name of Wells Fargo and consumer trust in banking for years to come.

When the city attorney of Los Angeles filed suit against Wells Fargo over alleged sales practices in retail banking stores in California, an email from Wells Fargo Teamworks was sent to all employees from John G. Stumpf, Chairman, President & CEO on May 5, 2015. The following is how Mr. Stumpf responded to the Los Angeles lawsuit, in a letter to employees headlined: "CEO: Lawsuit does not 'reflect our values or principles'"

I quote one of the paragraphs in Mr. Stumpf's letter, leaving it to the reader to determine what he meant. I consider his words a marvel of ambiguity. "As I stated in the shareholder letter of our 2014 annual report, we put customers at the center of everything we do. The reason our team members go to work each day is to help customers. The result is that Wells Fargo makes money, not the other way around."

The LA lawsuit was just the beginning of the horrific publicity that had a huge negative affect on all of the Wells Fargo Advisors' business. Some of my clients who also had Wells Fargo checking accounts switched brokerage firms, telling me as they did so, how much they hated doing business with the bank.

While I was on a short vacation, my partner, Rany, called me about an account that had taken out an equity loan using their stock brokerage account as collateral. Neither Rany nor I had ever been involved in equity loans before. Management insisted that we input detailed information of the loan into the client's account profile. The loan had been issued from a local Wells Fargo Bank, so before adding information about the loan, I needed more facts, especially since I had not approved the loan.

I returned to my office on June 15, 2015, and, during a meeting with Rany, Mike Origlia came into my office to remind me that I had to update my client's account with regard to the loan. Things got heated when I asked Mike "What was I expected to input on Smart Station (Wells Fargo Advisors computer system) regarding my client's equity loan? I didn't write the loan, knew nothing about it and the banker never called Rany to go over the equity loan with him before approving it. Mike accused me of being confrontational. I then advised him of my liability concerns and, once again, asked him what I should input into Smart Station. He told me that I should call my client to discuss the loan and input the conversation into the computer. Mike claimed I did not have liability, however Rule Number One in my business is "Know Your Client." In my opinion, by acknowledging the equity loan, I could have liability if the client's brokerage account suffered a huge drop in equity before shares could be liquidated and left the account with negative equity. I'd seen it happen to other brokers in the October 1987 stock market crash. It wasn't pretty.

32

WELLS FARGO ADVISORS:
THE KNIGHTS OF THE STAGECOACH

With just 15 months to retirement, I knew I had to keep a cool temperament, because management would use any excuse to nullify my succession agreement with Rany. This way they could avoid paying my retention bonuses that would be due in a few years and at the same time steal my book of business. I took Mr. Berrol's earlier threat very seriously. I avoided Mike like the plague and totally concentrated on taking care of my clients.

At the same time Wells Fargo was dealing with a constant onslaught of bad press hitting the financial news weekly, management was also devising new ways to confiscate commissions from their advisors. The firm claimed to need better compliance for monitoring clients' mutual funds that were not physically held at Wells Fargo Advisors, even though Wells Fargo Advisors was listed as the broker dealer. My affected clients' mutual fund statements displayed my name as the representative on the accounts.

Back in the 1980s and through 2005, most brokerage firms did not have the software to hold mutual fund positions in a client's regular brokerage account. When a client purchased a mutual fund, the client would receive a confirm from the brokerage showing the transaction. The mutual fund shares were either held at a depository company or registered in the client's name and mailed to that client, who was then responsible for the safekeeping of their shares. Logistically, the latter method created a problem if the client wanted to sell those shares. They would have to return the shares to the brokerage firm or mutual fund company and have them deposited into their mutual fund account before a sale could take place. I encouraged my clients to keep the shares in their account at the mutual fund depository and not run the risk of misplacing the shares and being unable to sell them in a timely manner.

Through the years, financial advisors were paid a small fee (known as 12 B-1 fees) by each mutual fund company as long as the financial advisor was listed as the representative on the account. Those fees were sent to the broker-dealer (i.e. Wells Fargo Advisors) who in turn would pay the financial advisor about 50% of those 12 B-1 fees. In return, the advisor stayed in touch and maintained a relationship to answer questions and advise the client.

It seems the company came up with another brilliant idea to steal their advisor's 12 B-1 fees and pocket them for Wells Fargo Advisors. I guess they thought 100% of the fees are better than 50%. Wells Fargo Advisors claimed they adopted a new policy in order to comply with numerous regulatory obligations including Anti-Money Laundering (AML), Know Your Client (KYC), various supervisory responsibilities and books and records requirements (BRR). I asked our compliance group if this was a new FINRA rule that we could no longer have advisors as representatives on mutual funds that were held away from the firm. The email response was "There does not appear to be a specific FINRA rule that states no more level zero." Level zero stood for the networking category that Wells Fargo Advisors decided to eliminate from the firm. Or did they?

In October 2015, advisors began to receive more detailed information about eliminating the clients' level zero mutual funds from the firm's books. I had about 20 clients holding at least 40 mutual fund positions valued at over 2 million dollars. I convinced about 50 percent of them to move their mutual positions into their existing brokerage accounts or open a new one, if necessary. Effective November 1, 2015, Wells Fargo Advisors stopped paying the 12 B-1 fees to advisors on the mutual funds that did not transfer directly into Wells Fargo Advisors. Most of the clients who did not transfer their mutual funds wanted to keep their mutual funds separate from their stock and bond accounts. Often, when a client did move the mutual fund to be held by Wells, the cost basis did not come over from the mutual fund company which created a tax nightmare when the funds were sold. In many cases, my posting sheets were the only source for date of purchase and cost information, which was valuable to my clients who did not keep their trade confirmations.

Although I stopped receiving the 12 B-1 fees after November 1, 2015, my name was not removed from my clients' statements, despite Wells Fargo Advisors insistence that it would be. As 12 B-1 fees continued to be paid to the firm with my name shown as the representative, I began to question why my name had not been removed and what happened to the fees Wells Fargo Advisors had received. First, I was told Wells would send them back to the mutual fund companies. I checked, never happened. Then I was told they were going to give the monies to charity. I checked, and that never happened. When I asked which charities, I received no answer.

By June 30, 2016, my name was still listed as the representative on the clients' mutual fund statements. Furthermore, I was getting compliance emails requesting my help in updating personal information on the accounts that I was no longer getting paid on. All of those mutual accounts that Wells Fargo kept the 12 B-1 fees on had been clients of mine for 15–25 years. Because of threatening compliance emails, I provided whatever information I had. I didn't need any further problems being so close to retirement. I continued to cooperate with them even though I felt they had hurt my client relationships and cost me thousands of dollars.

My name was finally removed from the mutual fund statements just prior to retirement. Theft was one thing I always had a hard time tolerating. Wells turned out to be an expert at it.

To prove my point, it is over five years since Wells took away the 12-B1 fees under the falsehood of Anti-Money Laundering, Know Your Client and Books and Records requirements. I say that because, to the best of my knowledge, Wells Fargo Advisors is still listed as broker-dealer on those accounts and they *continue to collect* the 12 B-1 fees. They didn't know my clients and if they had, they would have known they were not involved in money laundering. But they did know that receiving 100% of the 12 B-1 fees was better than 50%.

After reading the bad press about Wells Fargo and now seeing them outright stealing commissions, I sensed that something else must have been going on in the firm to deviate from its proud history. Could it be that Wells Fargo was hand picking executives from each category of their banking, stock brokerage and wealth management divisions and sitting them at a round table with their goal to come up with ideas for growing profits any way they could? In this scenario, I'd call them *The Knights of the Stagecoach* instead of the Round Table. It may be only imagination, but one thing is for sure: the actions Wells Fargo took devastated their once-great name. I hope they return to their old glory, as I still enjoy watching the "Tales of Wells Fargo" on television.

On September 6, 2016, I received an email from Tony Saponaro, Regional President which read "Congratulations on your 22-year anniversary this month. Thank you for being part of the success in Boca Raton. Your commitment and dedication to your clients is not only important to them, it is also important and appreciated by your colleagues at Wells Fargo Advisors."

I replied, "Thank you. After generating 6.6 million in gross commissions over the 22 years and serving in management, my retirement begins October 1, 2016." After reviewing Tony's email, I noticed Kathy Breidenstein wrote the email on behalf of Tony Saponaro. I was not surprised as I was once told by my former branch manager, Jeff, that "Tony doesn't return phone calls." I found that to be a true statement, so why would he take two minutes to write a congratulations email. Naturally, he did not respond to my retirement notice, either.

During my final seven weeks with Wells Fargo Advisors, Wells Fargo was bombarded with non-stop negative press. There were settlement announcements with the Consumer Financial Protection Bureau, the Office of the Comptroller of the Currency and the Office of the Los Angeles City Attorney over alleged sales practices. Those were just the beginning, followed by numerous claims of fraud that would be handled at the Federal level. John G. Stumpf, the CEO, sent all team members a message.

I got a chuckle when I read what he wrote "As you know, every Wells Fargo team member is expected to adhere to the highest possible standards of ethics and business conduct, which are spelled out in our Code of Ethics." It would seem such high aspirations did not apply to him and other executives. There was a "clawback" of bonus monies paid to Stumpf following his departure from Wells Fargo.

On September 23, 2016, just one week from my retirement, a local Sun Sentinel Editorial read, "New Wells Fargo CEO: Jesse James." The article revealed that during testimony Senator Elizabeth Warren ripped Stumpf apart and he could barely answer a question. On the same day, *Financial Advisor* magazine wondered "Should FAs (Financial Advisors) Call for Wells Fargo CEO's Head?" It was a headline I could have written myself if I hadn't already been threatened. Finally, it took the *Financial*

Advisor magazine to bring to light how much damage had been done to Wells Fargo Advisors' image because of the fraudulent actions by Stumpf and Wells Fargo Bank.

The last correspondence I received before retiring was a message titled "Wells Fargo I Know and Love. . ." from Derek Jones, Regional President Central Florida Community Banking. The email, dated September 29, 2016, thanked us for the job and suggested we share stories about the "Wells Fargo we know and love." The fawning email was sent to all the advisors in our office. After the hell we were dealing with, I wondered what planet he was living on.

Previously in a conference call with a member from the retirement team, Mike Origlia had agreed to split the cost of lunch meetings where my clients were introduced to Rany. Mike's share of the cost would have been about $300. Just before I retired, Mike reneged on that commitment. Once again, it was no surprise, but I told his assistant, Julie, that if Mike did not honor his commitment, I did not want a cake to celebrate my retirement on September 30th.

On my final day, which was unannounced to the branch, Mike did not come to my office to congratulate me on my retirement. Considering our prior hostility, there was no reason to expect him to show up. I planned to work until the market closed at 4:00 P.M. as I rarely left the office earlier. To my surprise the building's handyman showed up at my door at 3:00 P.M. and said "I am here to remove your computer and replace it with another advisor's computer." Apparently, my neighbor next door was moving into my bigger office. Normally, that change would take place on a Saturday or well after the retiring advisor was completely out of the office. I told the handyman "I am still working. Do not touch my computer or any of my belongings until I am out of my office." He continued to work in my office, but did not touch my computer or belongings. Was I being baited into a fight? Was this a last chance effort to void my succession agreement and steal my accounts? It may sound paranoid, but Wells knew I had a temper. Still, I kept cool and worked to 4:00 P.M. My final trade was a purchase of 500 shares of Verizon for a client @ 3:55 P.M. just before my 48-year stock brokerage career came to a close.

Before retiring, I mailed out a letter to all my clients. August 14th was always a special day for me as my letter explains.

> August 14th, 2016
>
> On August 14th, 1967 at the age of seventeen, I first began my Wall Street career as a margin clerk trainee with Paine, Webber, Jackson & Curtis. Wall Street soon became part of my bloodstream. During my long career, I was very fortunate to have fine mentors along the way. Most of all, with my great client relationships, we both were able to navigate through both treacherous bear markets and enjoyable bull markets. What a satisfaction it is to advise generations of client families these forty plus years.
>
> After long discussions with Catherine, my wife of forty years, I have made the decision to retire September 30, 2016. We intend to continue our world travels as ambassadors of our great country.
>
> I am pleased to say that my partner and dear friend Rany Janover, Senior Vice President-Investments, will be taking over my business. You can expect Rany to be an extension of me. He is experienced, honest, caring and, most important; he will put your interests first. Rany is looking forward to continuing the relationships I have had with you. If at all possible, we would be pleased to get together and review your investments. Please call my office at 561-347-3825 for an appointment.

I cannot thank all of you enough for allowing me to advise you and service your accounts. It has been a very special experience. I wish you all the best for the future.

Best Regards,
Jerry A. Wolff
Vice President-Investments

33

UNCORK THE CHAMPAGNE

A s soon as I arrived home, I kissed Catherine and said "It is time to pop the cork on the James Bond 007 Champagne." A bottle of this special Bollinger had been sitting there in the refrigerator for over a year. I was just waiting for the perfect moment and now it had come. Let the fun and adventures begin. I was so happy and excited I had tears in my eyes. I knew my retirement would be very special for the two of us. Now the world was ours to explore and we did.

On October 22, 2016, we flew to Barbados and spent a week at The Club Barbados Resort & Spa Timeshare. It was all inclusive and right on the beach. The food and drinks were very good. Best of all was their live nightly entertainment. Aside from the professional singers, they had two Karaoke nights in a neat little pub complete with a DJ. Catherine and I had performed Karaoke once before on a NCL cruise to Alaska. After a few drinks we were ready to have a blowout night celebrating and singing. I did three soul music songs solo and a duet with Catherine that featured Al Green's "Let's Stay Together." From there we flew directly to St Kitts for another week stay at my timeshare, also on a beautiful beach.

I could have named this chapter "The Beginnings" as we both knew what joy my retirement from Wells Fargo Advisors would bring to us. From December 2016 through November 2019, we would sail on six Seabourn cruises. Our travels took us to six continents and too many ports to count. We had the pleasure of meeting and listening to an incredible group of lecturers during our sea days.

There was one very special lecturer named Lawrence Blair, author of Ring of Fire. This anthropologist, explorer and film maker exposed us to a world very few get to see. With a patch on one eye, he rather resembled a pirate and was, indeed, a most fearless person. His underwater explorations and cultural adventures in places like Papua New Guinea inspired me. On ship, I purchased a set of DVDs entitled Myths, Magic & Monsters that encompassed some of his adventures. If you ever get the chance to see them, make sure you have your favorite drink next to you. You will need it.

Some of the other lecturers included mountain climbers, famous bikers, authors, anthropologists, former CIA heads, ambassadors from the U.S. and other countries. The wildlife we witnessed in Africa, Asia and South America was spectacular, but nothing could top the cultural experience of mingling with the locals.

Unfortunately, Covid-19 would bring the world to a halt in 2020. At this writing, I get sick just thinking about the thousands of U.S. lives lost along with another 2.7 million deaths from around the world. Families who suffered with Covid-19 can't replace what was lost. As a nation and the world, we all lost something of ourselves.

For Catherine and me, our travel dreams were merely delayed. When it is safe to travel again, we will continue our world journey as informal ambassadors of the United States. With our great pharmaceutical companies producing Covid-19 vaccines, I believe the world will soon be one again.

In summary, my exposure to racism, violence, assault, ignorance, fraud, corruption and corporate retaliation may have given me a few "chips on my shoulder". The point is that I refused to allow that mindset to take over my life.

With the exception of numerous basketball related surgeries, basketball has always played a role in keeping me mentally stable. The thrill of competition, scoring and blocking shots always makes big problems seem smaller. I hope to still be shooting 3-pointers at age 100.

My greatest loss was the passing of my son, Nathaniel. Anytime I get depressed for any reason, all I have to do is think of him and remind myself how brave and strong he was. I know I have to follow his lead.

On the other hand, Catherine and I celebrated our 45th anniversary recently with another bottle of Bollinger James Bond 007 Champagne. It won't be too long from now, that we'll be lifting anchor on a Seabourn cruise and I'll be saying to the bartender "Pour me a glass of champagne and just keep on pouring." Life is a great pour.

ACKNOWLEDGMENTS

I want to acknowledge my hardworking parents who allowed me the freedom to be myself and trusted me to do the right thing. I want to thank my P.S. 183 sixth grade teacher, Mr. Safran, who introduced me to numismatics. Special mention, as well, must be made to two seventh grade P.S. 252 teachers: Mr. Freidlander, who taught math and science, along with Mrs. Weinberg, who played a big role in improving my reading level.

I want to thank George Walsh, Senior Partner at Paine, Webber, Jackson & Curtis for listening to a 17-year-old and giving me the opportunity to learn the stock brokerage industry in a comprehensive way that few individuals ever get to do. Thanks go out to Mark Cimino, my first mentor in the stock brokerage industry who taught me about margin accounts and how to deal with my co-workers.

I would like to thank the Ted and Mary Kata family for allowing me to continue my stock brokerage career during the seventies when most financial advisors were dropping out of the industry. Their kindness and helpfulness will be remembered forever.

Thank you, Rany Janover, for being a good friend and helping me get through those final two nightmare years at Wells Fargo Advisors.

My special thanks go to Catherine, my love, partner, educator, adventurer and fellow world traveler. Catherine edited the entire book, page by page, correcting my grammar, but never altering my thoughts. I am certain that parts of the book were difficult for her to read, but she never wavered. Without her support, I would not have written my autobiography.

ABOUT THE AUTHOR

After surviving 48 turbulent years in the financial industry and speaking out against fraud, Jerry Wolff intends to enjoy the rest of his life with family and friends. The world is his to explore.

www.ingramcontent.com/pod-product-compliance
Lightning Source LLC
Chambersburg PA
CBHW060903120626
46553CB00001B/193